EDINBURGH

10 WALKS IN THE HISTORIC OLD TOWN

EDINBURGH

10 WALKS IN THE HISTORIC OLD TOWN

Euan MacInnes

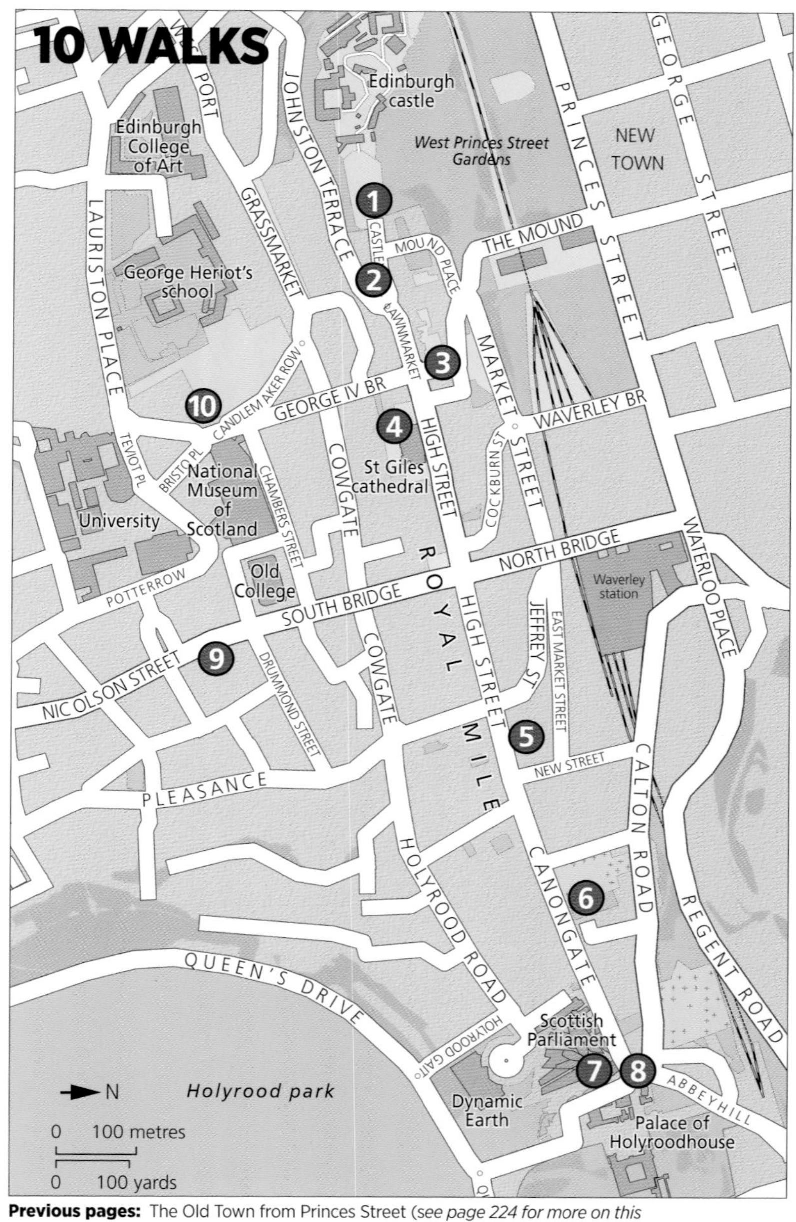

Previous pages: The Old Town from Princes Street (*see page 224 for more on this intriguing photograph*).

CONTENTS

ADVOCATE'S CLOSE
ADVOCATE'S CLOSE

A WARM WELCOME

I have no idea if you are a tourist in Edinburgh for the first time, a seasoned visitor to Auld Reekie or a local wanting to learn a little bit more about the city you live in; whatever your background, welcome. I hope this book provides with all you need to delve a bit deeper into the Old Town's past, uncover a few of its secrets and experience your own special moments in and around the Royal Mile. I love the Old Town of Edinburgh and I am very happy to have the opportunity to share it with as many people as possible.

As a student of history, then a tour guide and now a writer of Scottish history, what has always struck me about the Old Town is that it is not some museum piece, but a living, breathing part of Scotland's capital. The streets people walk down today are the ones their ancestors used centuries before: from the narrow closes that give a taste of the cramped, claustrophobic conditions of Edinburgh during the plague, to the grand vistas that inspired nineteenth-century writers and twenty-first century Instagrammers alike, the Old Town of Edinburgh is a place where you can feel history and relive the past.

The more I research Edinburgh's past the more I gain not only as a writer and guide but also when I find myself walking through the Old Town in my free time. This is what I want to share.

In this book I want you to be able to feel a part of Edinburgh's past as well as its present. To show you the parts that are the prettiest, most interesting and give you the best chances to connect with everything the Old Town has to offer. I hope that you too can have moments like I do when I discover something new and fall in love more deeply than before.

The ten walks in this book include a mixture of tourist hotspots and famous sights as well as underappreciated locations and hidden gems. The focus is on the Royal Mile and the closes that peel away from this famous thoroughfare, but rather than limit ourselves, the walks also stray outside the historic city limits, when the buildings we can visit, the view we can admire or the insight we can gain, is just too good to pass up.

Every walk starts at a major Old Town

Facing page: Advocate's Close, which affords a spectacular view of the Scott monument and Princes Street. The close has been significantly, and impressively, refurbished in recent years. (*see Walk 4*).

The charming Ramsay Garden

location that is easy to locate, then winds its way through closes, squares, staircases and garden paths before returning you to where you started. This way you can visit the attraction either before or after undertaking the walk and all your efforts will be focused on having the best time you can, not working out how to start, or worrying about getting back to where you were.

The walks are around the same length and at a leisurely pace you should be able to complete any of them in about an hour. Like most of Edinburgh, the Old Town is built on a hill so avoiding slopes and staircases was impossible. Instead every effort has been made to guide you down the steepest streets, returning by more gentle climbs. You should be able to do as many walks as you want in a day and when one finishes the next starting point will be just a couple of minutes away. The history and architecture should get your pulse racing, not the intense workout.

Starting with walk one, which explores the area around Edinburgh castle, each route has a different feel and explores a separate part of the Old Town; very rarely will you find yourself retracing steps you made on a previous walk. As we wander along the routes the text will point out the features you should look for, guide you towards the less noticeable elements and provide background and insight into how and why things are as they are. Each walk is also supplemented by other stories and summaries which provide more information about the most interesting people, places and events connected to the locations we journey through.

Edinburgh is a city that changes depending on when you visit, and, unsurprisingly, that affects our walks. In winter the trees are bare and as well as giving Edinburgh a more haunting and austere look, this also makes many more buildings and monuments visible. Return to the city in the summer and the verdant vegetation

The clock, Canongate tolbooth, a real Old Town landmark

may mean you have to push past the trees to see the same sights you viewed from afar.

Beyond the natural changes, events in Edinburgh may also change what you can visit. Certain streets are closed on Sundays and the many festivals in August also limit access to certain locations; most significantly the Edinburgh Military Tattoo and the concerts at the castle in July mean that the many monuments on the castle esplanade are hidden behind banked seating. When we can, the walks provide alternatives and at every stage we will help you get the most out of each walk, whatever day, month and, this being Scotland after all, climate, you find yourself in.

Now we are ready. Let us begin our journey.

Euan MacInnes,
Edinburgh, August 2018

THE OLD TOWN
A SHORT HISTORY

In the beginning

During the Ice Age a huge ice sheet passed over the area that is now Edinburgh, rolling over hills to form gently rounded slopes. However, when it reached the basal plinth of what is now castle rock, the ice sheet was forced to split, at which stage it produced the deep hollows of Grassmarket, Cowgate and Princes Street Gardens. The result was the creation of a typical geological feature, the crag-and-tail. The crag, composed of rugged rock, is of course castle rock, while the tail, of softer rock, constitutes the gentle west–east slope of what is now the Royal Mile.

There is archaeological evidence that the castle rock, a natural fortress on three sides, was inhabited as long ago as 850 BC, although evidence from other sites in the east of Scotland has led historians to conclude that humans were present here more than seven thousand years ago. These Bronze Age settlers lived in clusters of large roundhouses, spread across the rock. By the time the Romans arrived, in AD 78, a powerful local tribe, the Votadini, later known as the Gododdin, was in control. The castle rock was first recorded around AD 600, when it was known as *Din Eidyn* or the 'stronghold of Eidyn', although there are no clues about who, or what, Eidyn was.

Two burghs

There was a royal castle on the great rock as early as 1093 and it became a major fortress during the reign of David I, which began in 1124 (*see 'Discovering Edinburgh Castle' for more on the development of the castle*). The settlement that would develop into the town of Edinburgh was also beginning to grow: from its beginnings at the top of Castlehill, but at a distance from the castle, it spread eastwards down the slope, into the areas that are now Lawnmarket and High Street. It is not known for sure when the town became independent from the military establishment on the castle rock, nor when it became an independent burgh, but there is documentary evidence that burghal status was likely to have been achieved by Edinburgh no later than the twelfth century.

It is of course important to note that the Old Town consisted of two distinct and independent burghs for hundreds of years. In c.1143, David I granted the Augustinian canons of Holyrood abbey the right to create a burgh on the ground between Calton Hill and Arthur's Seat, which led to the foundation of the burgh of Canongait ('the way or street of the canons'). Before long, Canongate, as it was later known, expanded up the ridge of the Royal Mile, with a demarcation point between the two burghs at the Netherbow Port (port is the old Scottish word for gate). It was only in 1856 that Canongate was formally integrated into the city of Edinburgh.

While the earliest Old Town dwellings were made of wood, by the late fifteenth century there is clear evidence that, thanks to advances in building technology, many houses were being constructed of stone. Public buildings and spaces were also impressive. The parish church of St Giles, begun in the twelfth century, was large and imposing. There were three powerful religious foundations: the monasteries of Greyfriars and Blackfriars and Holyrood abbey. The main thoroughfare, the *via Regia*, or King's Way, now the Royal Mile, had stone paving by the early sixteenth century, prompting a visitor in 1618, English poet John Taylor, to describe it as 'the fairest and goodliest streete that ever mine eyes beheld'.

As the population grew there was a need for more accommodation but the main problem was lack of space. The Old Town's geography militated against easy expansion: it was bounded to the north by a body of water – the Nor' (or north) loch

Previous pages: A wintry Old Town, viewed from Edinburgh castle

– and to the west and south by steep slopes. The need to secure the town against English incursions made the problem even more pronounced. There had been earlier defensive walls but the Flodden wall, constructed after the disastrous defeat at the eponymous battle in 1513, was on a different scale. It ran for almost one-and-a-half miles around the Old Town and was five-feet (1.5m) thick and twenty-five feet (7.6 m) tall. The Flodden wall – along with its extension, the Telfer wall of 1620 – might have been a necessary bulwark against aggressors but it constrained development for 250 years. New houses were built but they were predominantly tenements, built ever higher. Edinburgh was growing upwards, not outwards.

The land contours of the Old Town also dictated the unique pattern of its streets. It is an area characterised by narrow closes, wynds and courts leading off the spine of the Royal Mile, and forming a herringbone shape, one that is still very much in evidence today. There are also dramatic changes of level, not only in its streets but also within individual buildings, some of which have a different number of storeys at the front and back.

Life in the old closes

An Old Town close today is a very different thing to those of the past. A close in the twenty-first century is considerably cleaner, more open and in many cases shorter, leading to a courtyard, garden or sometimes just the back of a pub or restaurant.

Old Edinburgh closes were very narrow, often only three or four feet (1m) wide, and very cluttered. There were also animals wandering around, especially pigs, and there are many references to neighbour disputes caused by the control of livestock. However, one resident, Lord Gardenstone, an eighteenth-century judge, was careful to ensure that he did not upset his neighbours. He treated his pet pig like a dog, keeping it indoors and even letting it sleep in his bed, at least until it became too large at which juncture it slept on the floor on a pile of clothes. This arrangement suited the noble lord; it meant his judges robes were nice and warm in the morning.

The Lord Gardenstone story reminds us that until the New Town was built, different social classes lived cheek by jowl in these narrow alleys. Many of the names of Old Town closes are drawn from the prominent families who lived there, for example Lady Stair's Close, which is just off Lawnmarket, or Baron Maule's Close, next to Jeffrey Street. Rich and poor, quite literally, lived on top of each other. Over the centuries, as the population of Edinburgh grew, new houses were sourced by the simple expedient of building taller and taller tenements. Up to the fifteenth century, these were invariably wooden structures with thatched roofs and could be over ten-storeys high. Given the Old Town slope, a tenement could be up to fourteen storeys tall if measured from the lower side of the hill.

Wealthier residents of a tenement building would avoid living too close to street level, where the smells were hard to avoid, or too high up, which meant not only a lot of stairs but also a more dangerous residence. A wooden structure of more than four storeys was very unsafe; top floors could collapse or be blown down in strong winds, and, if fire broke out, it was much more difficult to escape.

One tale exemplifies what sharing these tenements could be like. Lord Coalstoun, an important judge in the mid-eighteenth century, liked to lean out of his

Overleaf: Published in *Civitates Orbis Terrarum*, an atlas of the world's cities, in 1582, this is one of the earliest images of Edinburgh. It shows the castle, St Giles, the Netherbow port, Kirk o' Field and the Flodden wall.

Castrum puellarum
EDE
EDENBURGUM,
SCOTIAE
METROPOLIS.

VRG.

window in Byres Close and discuss matters with lawyers on their way to the courts. On one occasion two girls were playing a game upstairs, which involved lowering a kitten on a piece of cord out of the window. The frightened creature landed on Lord Coalstoun's head, reached out with its claws and when the girls pulled it up the judge's wig came with it, forcing him to wrestle it out of the kitten's grasp. People of his ilk were probably very grateful when the New Town was built.

The decline of the Old Town

At the start of the seventeenth century, the Old Town was in an enviable position. It was the home of Scotland's sovereign, then James VI, resident in Holyrood palace, and around his royal court were clustered the grand houses of the nobility and senior churchmen in places like Cowgate and Canongate. The most important civic institutions were to be found in the Old Town, including the Scottish Parliament and the Court of Session, the country's supreme law court, while the institution that grew into the University of Edinburgh had been established in 1583. In addition, Edinburgh was now officially recognised as the capital of Scotland.

The first blow was the Union of Crowns of 1603, which saw James VI of Scotland become king of both Scotland and England, where he was designated James I. James promptly decamped to London, taking his court with him, as well as important royal financiers like the fabulously wealthy George Heriot. The departure of the royal court was an undoubted setback for the Old Town, both in political and economic terms, but there were some compensations during the century that followed. Edinburgh's chief magistrate was granted the title of Lord Provost, a new Parliament house was built on the Royal Mile between 1632–40 while the College of Edinburgh (Edinburgh University) was greatly expanded.

A more significant event than even the Union of Crowns occurred in 1707, when the Treaty of Union saw Scotland lose its status as an independent nation. With the legislature now also based at Westminster, there was no longer a need for a Scottish parliament and therefore no need for the governmental classes to maintain homes in Edinburgh. The result was that many Old Town houses were subdivided and let to poorer tenants, who could not afford to maintain them, creating a spiral of decline.

During the eighteenth century, as the population continued to increase, overcrowding in the restricted space of the Old Town grew exponentially, bringing with it associated problems like fire and infectious diseases. There was pressure from the more affluent classes for higher quality accommodation, and so, in 1767, the town council launched a competition for the design of new suburbs to the north of where Princes Street now stands. The winner was a young architect, James Craig, whose simple, yet brilliant, plan resulted in perhaps the finest example of urban planning anywhere in the world: the New Town.

While significant parts of the New Town were later redeveloped for commercial use, the original aim was to provide fine homes for the middle, and upper-middle, classes. Sweeping terraces and grand squares in the classical style sprang up and were complemented by fine gardens and elegant public buildings. With an earthly paradise on its doorstep, the Edinburgh elite quickly abandoned the Old Town, among them the great philosopher and historian, David Hume, who built a grand house in the New Town's St Andrew Square.

Disaster and rebirth

In the early hours of 24 November 1861, a building above Paisley Close, also known as East Bailie Fyfe's Close (which is on the north side of High Street, between John

The so-called 'Heave Awa' disaster of 1861 shocked Edinburgh and led to much-needed improvements in the Old Town.

Knox house and North Bridge), collapsed. Of the close's seventy-seven residents, thirty-five would either die that night or later in hospital. It was an event that became known as the 'Heave Awa' disaster because rescuers heard a survivor, Joseph McIvor, shouting 'Heave awa lads, I'm no' dead yet'. The replacement building has a memorial to those who died.

What happened that November night shocked Edinburgh, but, with hindsight, such a cataclysm was almost inevitable. In the mid-to-late nineteenth century, living conditions in the Old Town were, for too many of its people, appalling. The population of the inner-city had more than doubled from 82,000 in 1800 to around 170,000 by 1861. Overcrowding had reached critical proportions and it was not uncommon for fifteen families to be crowded into tenements just a few storeys high. Windowless dwellings were common, while sanitation was primitive and clean drinking water almost non-existent. Many of the old tenements, like the one that collapsed in Bailie Fyfe's Close, dated from the sixteenth century and were constructed mainly of wood.

Thanks to pressure from the public, action followed swiftly. By 1862, the first medical officer of health for the city, Henry (later Sir Henry) Littlejohn, was appointed. He set about his duties with the utmost vigour, collecting a huge amount of data on the effects that poor housing, lack of proper sanitation and overcrowding had on the health of Old Town residents. His report, published in 1865, was ground-breaking and showed, for example, that death rates in the Old Town were double those in the affluent New Town just a short distance to the north. To his credit, Edinburgh's Lord Provost, William Chambers, took the report very seriously. Bringing all

LoullyMakes
NICOLSON

of his political skills to bear, he promoted new legislation, which resulted in the City Improvement Act of 1867.

The Act led to huge changes. Many of the old slums were demolished and replaced with new thoroughfares like Chambers, Jeffrey and Market streets. Systems for water supply and drainage were introduced, new powers to inspect dairies, bakeries and meat markets were introduced and the reporting of infectious disease became compulsory. The reform programme proved to be highly effective: within a few decades, mortality rates more than halved.

At around the same time, the ideas of the man who became known as the 'father of town planning', Sir Patrick Geddes, were beginning to bear fruit. Geddes, an academic, promoted the concept of 'conservative surgery', which emphasised conserving and refurbishing older properties where this was feasible. With his guidance, many of the old courts and closes were improved, including James's Court, Wardrop's Court and the project most associated with him, Riddle's Court. However, Geddes was also involved in the provision of new housing and his development of the visually striking Ramsay Garden, which incorporated the eighteenth-century house of poet Allan Ramsay, is perhaps the best example of this (*see Walk 2 for more on Geddes*).

The campaign to improve the Old Town continued into the twentieth century, especially after the Second World War. Much of the credit must go to Ebenezer MacRae, the highly energetic city architect who did so much to shape modern Edinburgh. There was a particular focus on Canongate, where the eminent conservation architect, Sir Robert Hurd, worked to restore many of the older tenements. The photograph opposite, of 189–191 Canongate, which was built in the seventeenth century, shows how effective that work was. It also helped that Edinburgh's municipal authorities established the Old Town Conservation Area in 1977.

However, despite these efforts, the Old Town continued to decline with the number of gap sites on an upward trajectory and the population falling to a new low in the 1981 census. As a result, the Edinburgh Old Town Renewal Trust was founded in 1985 to coordinate the work of a range of agencies. Since then, many older buildings have been refurbished and there is a strong desire to ensure that new development respects the history and traditions of Scotland's most historic area.

World Heritage Site

The work done by Geddes, MacRae and others is cited by UNESCO as one of the reasons that the Old Town, along with the New Town, was designated a World Heritage Site in 1995. As UNESCO points out, along with the other sites worldwide, Edinburgh's two outstanding and very different towns are of 'outstanding value to humanity'. One is an example of 'organic medieval growth' while the other grew out of 'eighteenth and nineteenth century town planning'.

The important work of preserving and maintaining the historic buildings of the Old Town is an ongoing process. The World Heritage designation is undoubtedly a bulwark against unsympathetic development.

Opposite: The renovated 189–191 Canongate

THE WALKS

Facing page: Acheson house, which dates from the seventeenth century and is one of the finest buildings in the Old Town

NEMO ME IMPUNE LACESSIT

WALK 1
THE ESPLANADE, EDINBURGH CASTLE AND THE CASTLE ROCK

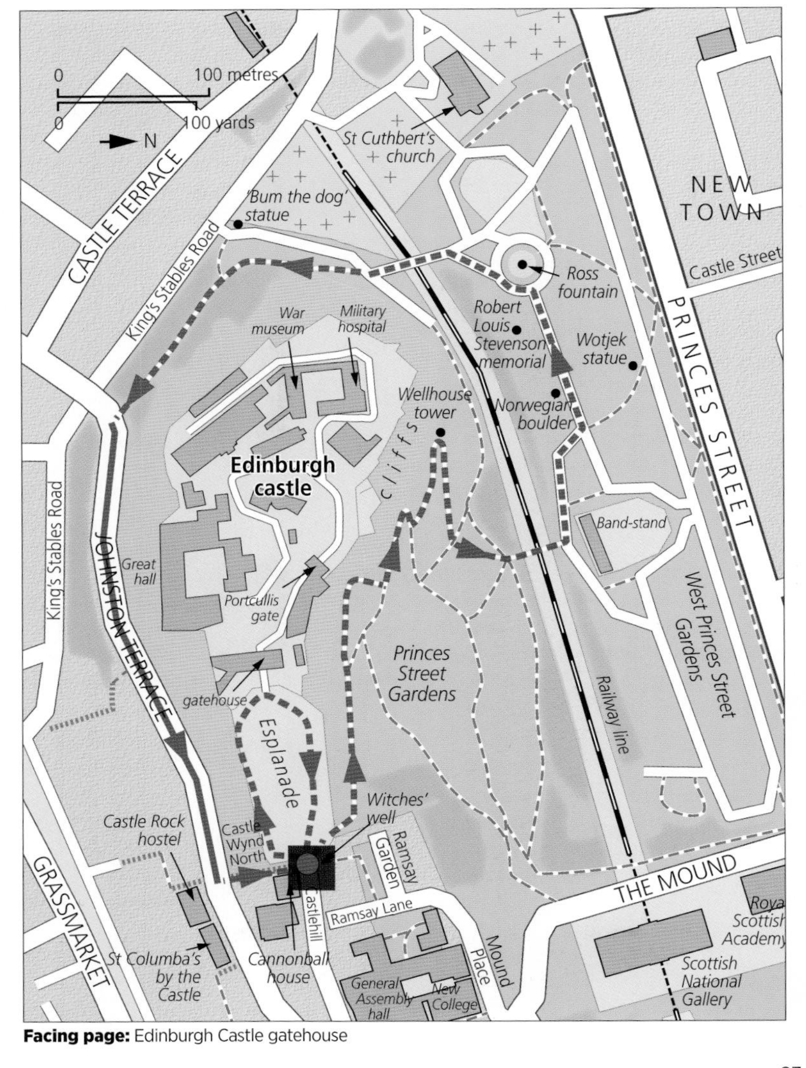

Facing page: Edinburgh Castle gatehouse

Start Esplanade, east side, at the top of Royal Mile.

Summary After a walk around the esplanade, with its impressive military monuments and statues, we circumnavigate Edinburgh castle and its forbidding volcanic cliffs. Along the way we take in Princes Street Gardens, as well as superb views of the Pentland hills, the New Town and Fife.

Highlights Edinburgh castle • Esplanade military monuments • Robert the Bruce and William Wallace statues • Castle cliffs • Wellhouse tower • Princes Street Gardens (west) and statues • Ross fountain • Historic churches • the Robert Louis Stevenson story • Cannonball house • In-depth: Witchcraft in Scotland.

The Walk

We begin at the entrance to the esplanade at the top of the Royal Mile. The esplanade was first built in 1753 as a parade ground and was significantly enlarged during the nineteenth century. Today it is best known as a venue for concerts and ceremonial events, and, in particular, as the home of the world-famous Edinburgh military tattoo, a spectacular event staged annually, in August.

Before we start walking, face the castle.

From here we can see the gatehouse, the entrance to the castle, and above and behind it the curved shape of the half-moon battery. This was built after the *lang* (long) siege of 1571–3, when much of the castle was destroyed during a stand-off between the supporters of Mary, Queen of Scots and the Earl of Lennox, regent to her infant son, James VI *(see 'Discovering Edinburgh Castle')*. The mighty David's tower – built in the late fourteenth century by King David II, the son of Robert the Bruce – was the most important part of the structure lost in the siege.

Turn left and walk to the edge of the esplanade. The view south includes several interesting buildings, such as George Heriot's school, a seventeenth-century Scottish Renaissance masterpiece funded by the eponymous royal goldsmith and banker, 'Jinglin' Geordie Heriot. Note also the red sandstone, Beaux Arts-style Edinburgh College of Art of 1906 (by architect J. M. Dick Peddie). Further south you can see the Pentland hills; the white lines on the hill to the south-west are the artificial ski slopes of the Midlothian snow-sports centre.

Turn right and walk beside the south wall of the esplanade. Here we will pass three monuments of interest, all commemorating Scottish regiments.

The first is a bronze plaque dedicated to David Leslie, Earl of Leven and the regiment he raised in 1689, which would be later known as the King's Own Scottish Borderers. Leven's Regiment of Foot was created to support William and Mary against the Jacobite forces of the deposed James VII, and, despite being routed in the battle of Killiecrankie just five months after its inception, Leven's regiment carried on, acquiring a sterling reputation. Like many famous Scottish regiments its legacy lives on today as the 1st battalion, the Royal Regiment of Scotland.

The next plaque honours the Gordon Highlanders, specifically those men who died

David Leslie plaque

Gordon Highlanders memorial plaque

in the Second Boer War of 1899–1902. Alongside a list of those who fell is the stag's head, a representation of the unit's cap badge, and the Gordon motto *Bydand*, the Scots word for 'waiting', as in the English phrase 'to bide your time'. The Gordons suffered heavy casualties in the conflict but were justifiably lauded for their efforts in defending the town of Ladysmith and at the Battle of Doomkop. It was here that Winston Churchill, then a young war correspondent, described the Gordons as 'the finest regiment in the world'.

Argyllshire Highlanders/Princess Louise fountain

The final memorial on this side of the esplanade is a decorative drinking fountain/horse trough that emphasises the links between the 91st Argyllshire Highlanders and Princess Louise, the fourth daughter of Queen Victoria. The 91st had formed the honour guard at the 1871 wedding of Louise and John Campbell, the future Duke of Argyll. A year later the regiment changed its name to Princess Louise's Argyllshire Highlanders and added her coronet to Campbell's boar-head emblem, both of which are carved into the memorial. In her will Princess Louise left the Lorne jewels (a diamond-and-pearl necklace and a locket) to the Scottish people and they are on display in the castle alongside the crown jewels.

Following the wall of the esplanade, we reach the gatehouse. This was a relatively late addition to Edinburgh castle, built in 1888. The trench under the bridge is much older: it was dug by the castle garrison in 1714 after Queen Anne's death, due to concerns about a Jacobite rebellion.

On the gatehouse, there is a crown, a brightly coloured lion rampant and the Latin phrase *nemo me impune lacessit*. The first two are royal symbols and the use of the lion rampant as the royal standard of Scottish monarchs goes back to the eleventh century. The Latin phrase means 'nobody cuts me with impunity' and can be dated back to coins minted during the reign of James IV, although it might be even older. The two statues on either side of the bridge that leads to the gatehouse are of Scotland's two great heroes: King Robert the Bruce (*left*) and Sir William Wallace (*see photo on page 22*) and were unveiled in 1929. The flags on the poles sometimes change though most commonly you will find the Scottish saltire, the lion rampant, the Edinburgh castle logo and the flag of the military garrison, which is red and green with a castle in the centre.

It is possible to enter the gatehouse and outer courtyard before having to buy a ticket. Look for the carvings of cannons, soldiers

72nd Highlanders monument

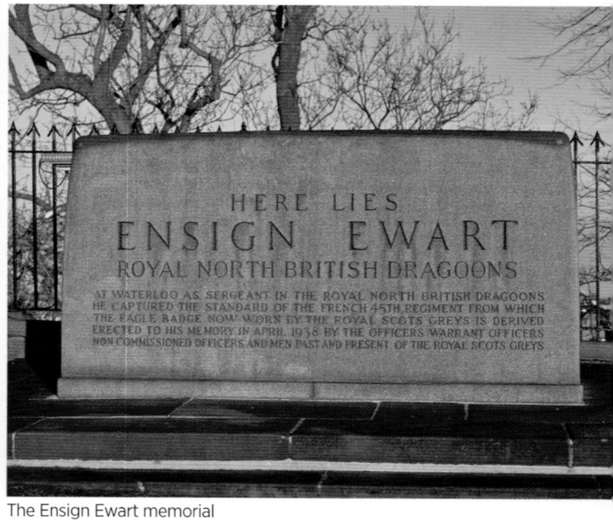

The Ensign Ewart memorial

and other military weapons on the walls to the left and right as you walk through the gatehouse. When you reach the outer courtyard, you should investigate the sixteenth-century Portcullis gate, which, like the half-moon battery, was built after the front of the castle was devastated during the *lang* siege. (*see 'Discovering Edinburgh Castle'*).

Return to the esplanade and continue following the esplanade round.

On the left, just after the gatehouse, a plaque explains that some of the land underfoot is part of Nova Scotia. This is because in 1625, Sir William Alexander of Menstrie, Earl of Stirling, became Baron of Nova Scotia. A ritual part of receiving this honour involved taking 'sasine', which meant symbolically receiving earth and stone from the land he now possessed. Rather than go to the trouble of travelling to North America, part of the Castlehill was decreed to be Nova Scotia, and that was the ground the Earl was given.

We will now walk past the military monuments on the north side of the esplanade.

The first is a pink granite obelisk of 1883 (McDonald, Field and Co.), sometimes known as the Afghan Needle, which honours the fallen of the 72nd Duke of Albany's Own Highlanders regiment in the Afghan war of 1878–80. The 72nd distinguished itself, winning four battle honours, including at Kandahar where it routed the enemy despite having endured a gruelling 320-mile march from Kabul. Initially known as the 78th Highland Regiment of Foot when it was raised in 1778, the unit was renamed in honour of Frederick, Duke of York and Albany (*see Frederick's biography below*). The regiment has had several iterations since then, including being part of a later amalgamation that created the Seaforth Highlanders.

A granite slab (William H. Kininmonth, 1938) marks the burial place of Charles Ewart (Ensign Ewart), one of Scotland's greatest heroes. The plaque details the heroics he performed at the Battle of Waterloo in 1815 (*see Ewart panel on page 29*).

The next monument we come to is a bronze statue (Thomas Campbell, 1839) of Frederick Augustus, Duke of York and Albany (1763–1827), second son of George III and commander-in-chief of the army between 1798 and 1809. The statue depicts Frederick

Frederick, Duke of York

Scottish Horse monument

Colonel MacKenzie cross

in heroic pose, wearing the robes of a Knight of the Garter with the baton of a field-marshal in his right hand. In reality he was unsuccessful in battle, losing badly to the French in Flanders in 1794, and again in Holland in 1799. The mocking nursery rhyme 'The Grand Old Duke of York' is said to have been written with Frederick in mind. His real interest was military administration, a field in which he excelled, but he was forced to resign as commander-in-chief in 1809 when his mistress, Mary Anne Clarke, was found to have been selling army commissions. Frederick has a strong connection to Edinburgh, despite never visiting the city, being one of the two princes after whom Princes Street is named (the other is his older brother, the future George IV).

Next to the Duke is a memorial (Stewart McGlashan and Son, 1905) to those members of the Scottish Horse regiment who died in South Africa in the second Boer War of 1899–1902. A pink granite Celtic cross, it features a lion rampant on a shield, a carved sword, detailed scrollwork, a battered rock-cut plinth made from Peterhead granite and plaques on three sides. The memorial also incorporates the regimental motto, *nemo me impune lacessit,* the same as on the Scottish coat of arms, and a list of those who died, including the names of several Zulu scouts. The history of the Scottish Horse begins in 1900 when army commander Lord Kitchener sanctioned the raising of two new regiments of mounted infantry. These consisted of Scots, or those of Scottish heritage, living in South Africa, with their ranks supplemented by men from other parts of the British Empire, most notably Australia. Amongst many notable honours the Scottish Horse received was the award of the Victoria Cross to an 18-year-old lieutenant, William English.

The next monument is another Celtic cross. These are modern recreations of the many Pictish crosses in Scotland and are the earliest evidence of the conversion of the Picts. The National Museum of Scotland has some of these ancient crosses on display. This one (Sir John Steell, 1875) commemorates Dundee-born Colonel Kenneth MacKenzie (1811–73), who served for a combined forty-two years in the 92nd Highlanders and on the army staff. The memorial to the respected soldier, who fought in several

Ensign Charles Ewart

In June 1815 a small town in Belgium gave its name to the most famous battle in history: Waterloo. Two mighty armies – one under the command of Napoleon Bonaparte and the other led by the Duke of Wellington – would fight to the death to determine the fate of Europe. As might be expected, there were many Scots in Wellington's army, including Ayrshire-born Charles Ewart, a sergeant in the 2nd Royal North British Regiment of Dragoons, otherwise known as the Scots Greys. At 45, he must have been one of the oldest combatants on the field, yet age was no handicap to Ewart. During fierce hand-to-hand combat, the valiant sergeant – said to be a giant of a man – slew several French soldiers before capturing the imperial eagle of France from the crack 45th *regiment de ligne*, known in the French army as the 'Invincibles'. Made of gilded bronze and commissioned by Napoleon Bonaparte himself, the imperial eagle, the aigle eployée, was a hugely significant symbol for the French army.

It is said that Ewart was even prouder of the heroics he performed before capturing the eagle. Engaged in a joust with a French officer who was an expert swordsman, Ewart disarmed his foe and would have dispatched him but for the intervention of his superior, Cornet Francis Kinchant, who ordered the mighty sergeant to show mercy. Ewart complied, at which juncture the Frenchman gratefully surrendered his sword to Kinchant and was told to go to the rear. However, as Ewart wheeled away to re-engage the enemy he heard the sharp report of a pistol. Turning around, he saw Cornet Kinchant fall from his horse, fatally wounded, while the French officer whose life had been spared was tucking a pistol into his coat. Enraged by such a dastardly act Ewart decapitated the Frenchman with a single swing of his sword.

In the immediate aftermath of the battle Ewart was promoted to lieutenant, and later to the rank of ensign, and was also awarded the Waterloo medal. His regiment redesigned its badge to honour the capture of the eagle standard, which is now on display in the regimental museum in Edinburgh castle. There is also a marvellous painting in the great hall of the castle that celebrates Ewart's heroism: *The Fight for the Standard* by the Victorian artist, Richard Ansdell (reproduced on facing page).

When Charles Ewart left the army, he moved to the north-west of England, perhaps because his wife hailed from Stockport. He died in 1846 at the age of 77, in Salford, and was buried in a churchyard in that city. When a factory was built on the site of the churchyard, Ewart's grave was lost for decades until it was discovered after an exhaustive search by a sergeant-major in the Scots Greys. Thus, in 1938, his body was exhumed, transported home to Scotland and reinterred with full ceremonial honours on the Castle esplanade. It was a fitting tribute to one of Scotland's greatest-ever heroes.

Facing page: *The Fight for the Standard* by Richard Ansdell

India Cross

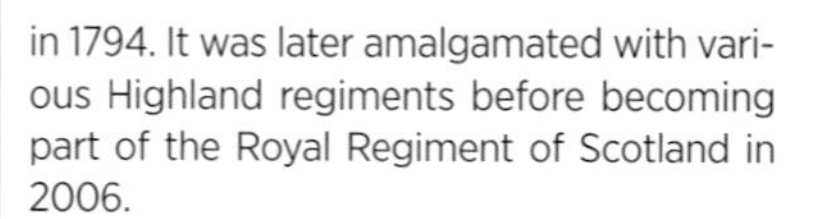

Witches well

theatres including the Crimean war of 1853–6, was paid for by his friends and colleagues. The richly carved cross sits on a rubble plinth and features a sword and images of wild and fantastic beasts.

The final Celtic cross here (Sir Robert Rowand Anderson, 1861) is sometimes known as the India Cross and commemorates soldiers of the 78th Highland regiment who fell in the battles of 1857–8, known at the time as the Indian Mutiny, but also as the First War of Indian Independence. In that conflict the regiment as a whole won the Victoria Cross for its heroism in relieving the city of Lucknow. The elephant motif on the cross relates to an older Indian campaign, of 1803, and it became an important of the regiment's identity, so much so that, in the 1830s, an elephant was even brought to Edinburgh by the 78th: the great beast led parades through the city, slept in the castle stables and drank beer through the canteen windows. Sometimes known as the Ross-shire Buffs, the 78th Highland was formed by F. H. Mackenzie, 1st Baron Seaforth, in 1793 and first saw action against the French in 1794. It was later amalgamated with various Highland regiments before becoming part of the Royal Regiment of Scotland in 2006.

Before leaving the castle esplanade, turn to the right and walk across to the wall of the building which sits at the front of the esplanade entrance.

On the wall is a small drinking fountain and a plaque. This is the witches well, which remembers the more than three hundred people, mostly women, who between 1479 and 1722 were executed within a few feet of this spot for the 'crime' of witchcraft (*see 'Witchcraft in Scotland' pp. 38–9*). The fountain was sculpted, in 1894, by John Duncan, a leading figure in the Celtic revival movement, and consists of two heads, one wicked, one helpful, the flowers of the foxglove and snakes. These symbolise dual purposes, evil and wisdom.

Turn left, walk past the picturesque residences of Ramsay Garden (*see Walk 2*) with the carved cherub on the wall, and exit the esplanade via the gate that leads to the northern slopes of the mighty hill.

Wellhouse tower

'Wotjek the bear' statue

As you walk down the path you have an opportunity to appreciate the sheer cliffs of the castle rock and the size of the castle's battlements as well as an excellent view of the gardens and the New Town and beyond that to Fife.

At the first fork, take the right. At the junction, go left and when you reach a dead end go down two sets of stairs, going left until you reach a group of ruins.

These ruined buildings are the remnants of the Wellhouse tower, built in 1362 by burgess Roger Hog to protect St Margaret's well, which was named for Queen Margaret (*see 'The Old Town: A Short History'*), a natural spring that supplied fresh water to the castle. Look up and you can see the remains of the foundations, from which a crane lifted up the water buckets. The well was of such importance to the castle that, during the *lang* siege of 1573, the troops commanded by Regent Morton (who had replaced Regent Lennox) went to great lengths to prevent its use, including heavy artillery bombardment and arsenic poisoning. By the seventeenth century the tower was a virtual ruin, and, apart from making the structure safe, little has been done since. Around the front of the structure a stone plaque gives more details.

Continuing along the path you reach a bridge over the railway tracks; go over it.

This area is Princes Street Gardens. Originally marshland, in 1450 watercourses were diverted and the area became a shallow lake, the Nor' loch. The loch was slowly drained during the course of the eighteenth and nineteenth centuries and the beautiful gardens were created.

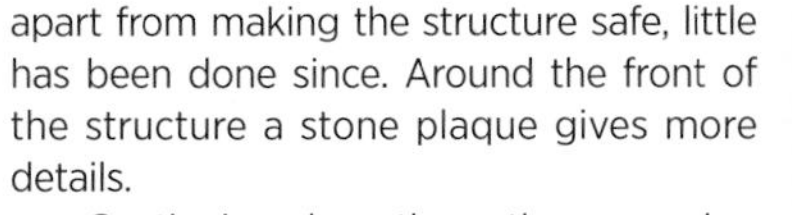

When you cross the bridge, turn left.

The Ross bandstand on the right has been the venue for concerts since 1877. At the time of writing, plans are being discussed to renovate the venue to show more entertainment such as the concerts and firework displays during Hogmanay and the Edinburgh International Festival.

When you reach the main path, turn left and walk along it.

On the path to our right, which leads up to Princes Street, you may be able to see a statue of a soldier – and bear. This is Wojtek,

Robert Louis Stevenson memorial

a Syrian brown bear acquired by Polish troops in Iran during the Second World War and who became a favoured friend of the unit. Indeed, the badge of the 22nd artillery supply company of the Polish 2nd Corps is that of a bear carrying a missile, a design adopted after Wojtek apparently helped troops carry shells during the Battle of Monte Cassino in 1943–44. Because Wotjek had been adopted by the Polish soldiers when he was a cub he came to regard them almost as his parents and was never a danger to humans. He loved cigarettes, which he ate, and also beer, and would peer down the bottle after it was empty, looking for more. After the war Wojtek came with his Polish troops to the Scottish Borders and for the final years of his life lived in Edinburgh zoo. A plaque gives more information.

Continue along the main path, and, on the left, there is a boulder, transported from Norway and placed in the gardens as a memorial to the solidarity between Norwegian and British forces during the Second World War.

Also on the left is a path that leads to a small gravestone surrounded by silver birch trees. The inscription, 'R.L.S. A MAN OF LETTERS 1850–1894', is the only indication that this is dedicated to the great writer, Robert Louis Stevenson. According to the Stevenson Trust, which erected the memorial (designed by Ian Hamilton Finlay) in 1987, Stevenson's letters reveal that he did not want a statue, and this modest stone is for a modest man (*see Stevenson panel below*).

When you reach the Ross fountain, stop, and look up at the castle on the left.

From here we can see the former military hospital and just behind it the Scottish National War Museum (*see 'Discovering Edinburgh Castle'*).

The Ross fountain was cast in Paris and installed in 1872, having been on display in London ten years earlier. The gun-maker Daniel Ross bought it and gifted it to the city. When it was unveiled the hierarchy of the nearby churches of St Cuthbert's and St John the Evangelist were said to be displeased at the fountain's celebration of nudity. The four nymphs under the naked woman at the top represent arts, science, poetry and industry and below them are mermaids. In 2001 the fountain was restored but by 2015 it had fallen into disrepair and funds were found to restore it to working order. Following repair work the fountain, now fully functional, was returned to site in 2018.

Behind the fountain, you can see the backs of St Cuthbert's church, and, further to the right at the west end of Princes Street, the nineteenth century Episcopal church of St John the Evangelist. St Cuthbert's occupies a site that, it is said, has had a Christian place of worship since the eighth century. The structure we see today is by Hippolyte J. Blanc and dates from the 1890s although its steeple is a survivor from a predecessor church of the late eighteenth century. St John is a wonderful Gothic design of the late nineteenth century by William Burn.

Go left, take the left path and walk over the bridge.

After crossing the bridge, a sign on the right gives information about the plants in the area. Take the left path leading up round the foot of the cliffs of the castle rock.

Ross fountain

From this higher position, looking right you can see the top of the large, redbrick Caledonian hotel which was built as part of the much-loved Princes Street railway station, once the largest station in Scotland but which closed in 1965. To the left, and closer to us, is the back of the more modern Traverse theatre, which, with the Usher hall and Lyceum theatre, is part of a significant cultural hub. This grand, purpose-built facility hides the Traverse's beginnings. It started in the 1960s in a former brothel in the Lawnmarket and as well as experimental theatre it became known for accidental stabbings during performances in which real knives were used.

Follow the path round. On your left, next to signs prohibiting climbing the castle rock, is a small plaque on an aspect of the surrender of the castle in 1689 to troops loyal to William of Orange in the wake of the Glorious Revolution of 1688 (*see 'Discovering Edinburgh Castle'*). This is a reconstruction of another plaque, which you can see up on the castle walls above a small gate.

To the right, on the path below, there is a bronze statue of a dog (King's Stables Road entrance to Princes Street Gardens). It is of 'Bum', a St Bernard-spaniel cross from San Diego, California. San Diego has been Edinburgh's twin city since 1978, and, in 2008, to promote the link a statue of Bum was erected in Edinburgh while at the same time a statue of Edinburgh's very own legendary dog, Greyfriars Bobby, was erected in San

'Bum the dog' statue

Robert Louis Stevenson

Along with Sir Walter Scott and Robert Burns, Robert Louis Stevenson (1850–94) is one of Scotland's three great literary figures. Very popular during his lifetime, his work is still widely read, in particular the novels *Treasure Island*, *The Strange Case of Dr Jekyll and Mr Hyde* and *Kidnapped*. While some academic critics have been less than kind about his oeuvre, Stevenson had many notable admirers, among them distinguished contemporaries such as Henry James, Rudyard Kipling and Mark Twain.

Robert Lewis (later Louis) Balfour Stevenson was born into Edinburgh's upper-middle class. His father, Thomas Stevenson, was a scion of the eminent 'Lighthouse Stevensons', while on his mother's side he was descended from Church of Scotland ministers and university professors. When Robert was seven the family moved to 17 Heriot Row, one of the most prestigious addresses in the New Town, home to the city's *haute bourgeoisie*. While he would later characterise his childhood as a golden age the realty is he was a sickly child who suffered from bronchitis, pneumonia and feverish colds. It was during the long periods confined to bed that his imagination was fired, helped in no small measure by the storytelling talents of his nurse, Alison Cunningham, whom he called 'Cummy'. Even before he could write he was dictating stories to his mother and Cummy.

In 1867 Stevenson went up to Edinburgh University where – under the influence of his father – he read engineering. It was a subject for which he displayed considerable aptitude and he loved to visit the harbour and lighthouse projects being undertaken by his father's firm. However, other aspects were anathema to him, and he had a particular dread of being cooped up in an office. He confessed to his parents that he cared for nothing but literature and that he intended to devote his life to writing. To please his parents, and strictly as a compromise, he switched to the law, and, in 1875, was called to the Scottish bar. But he practised only briefly as an advocate; the lure of the literary world was too strong.

Now free from what he considered the stifling morality of the professional classes, the persona and lifestyle he adopted was that of the bohemian; he wore his hair long and favoured velvet jackets and other flamboyances. Frequently found in Edinburgh's many pubs and brothels – much to the annoyance of his strict Presbyterian father – he enjoyed the company of seamen, chimney sweeps and thieves. It was at this time he rejected the strict Presbyterianism espoused by his family, although its Calvinistic principles would inform much of his work.

By the late 1870s Stevenson had made tentative forays into the world of literature, and his work appeared in a range of magazines. In 1878, his first book, *An Inland Voyage*, was published and proved to be a critical success. This was followed a year later by *Travels with a Donkey in the Cevennes*, the most acclaimed work from his early period. It was in France at this time that he met the great love of his life, Fanny Osbourne, an American woman, ten years his senior, who was married with two children. When Fanny returned home in 1879 Stevenson made the rash decision to follow her. It was an arduous journey, particularly for someone in poor health: from Glasgow to New York by sea and then overland to California. In fact, he almost died due to a lung haemorrhage and only pulled through thanks to Fanny's devoted nursing. He would be a virtual invalid for the rest of his life.

After Fanny divorced

Robert Louis Stevenson

the couple married and they returned to Scotland where Stevenson began a novel, *Treasure Island*, published in 1883. It was inspired by a map he had drawn to amuse his stepson, Lloyd Osbourne, and it tells the story of an epic sea voyage to recover treasure buried by Captain Flint, a pirate. It is a thrilling read, full of memorable characters like Long John Silver, Ben Gunn and Jim Hawkins. Perennially popular, the book has never been out of print and has been adapted many times for the big screen, television, radio and the stage, its influence clear in swashbuckling films like *Pirates of the Caribbean*.

However, it was his next novel, *The Strange Case of Dr Jekyll and Mr Hyde* (1886) that brought him worldwide fame. Drawing on Stevenson's fascination with the good and evil parts of a man's character it relates the story of the respectable physician, Dr Jekyll, who discovers a drug that transforms him into an evil-doer, Mr Hyde. It was an instant best-seller and highly influential, with the phrase 'Jekyll and Hyde character' becoming proverbial. Stevenson's reputation soared even higher with *Kidnapped*, also published in 1886, a novel that perfectly captures the febrile state of Scotland after the Jacobite rising of 1745.

Still in his mid-thirties, Stevenson's reputation as a great writer was now secure. Yet his health continued to deteriorate and he looked for more agreeable climes. In 1888 he embarked on the first of his Pacific voyages, visiting Hawaii, Tahiti and Samoa. He would spend the last four years of his life in Samoa, on the beautiful plantation of Vailima with its stunning views of the ocean. He had great empathy with the Samoans, who nicknamed him Tusitala (writer of tales), and his time on the island was highly productive. The sequel to *Kidnapped*, *Catriona*, was penned there as was his unfinished masterpiece *Weir of Hermiston*. Robert Louis Stevenson died in December 1894 and was buried, according to his wishes, in Samoa, at the summit of Mount Vaea.

Left and right: Cannonball house.

Diego. Bobby and Bum are located next to each other in San Diego while in Edinburgh, because of a council decision, they are separated by the length of Grassmarket.

Bum appears to have arrived in southern California from San Francisco in the late 1880s without an owner. In San Diego, he roamed freely, developed a taste for beer, gave rides to small children and gained popularity for his independent spirit, becoming an unofficial city mascot. Bum was a local celebrity; his exploits were documented in local newspapers and his image was reproduced on city dog licences. His popularity reached new heights after a railyard fight with a bulldog, during the course of which he was hit by a train and lost part of his right foot. However, from then until the end of his life he was well looked after by the people of San Diego.

As you round the castle rock the path leads up the hill to Johnston Terrace. Enter the terrace, turn left and continue up the hill with the castle esplanade now on your left. If you cross the road you will be able to look down onto Grassmarket and at the same time have a good view of south Edinburgh.

When you reach the base of the Castle Wynd North stairs you have nearly finished the walk. All that remains is to look to the right at two interesting structures: Castle Rock hostel (15 Johnston Terrace), built in 1846 and turned into a backpackers' hostel in 1997, and St Columba's by the Castle (14 Johnston Terrace), a small church of 1846 in the Gothic style, designed by John Henderson for local Episcopalians. Then go up the Castle Wynd North stairs on the left.

Near the top, look at the building on the right (356 Castlehill). It dates from the late sixteenth century, although it has been much remodelled since, and is known as Cannonball house. Just below the top two windows a metal ball is lodged into the west wall. A romantic story claims it is a cannonball fired from Edinburgh castle at Bonnie Prince Charlie's temporary residence, Holyrood palace, during the Jacobite occupation of Edinburgh in 1745. However, the truth is more prosaic. The ball marks the gravitational height of water pumped from Comiston springs to the Castlehill reservoir on the other side of the street.

We have now reached the end of our walk. Perhaps you would like to try another. In which case the starting point is just down the Castlehill and on the right.

The massed pipes and drums of the Royal Edinburgh Military Tattoo, castle esplanade

The Tattoo is staged every August on the esplanade and with marching bands, dancers and musicians it is one of the most spectacular shows of its kind anywhere in the world. It began in 1950 and, thanks to its continued popularity with audiences, sells out year after year. It is estimated that fourteen million people have seen a performance, with more than two hundred thousand attending annually. Although dominated by Scottish themes, complemented by a significant input from across the armed forces of the United Kingdom, the Tattoo has long been a cosmopolitan affair and by 2018 performers from forty-eight countries had taken part. In this photograph, the massed pipes and drums are led by Brian Alexander, senior drum major.

IN DEPTH

Witchcraft in Scotland

Although Scottish people had long believed in the existence of witches it was not until the Protestant Reformation in the mid-sixteenth century that the practice of witch-hunting took hold. In 1563 an Act designating witchcraft as a capital offence was passed and from then until the late seventeenth century Scotland experienced five great witch panics, which saw between three and four thousand people being charged with this 'crime', with most tried in Edinburgh. Around half of those accused were executed, usually by strangulation, burning or drowning.

THE DEVIL'S MARK AND 'WITCH-PRICKERS'

It is estimated that nine out of ten of those accused of witchcraft were women, most of them older and poorer than the general population. According to the beliefs of the time, women were turned into witches at satanic courts, which were held in graveyards, especially those with a ruined kirk. The devil would say a black mass and then 'lie carnally' with the aspiring witch, before cutting her and baptising her with her own blood. From that day on the witch bore the 'devil's mark', the place from where the blood had been drawn. It led to a bizarre new profession: that of 'witch-pricker', men who used used long pins to poke the bodies of accused witches, hoping to find the 'devil's mark', on which it was thought the witch felt no pain. Prickers were only paid if they found this spot, and, unsurprisingly, they almost always did.

THE ROYAL CONNECTION

James VI (1566–1625), son of Mary, Queen of Scots, is widely regarded as Scotland's most successful sovereign. Highly educated and possessed of a keen intellect, he was also sufficiently calculating to manoeuvre himself onto the English throne in 1603, becoming James VI of Scotland and James I of England. Despite his intellectual sophistication, he was a believer in the occult and witchcraft, even penning a book, *Demonologie*, on the subject. When, in 1590, his return to Scotland with Anne of Denmark, his new wife, was disrupted by storms James was convinced the bad weather was due to a witch's spell. It led to his active participation in the most notorious and wide-ranging trial of them all, that of the North Berwick witches, held from 1590–1.

THE SAD CASE OF GEILLIS DUNCAN

During the period 1590–1 almost one hundred people were tried for the crime of witchcraft in the Old Town. The whole process started when Geillis 'Gilly' Duncan, a serving maid from Tranent in East Lothian, was suspected by her employer, David Seaton, a local official, of being a witch. He had heard stories of Gilly's healing powers and when he discovered that she was absent from her room nearly every night he became convinced that his young servant was a witch. Seaton tortured her and found a small blemish on her throat, which he claimed was the devil's mark. After suffering even more barbaric torture, Gilly, now driven to distraction by fear and pain, named many others as witches.

THE GREAT WITCH TRIALS OF 1590–1

King James, on being given the names of those implicated by Gilly Duncan, immediately ordered that they be brought to Holyrood palace. One of the unfortunate accused, Agnes Sampson, was tortured and although she at first denied all the charges she eventually could take no more and confessed that along with many others she took part in a 'Witches Sabbat' in North Berwick on Halloween night, 1590. Held in a haunted church, Agnes told how two hundred witches had convened with the Devil himself and that during the proceedings had discussed the best way to kill King James. One method involved extracting the venom from a black toad to cast a death spell on the King. When the King, who was present at the trial, declared that her account was too far-fetched Agnes did her best to prove she was telling the truth: she whispered to James the exact words he had spoken to Anne of Denmark on their wedding night. James, now convinced she was telling the truth, ordered her to be executed.

As the court proceedings continued close to a hundred people were dragged into the net, including the Earl of Bothwell. Most were tortured, invariably in the cruellest way possible. Dr John Fian, a schoolteacher and Bothwell's secretary, had his fingernails pulled out and needles plunged into the quicks of his

King James VI interrogating Agnes Sampson and three of her fellow witches.

fingers; he was then subjected to the 'boot', a device in which the legs were encased and then crushed. Finally, Fian, after confessing, was strangled and then burned on the Castle Hill.

AGNES FINNIE: EDINBURGH'S MOST NOTORIOUS WITCH

Agnes Finnie was a widow who lived in Potterow on the southern limits of the Old Town, in the parish of Greyfriars. Her accusers described her as being bad-tempered, spiteful and quick to curse her adversaries. Agnes was also accused of causing illness, striking people dumb and summoning the Devil to bite a chunk of flesh from those who confronted her. It is certainly true that many people who crossed her lived to regret it, almost immediately (though obviously coincidentally) going down with unexpected ailments.

In common with many other cases of the time, the motives for Agnes Finnie's anger were local and domestic. She was a shopkeeper and small-time moneylender, which naturally led to disputes. It is said she refused credit to some and fought with others over the lending terms. Each time it was said that Agnes swore revenge, cursing those who treated her badly. This was what led to her trial in late 1644.

The case was a complicated one and she argued strongly that the complaints against her were both false and malicious. Sadly, for Agnes, she was found guilty and sentenced to be strangled and burnt on the Castle Hill, a punishment that was duly carried out in March 1645.

EVENTS
CAFE
e Hub
TICKETS
BUSINESSES OPEN AS USUAL

WALK 2
CASTLEHILL AND THE TOP OF THE OLD TOWN

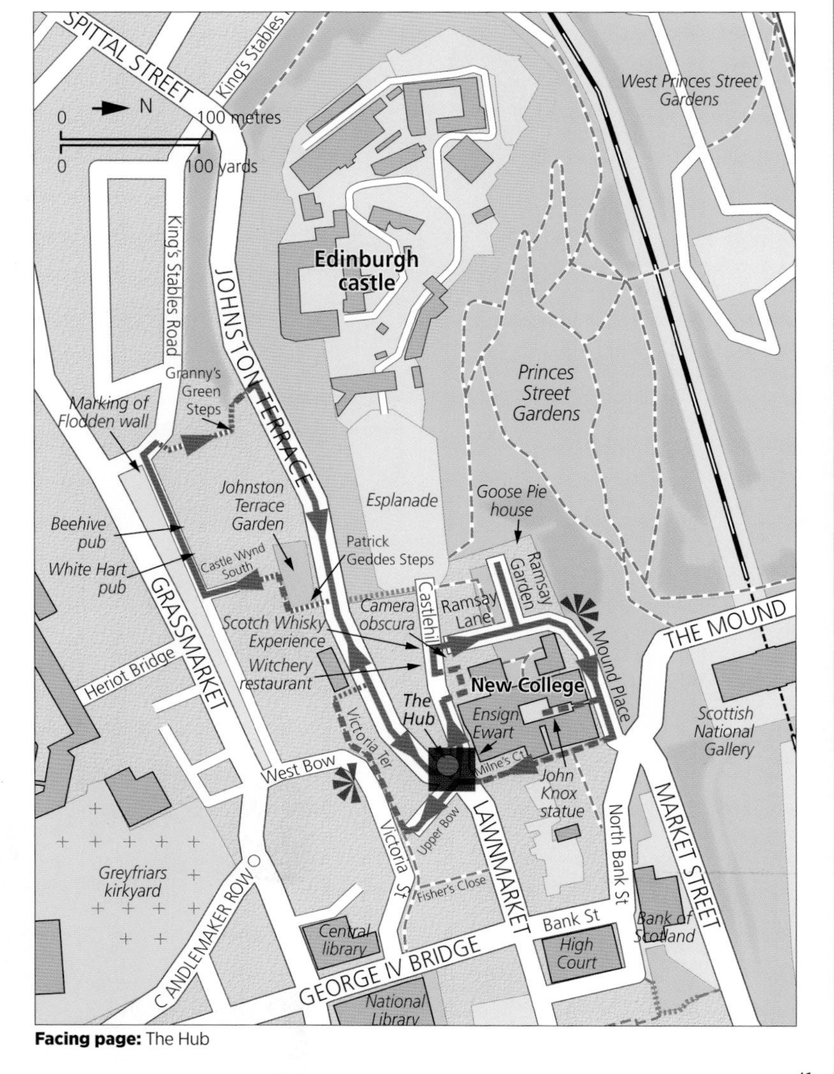

Facing page: The Hub

Start The Hub (formerly Tolbooth St John's church), 348 Castlehill

Summary We walk up Castlehill, taking in historic closes, and then view Ramsay Garden with its distinctive architecture. The walk moves onto the New College complex on Mound Place, a key site in Scottish history. The third and final part of takes us along Upper Bow, Victoria Terrace and a section of Grassmarket. Views of Scottish National Gallery, New Town and Fife.

Highlights The Hub • Historic closes • Boswell and Johnson plaque • Scotch Whisky Experience • Camera obscura • Sir Patrick Geddes story • Ramsay Garden • New College • Church of Scotland and general assembly panel • John Knox statue • The Mound • Milne's Court • Flodden wall remnants • Granny's Green Steps • In-depth: Lost Old Town

The Walk

Our walk begins at the Hub (*see page 40*), one of the finest Gothic buildings in Scotland, its soaring spire the tallest in the city at 241 feet/74 metres. Today it serves as a café, function rooms and the offices of the world-renowned Edinburgh International festival. Formerly Tolbooth St John's church, the Hub owes its elegance to the 1830s designs of the eminent ecclesiastical architect, A. W. N. Pugin. As a church it was the meeting place of the general assembly of the Church of Scotland until 1929 when that body moved to the assembly hall on The Mound. During the twentieth century, St John's conducted services in Gaelic and was renamed Highland Tolbooth St John's church in 1956 before this role was transferred to Greyfriars kirk in 1981. The church then fell into disuse until the renovation in 1999 that created the Hub.

When St John's was built, the intriguingly named 'Stripper's Close' had to be demolished. It has been suggested that criminals were stripped here before being publicly flogged through the town, from 'the Castle Hill to the Netherbow', often in a mobile pillory. The practice of public whipping was not abolished until 1822.

Face the Hub and turn right, cross the road and turn left up Castlehill. On the right, we pass Jollie's Close and arrive at the entrance to Semple's Close.

Inscription, Semple's Close

Although not initially inviting, Semple's Close is well worth visiting. At the bottom, there are the remains of a mansion built in 1638 for the Semple family. Above the surviving lintels, there are two quotes: 'PRAISED BE THE LORD MY GOD, MY STRENGTH AND MY REDEEMER ANNO DOM. 1638' and 'SEDES MANET OPTIMA COELO', which roughly translates as 'See. Heaven Remains Best'. The family crest carved next to the quotations remains unidentified.

Turn left and go up the short flight of steps.

This was once the back of Skinner's Close, named after the Incorporation of Skinners and Furriers, which had its premises here. On the right is the rear of Rainy hall, a building whose construction, in 1900, involved destroying the seventeenth-century mansion we just saw in Semple's Close. (Rainy hall is part of the New College complex and is covered in more detail below.) Turn left and return to Castlehill. Cross the road and turn right, up the hill. On the right, you will see a small white door. This, as the sign shows, was once Skinner's Close.

On your left, you will find the Witchery restaurant, which is in front of Boswell's Court. On the restaurant walls, there are boards displaying the menu and information on the Cadies and Witchery tours. There is also a plaque detailing a meeting between two celebrated literary figures: in 1770, James Boswell, who lived in the Old Town, and Dr Samuel Johnson, visiting from London, dined here. This may have been the beginning of Boswell's attempts to have his great friend accompany him on a tour of the Hebrides, an expedition that took place in 1773, and one that both men published a book about. Johnson, among his many other achievements, compiled the first English dictionary, this event and many more being covered in Boswell's celebrated biography, *The Life of Samuel Johnson* (1791). Boswell's Court, however, is named after Boswell's uncle, also James Boswell, who lived here in the eighteenth century.

The next building on the left was previously Castlehill school for boys, built in 1896 on the site of a mansion owned by the Duke of Gordon when he was keeper of the castle during the seventeenth century. It is now a visitor attraction featuring whisky, Scotland's national drink. The Scotch Whisky Experience (354 Castlehill) sells a wide range of whiskies and has guided tours available for those interested in the history of the drink, whose name comes from the Gaelic *uisge-beatha,* 'water of life'. The highlight of the tour is the collection of nearly 3,500 bottles of whisky, many of which are extremely rare.

Turn around, cross the road and go down Ramsay Lane.

On the right is the outlook tower (549 Castlehill), with its camera obscura, an instrument that uses lenses and mirrors to project images of Edinburgh and the surrounding countryside onto a large,

Boswell and Johnson plaque, Boswell's Court

Scotch Whisky Experience

Outlook tower, housing the camera obscura (note spectator on viewing platform)

circular dish. The building, spread over five floors, also has a rooftop viewing gallery, which affords excellent views over the city and beyond (entry fee charged). The tenement that houses the outlook tower was once owned by the Laird of Cockpen but was bought by Maria Short in the 1850s. She added two storeys and the camera obscura, renaming the building Short's observatory. In 1892 the observatory was acquired by sociologist, scientist and town planner, Patrick Geddes (*see Geddes panel*).

Continue down Ramsay Lane. On the right, above the entrance to the camera obscura is a coat of arms; its most noticeable details are a pelican, a shield with a blue stripe and red stars and the motto 'Giving and Forgiving'. This is the heraldry of the Biggars of Woolnet and once stood above the entrance to Woolnet house in Midlothian. In 1953, when the seventeenth-century property was demolished, the entrance was moved here. On the right there are two nineteenth-century school buildings. On the left, just before the entrance to Ramsay Garden, is a plaque with information about the street and its historic connections.

Turn left into Ramsay Garden.

These streets are named after one of Scotland's leading literary figures, Allan

Plaque, Ramsay Garden

Sir Patrick Geddes

Patrick Geddes has many notable achievements to his name: he was a brilliant scientist who played a leading role in the discovery of chlorophyll, the green pigment of plants; he pioneered the concepts of summer schools and interdisciplinary studies; his sociological writings were so influential that he is known today as the 'father of town planning'. For those who love Edinburgh, however, it was his tireless work to preserve historic buildings in the Old Town that is his greatest legacy.

The son of an army officer, Patrick Geddes (1854–1932) was born in Ballater and after an unhappy spell working as a bank clerk he enrolled at Edinburgh University in 1874 to read natural sciences. His life as an undergraduate would be short-lived: after just a week he made the impetuous decision to abandon his course. He would never take a degree, the ultimate paradox for one who contributed so much to academia.

Despite the lack of a formal qualification Geddes was able to find work in universities in London and Paris, where he specialised in microbiology. Although this was a field in which he excelled a period of temporary blindness meant that he could no longer use a microscope, forcing him to give up microbiology. In 1880 he returned to Scotland, and, while his main residence was in Edinburgh, he secured a professorship in botany at the University of Dundee, thanks largely to his ground-breaking book, *The Evolution of Sex*.

His academic duties in Dundee were not onerous, and, after moving to James's Court in the Old Town, he threw himself into the causes of conservation and social renewal. With sterling support from his wife, Anna Morton, he launched a plethora of initiatives. He founded the Edinburgh Social Union, as well as halls of residence for students, and then, in 1887, initiated the first summer schools ever held in Europe. In 1892, in a further ambitious move, he bought Short's observatory on Castlehill, renaming it the outlook tower, a principal aim being to show the relationship between town and countryside. His plans for the building went well beyond a camera obscura; he set up a museum and study centre in the building.

It was also in this period that he did so much to preserve what was best in the Old Town. Assisted by volunteers, mostly students, he undertook a number of renovation schemes. Geddes was opposed to the so-called improvers, who were bent on the destruction of old buildings. He wanted to conserve historic structures and where demolition was unavoidable he argued for their replacement by green spaces that would enhance the environment, a concept he called 'conservative surgery'.

The philosophy espoused by Patrick Geddes was highly influential throughout the twentieth century and informed the system of national planning introduced after 1945. Nor has he been forgotten in Edinburgh – in recent years the Patrick Geddes Centre was created in the Old Town, in Riddle's Court (*see Walk 3*), a sixteenth-century courtyard building that Geddes restored in 1892, as well as the location for his summer schools.

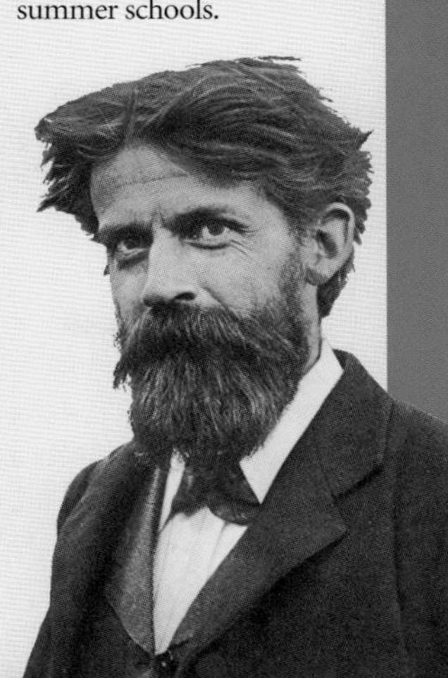

The quirky and colourful Ramsay Garden from Princes Street

Ramsay (1684–1758), who had a house built here in 1733. Ramsay was born in Lanarkshire and moved to Edinburgh in 1700, where he was apprenticed as a wigmaker. However, his love of literature soon took precedence. In High Street, he opened a bookshop and the world's first circulating library before becoming a theatrical impresario (he opened a theatre in Carruber's Close) and a noted publisher of Scottish poetry. Ramsay was himself a fine poet and his early verses, which betrayed marked Jacobite sympathies, were highly praised. However, the work for which he is best remembered is his drama, *The Gentle Shepherd*, of 1725, a pastoral comedy that deals with rustic manners and mores and which would later be produced as an opera. It was greatly admired by both Robert Burns and James Boswell. His son, also Allan Ramsay (1713–84), was one of Britain's finest portrait painters.

The colourful and picturesque Ramsay Garden was developed in the 1890s. The apartments here are highly desirable, especially those with a panoramic view of Princes Street, the New Town and much else besides. Ramsay's property, known as Goose Pie house because its octagonal shape was said to resemble a pie tin, is older and has been enclosed by later development. The best view of this eighteenth-century building is from The Mound or Princes Street.

The master plan for Ramsay Garden was conceived by the aforementioned Sir Patrick Geddes, who lived in a flat here as well as in other properties nearby. At the start of the street you will notice how Ramsay developed his ideas of light and space while incorporating traditional Edinburgh building forms, such as outside stairs. At the end of Ramsay Garden, you should look up and to the left to see the many carvings on each storey of the stair-tower. Ahead of us, above the entrance of another stair-tower, are cherubs representing a farmer, a mason and a blacksmith. Finally, turn back, but before leaving Ramsay Garden look up to your left to see carved-dragon corbelling.

Leave Ramsay Garden and turn left.

As the steep slope bends to the right look left across Princes Street Gardens to see the New Town and Fife in the distance, where, on a clear day, the peaks of East and

West Lomond can be made out. Down in the gardens you can see the Scottish National Gallery and next to it, facing onto Princes Street, the Royal Scottish Academy. Both neoclassical buildings were designed by the great architect, William Playfair, in the mid-nineteenth century, and remodelled in the twentieth. They are well worth a visit when you venture out of the Old Town. Like most museums and galleries in Edinburgh, the Scottish National Gallery and Royal Scottish Academy are free to visit, although for special exhibitions a charge is levied.

Follow the road as it curves.

The grand building on the right, in Mound Place, is the Tudor-style New College, designed by William Playfair and built 1845–50 before being expanded and remodelled in the 1880s and 1910s. Its twin towers are particularly impressive, dominating the main elevation, and can best be appreciated from Princes Street. New College was originally built as a church and school of divinity for the Free Church of Scotland, which was created after the historic split with the Church of Scotland in 1843 (*see Church of Scotland panel below*). Rather cheekily, the twin towers perfectly frame the spire of the church to the rear, which at the time was the headquarters of the rival Church of Scotland (and is now the Hub). However, today New College is associated with the Church of Scotland, which convenes here every year, in May, for its general assembly, held in the appropriately named assembly hall, completed in 1859 to plans by David Bryce. The complex is also home to Edinburgh University's highly regarded school of divinity.

In 1989 a hugely significant event took place in assembly hall when as part of the Scottish Constitutional Convention fifty-eight of Scotland's seventy-two MPs signed the 'Claim of Right for Scotland', a document advocating the creation of a Scottish Parliament. Then, from 1999 until 2004, the New College site was the temporary home of the Scottish Parliament before the new

New College, Mound Place

building in Holyrood was finished, with the assembly hall being used as the Parliament's debating chamber. Like countless other Old Town locations, it is also a festival venue during August and has seating for 1,250 people. To the left of the main gate there are plaques: one commemorating Revd John Witherspoon (1723–94), who was one of six Scots-born men to sign the US Declaration of Independence in 1776; the other celebrating the 150th anniversary of the laying of the foundation stone of the New College building.

Go through the entrance and enter the courtyard.

Revd John Witherspoon plaque

The Church of Scotland and its general assembly

The Church of Scotland is the established church of the nation and has been recognised as such by law since 1690. The process leading to that status was a long and turbulent one, which began in the mid-sixteenth century. Until then Scotland, like England, was predominantly Roman Catholic, but when the Reformation took hold in the 1560s, the old faith was swept away. Inspired by charismatic preachers like George Wishart (1513–46) and John Knox (c.1514–72), an alternative religion, based on Presbyterian principles, became dominant. The new church rejected Episcopalian forms of government (rule by bishops) and instead organised itself in a much more democratic way, emphasising the role of elections and courts.

Despite the sweeping changes brought about by the Reformation, the Church of Scotland would face many challenges, not least the desire of the Crown to influence how it was governed. The Stuart kings of the seventeenth century were themselves Protestant but they consistently attempted to restore the rule of bishops. This caused deep divisions in Scottish society and led to the national covenant – a document that flatly rejected episcopal-style governance – being unveiled at Greyfriars kirk in 1638 (*see page 186*). Copies were made and distributed to churches up and down the land and it is estimated that 300,000 Scots would eventually sign the covenant. Inevitably, the conflict between Crown and Covenanters, as they became known, turned violent. The bloodiest period was the so-called Killing Times of 1684–7 when government forces under John Graham of Claverhouse (later Viscount Dundee) ruthlessly repressed the Covenanters. The bold Graham, depending on one's sympathies, was nicknamed either 'Bluidy Clavers' or Bonnie Dundee. It took a new Presbyterian settlement in 1690 – in the wake of the Glorious Revolution of 1689 and the accession of William of Orange to the throne – to avert further bloodshed.

While the Church of Scotland was now dominant, internal divisions caused a number of schisms. The most serious was the so-called Disruption of 1843, which led to around one-third of its ministers and members leaving. Like the Covenanters, the dissenters of the Disruption were opposed to the influence of the government in the running of church affairs and to patronage, a process that led to the formation of the Free Church of Scotland. Scotland now had two major Presbyterian denominations and in 1847 this became three with the formation of the United Presbyterian Church. A slow process of reconciliation began and was helped by the abolition of patronage by Parliament in 1874. In 1900 the Free Church of Scotland and the United Presbyterian Church joined forces to form the United Free Church, which, in 1929, merged with the Church of Scotland. Although there were still active Free Church denominations – especially in the Highlands and Islands – the Church of Scotland was now restored to its historic position within Scottish society.

Today the Church of Scotland's most important body is the general assembly, which convenes for a week in May in the assembly hall on Mound Place. It is an important event in the life of the nation and one that was first held in 1560, the year of the Scottish Reformation. Around eight hundred commissioners (clergy, elders and other

The Princess Royal at the general assembly of the Church of Scotland

members) attend the general assembly, which by law, is the supreme court, legislative body and debating chamber of the Church of Scotland. The general assembly is chaired by the 'moderator of the general assembly of the Church of Scotland', a title carefully chosen to reflect the Church's belief that its true head is Jesus Christ and not a mere mortal. Such is the significance of the general assembly that the sovereign appoints a personal representative, the Lord High Commissioner, who, in assembly week, takes precedence after the Queen and the Duke of Edinburgh and before the rest of the royal family. Previous Commissioners have included cabinet ministers, High Court judges and senior members of the royal family, including the Duke of Rothesay (the official title of Prince Charles in Scotland) and the Princess Royal. The Queen – who took an oath at the Coronation to preserve the Church of Scotland – has herself attended the general assembly.

Guest speakers are often invited to address the general assembly, perhaps the best-known – and certainly most controversial – example being Margaret Thatcher in 1988. Never popular in Scotland, the former prime minister's speech was an unapologetic defence of her social and economic policies and was wittily nicknamed the 'Sermon on the Mound'. A majority of those present were staunchly opposed to 'Thatcherism' but they responded to her peroration with a respectful, if stony, silence.

In common with most Christian denominations in the developed world, the Church of Scotland faces the twin challenges of declining attendances at its services and an ageing membership. Despite these problems it still has 350,000 active members, who are served by 800 ministers and 1,500 ancillary staff. Although membership now constitutes less than 10 per cent of Scotland's adult population most people still have an empathy with the Kirk and for this reason it continues to be one of the most influential voices in society.

As well as marvelling at the wonderful architecture, you will notice a statue of John Knox on the left (John Hutchison, 1895). Knox was the single most influential figure in the Scottish Reformation and minister of Edinburgh's St Giles high kirk (*for more on Knox, see Walk 5*). If you are able to access the interior of New College, there is much of interest, including the aforesaid oval-shaped assembly hall with its tiered galleries. Leading to assembly hall is the iconic black-and-white corridor, which was originally open to the sky, but later remodelled as a cloister with depressed arches. Note, too, the splendid Rainy hall – named after a former principal of New College, Revd Robert Rainy (1826–1906) – which, with its high ceilings, wood panelling and coats of arms resembles an Oxbridge dining hall.

Retrace your steps out of assembly hall and arrive again on Mound Place.

The slope in front is The Mound, which has an interesting history. It occupies land that was once covered by the Nor' (north) loch, an artificial stretch of water created in 1450 to enhance Edinburgh's northern defences. As invasion fears subsided, and the city expanded, the loch was gradually drained, with all traces gone by the 1820s. The only problem was that much of the drained land was marshy and difficult to negotiate, making journeys between the Old Town and the burgeoning New Town to the north inconvenient. Looking for a way to create a workable link, a shrewd local tailor, George Boyd, had a eureka moment. In 1781, he proposed that the earth and rubble disturbed by the construction of the New Town could provide the solution. That is how a 'Mud Brig', or 'Earthen Mound' as it came to be known, linking the Old and New towns, came into existence. It was a huge undertaking, with more than 1.5 million cartloads of spoil being moved between the two parts of the city. Sir Walter Scott was not a fan: he remarked that the Mound was a 'huge deformity', the most 'hopeless and irremediable error . . . committed in the course of the improvements of Edinburgh'.

John Knox statue

Turn to the right and as we walk past the front of New College turn right and walk up the steps in front.

After a steep climb and a short tunnel, you arrive in the courtyard of Milne's Court, the oldest open square in the Old Town. It was completed in 1690, a speculative development by Robert Milne of Barfargie, master mason to the king, who, in 1670, worked on the extension of Holyrood palace. Milne (sometimes Mylne) built two huge blocks, one within the courtyard (north) and the other (south) with a frontage onto Lawnmarket. Due to its size, regularity and superior construction standards it was a complete contrast to the often-ramshackle properties in the vicinity and immediately became one of the most fashionable addresses in Edinburgh. A plaque at the end of the close gives more information.

Continue past the courtyard and you arrive back on Royal Mile.

On the right, there is the Ensign Ewart pub, which claims to have been established in 1680, though it is of course named after

Milne's Court

Ensign Ewart pub

Charles Ewart, hero of the Battle of Waterloo in 1815 (*for more on Ewart, see Walk 1*).

Cross the road, turn right, then left down Upper Bow.

From the fourteenth till the nineteenth century, different weigh-houses stood near this site, the last being destroyed to widen access to the castle. A weigh-house, or 'tron', was used to provide accurate weights and measures in a marketplace. Other weigh-houses stood in West Parliament Square and by the Tron kirk on High Street.

Go down Upper Bow, walk around the stairs to the notice board in front of the railings. Here you can see how the street was redeveloped in the 1830s along with descriptions of nearby buildings. The completion of Victoria Street was the last change to the Old Town street plan.

Turn right and walk along Victoria Terrace.

On the left is Victoria Street, which runs down the hill towards West Bow and Grassmarket. At the end of the terrace the view opens up and you can see the top of Grassmarket and George Heriot's school on the hill.

On the terrace, veer right and take the stairs on the right up to Johnston Terrace. At the top of the stairs, turn left.

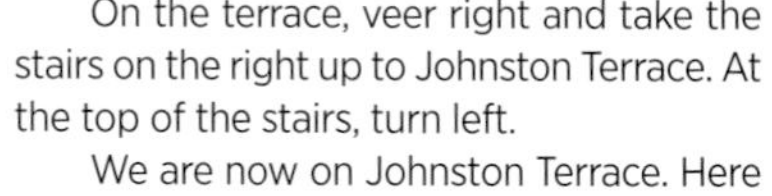

We are now on Johnston Terrace. Here you can see the back of the Castlehill school on the other side of the street, with the separate entrances for boys and girls.

Turn left and head along the terrace. Ahead is a wonderful view of the castle. Take the first left, down Patrick Geddes Steps.

Patrick Geddes Steps

The street signs on the left-hand side of Patrick Geddes Steps are decorated with Geddes's 'three doves': heart, hand and head. They represent his theory of education, which holds that we learn through sympathy (heart), synergy (hand) and synthesis (head).

On the right, you can see Johnston Terrace Garden, the smallest wildlife reserve operated by Scottish Wildlife Trust. The wild flowers that grow here are protected and access to the garden is by arrangement only.

At the bottom of the steps the alley turns right and then left into Castle Wynd South, which leads to Grassmarket, an area traditionally associated with markets of all kinds, including the sale of horses. It was a street of perpetual bustle as carters arrived with goods from across the country and taverns and lodging house sprang up to cater for their needs. To add to the tumult, Grassmarket was the site of public executions until 1785, with the gallows being particularly busy during the time of the Covenanters. More than a hundred Covenanters met their maker here, the last in 1688. The site of the gallows is marked by a cross set in cobbles and incorporated into the cylindrical Covenanters' memorial. Today Grassmarket is still a lively area with many interesting shops, cafes, restaurants and

Burns plaque, White Hart inn

pubs. It also plays host to regular events, such as the jazz festival, which is held in July.

Turn right and walk along the right-hand side of Grassmarket.

On your right are two interesting pubs, which claim to have been visited by Scotland's national bard, Robert Burns. A plaque next to the White Hart proclaims that the great man stayed there on his last visit in 1791, and the Beehive next door asserts that Burns whiled away the hours watching the cockfights in its predecessor establishment.

When you reach the end of Grassmarket look at the ground. Here you can see markings that show the position of the old

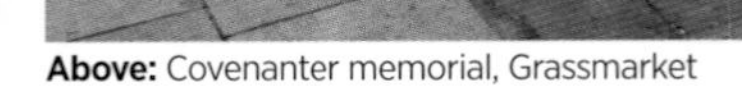
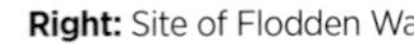

Above: Covenanter memorial, Grassmarket

Right: Site of Flodden Wall

Grassmarket

defensive buttress, the Flodden wall. It was built after Scotland's disastrous defeat at the Battle of Flodden in 1515 to replace the King's wall. The Flodden wall has mostly been destroyed but there are parts of it extant. The writing on the pavement describes how strong the Scottish position was before the battle began and is in fact an extract from Sir Walter Scott's epic poem, *Marmion: A Tale of Flodden Field* (1808).

Before we leave Grassmarket look at the buildings at the west end of the square. Above the shops there are the coat of arms of Glasgow and Edinburgh with their mottos, 'Let Glasgow Flourish' and 'Nisi Dominus Frustra'. This building was once a branch of the Glasgow Savings Bank. The Edinburgh motto translates as 'Except the Lord in Vain' and is a quote from Psalm 127:1.

Turn right and you see another set of stairs, with the marvellous name of Granny's Green Steps. Walking up the steps, you pass a lovely little park on the left as you head towards the castle. It is thought this is the green where old women dried washing, hence the name Granny's Green Steps. However, the steps themselves are a modern creation, completed in 2001.

At the top of Granny's Green Steps, cross the road and turn right. Follow Johnston Terrace back to where we started.

As you walk back on the right-hand side of the street, if you look above the shops and restaurants, you see the sign of W. M. Mackintosh, a former antiques dealer and underneath that, between the windows, you can see the remains of a painted sign promoting the firm of undertakers that occupied the site. Many of these signs still adorn walls in Edinburgh and it is always worth looking above the shops in the city to find these glimpses of history.

When you reach the Hub, our walk is complete. If you would like to start another, walk down Lawnmarket, turn left into Lady Stair's Close and enter Wardrop's Court.

Granny's Green Steps

IN DEPTH

Lost Old Town

MARY OF GUISE PALACE

Daughter of a powerful French nobleman, Mary of Guise married King James V in 1538 and bore him two sons (both of whom died in infancy) and a daughter. Following James's untimely death in 1542 the dowager queen doggedly upheld French and Roman Catholic interests in Scotland, serving as regent from 1554–60 while her daughter, Mary, Queen of Scots was in France. As regent, she had a palace to match her status, on Castlehill, roughly where the Hub sits today. The palace was lavishly decorated and came complete with an oratory, a secret chamber on the first floor and a 'deid' room for the deceased to be laid out prior to burial. Like many grand houses in the Old Town, it was divided into flats, before, in 1861, being demolished to make way for the Free Church of Scotland assembly hall.

UPPER/WEST BOW

This was a narrow, z-shaped lane that ran between Lawnmarket and Grassmarket. It is said that the upper floors of properties on opposite sides of the street were so close together that residents could take tea together without leaving home. Much of the middle section was lost in the 1830s due to a plan to improve access to the Old Town, although Bowhead house, seen here, survived until the late nineteenth century.

Upper Bow in 1878

THE OLD TOLBOOTH

Positioned prominently on High Street, at the north-west corner of St Giles cathedral, the old tolbooth was built in 1386. As the name implies, it was the place where tolls were collected but was also used as a meeting place for the town council and as a courthouse. However, with the construction of a new tollhouse close by, the old building gradually developed into a prison, which would be nicknamed 'Thieves Hole'. Those unfortunate enough to be incarcerated here had to endure hellish conditions in a building that had no ventilation, running water or toilet facilities and straw-covered stone floors in place of beds.

The tolbooth also had an 'iron room', in which prisoners sentenced to death were held. On the day of their execution they were led to a platform attached to the west gable, where gallows had been set up. Those hung here included the notorious Deacon Brodie.

LUCKENBOOTHS

Luckenbooths were 'locked booths', a medieval version of the shopping mall.

Located at the eastern end of the old tolbooth, the luckenbooths were located in a four-storey, timber-fronted tenement, which had the effect of narrowing the street to fifteen feet on its north side. It was here, on the first floor of the luckenbooths, that poet and playwright Allan Ramsay opened the world's first circulating library in 1726. Between the luckenbooths and St Giles there was a narrow passageway called the krames, or creams, effectively a bazaar packed with traders selling their wares from small pitches. Like the old tolbooth, the luckenbooths and the krames were demolished in 1817.

NETHERBOW PORT

This was the grandest of the six 'ports', or gateways, and it controlled entry between Edinburgh and the independent burgh of Canongate and was situated where Jeffrey and St Mary's streets intersect with High Street. Much more than a gate, it was actually a fine building with an imposing clock tower, spire, apartments within and even a blacksmith's forge. The tower also had a more sinister use: to display the dismembered limbs of those who had been hung for their crimes. In 1764, the Netherbow port was pulled down to ease traffic flows, a move opposed by many.

BLACKFRIARS MONASTERY

The monastery of the black friars, or Dominicans, was founded by King Alexander II in 1230. It sat within extensive grounds to the south of Cowgate, extending from Potterow in the west to Pleasance in the east. The monastery buildings were located at the bottom of Infirmary Street, and, close by, there was the collegiate church of St Mary's-in-the-Field (also known as Kirk o' Field), which stood on the site now occupied by the Old College of Edinburgh University. A wealthy institution, the monastery was much favoured by royalty, whose gifts helped it expand and prosper. As a Roman Catholic institution, the monastery was largely destroyed in 1559 at the time of the Reformation. While there is no trace of it today, an archaeological dig in 2013 revealed the skeleton of a knight and a thirteenth-century gravestone.

Old tolbooth, High Street

Lawnmarket, in the shadow of the castle, is the oldest part of the Royal Mile and connects Castlehill and High Street. The name derives from 'land market', because, following a charter granted by James III in 1477, this was designated as the place where 'inland' goods such as linen, coarse cloth and yarn could be sold.

WALK 3
LAWNMARKET AND GEORGE IV BRIDGE

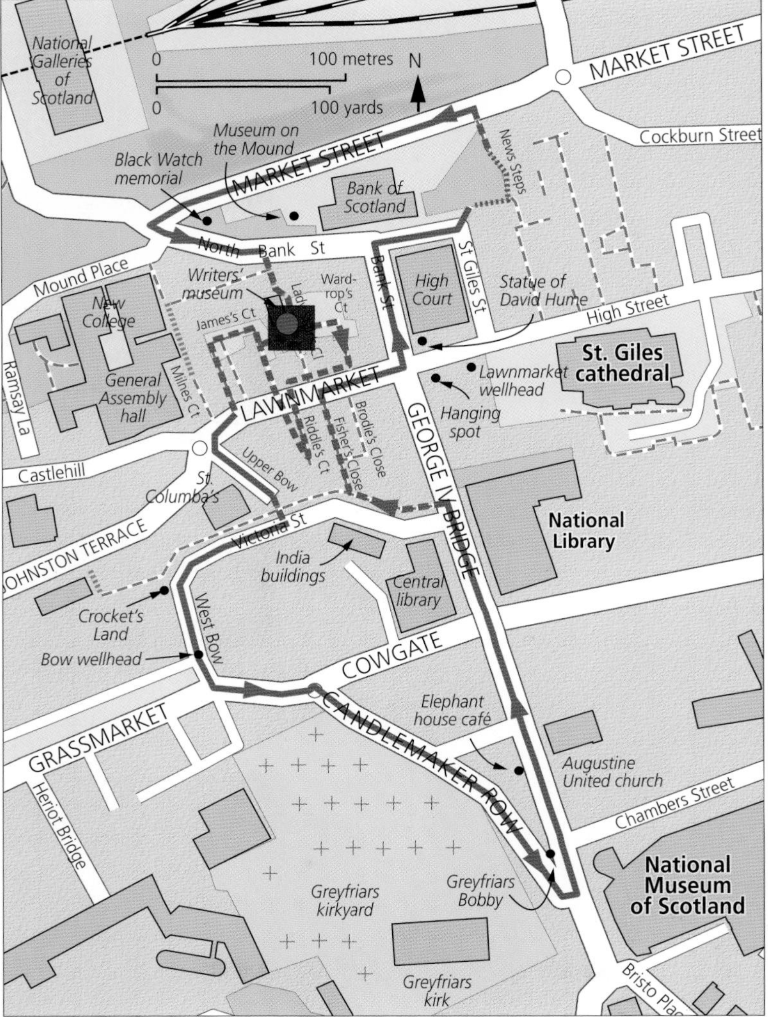

Start Wardrop's Court, facing the writers' museum (formerly Lady Stair's house). Access also through Lady Stair's Close.

Summary The focus is on Lawnmarket, with its many historic closes and houses. We also take in delightful Victoria Street, with its quirky shops, and parts of the lively Grassmarket, full of historic pubs and restaurants. There is a stroll along George IV Bridge, followed by a walk past the wonderful Bank of Scotland HQ.

Highlights Writers' museum • Makars' Court • Lady Stair story • Gladstone's Land • Riddle's Court/Patrick Geddes centre • James ('s) Court • George IV bridge • Harry Potter connection • Victoria Street's bijou shops • Crocket's Land • Ratho murderer • Edinburgh central library and National Library of Scotland • Deacon Brodie • Bank of Scotland building • Black Watch statue • In-depth: the Harry Potter trail

The Walk

We start facing Lady Stair's house (now the writers' museum), which was built in 1622 for Sir William Gray, a prosperous merchant. After falling into disrepair, the building was bought, in 1893, by the earl of Rosebery, who was acting on a suggestion by Patrick Geddes. Much restoration followed, including the demolition of three of the wings. However, significant parts of the original structure remain, including a spiral staircase. Inside there is another interesting feature: an uneven staircase with a trick step that was designed to catch out burglars sneaking around in the dark. Above the front door, the lintel is dated 1622 and carved with Gray's initials and those of his wife, as well as a quote from Proverbs 3:7.

Writers' museum, Lady Stair's Close

Today, the house is owned by Edinburgh City Council, in which it operates a writers' museum. The museum celebrates literary giants Robert Burns, Sir Walter Scott and Robert Louis Stevenson, and has many fascinating artefacts associated with their lives, such as letters and childhood toys, as well as first editions and even the printing press used to produce Scott's *Waverley* novels. It was the connection with Burns that led to the creation of the museum as the man from Ayr briefly stayed here in 1786, his first visit to Edinburgh.

In the courtyard, next to the museum, you will find Makars' Court. Look down and you will see quotes from Scottish writers carved into paving slabs. The quotes are drawn from a wide range of Scottish writers,

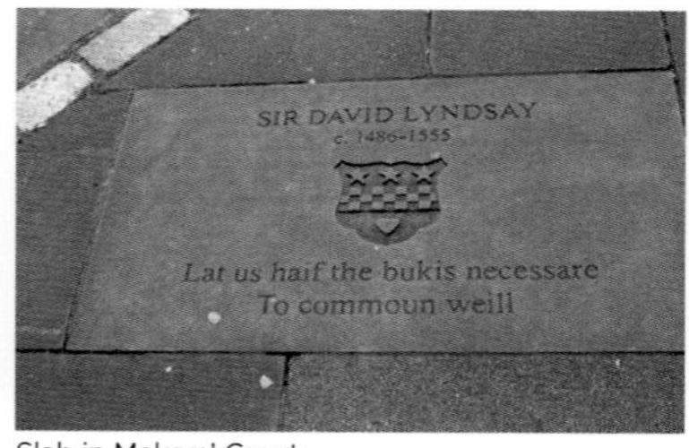

Slab in Makars' Court

The strange affair of Lady Stair

The married life of Lady Stair was truly astonishing, so astonishing that Sir Walter Scott based one of his short stories – 'My Aunt Margaret's Mirror' – on her matrimonial travails. Born Lady Eleanor Campbell, probably in the 1680s, she was a great beauty from a noble family and at a young age married James, Viscount Primrose. Her husband, however, was a drunk and a vicious bully and such was his temper that he came within a whisker of murdering his wife. One day, Eleanor was dressing in their Edinburgh town house, close to an open window, when his lordship sneaked into the room, a drawn sword in his hand. It was only a glance in the mirror that saved her life. Seeing the sword, and the evil intent in his eyes, she jumped out of an open window, half-dressed, and had the presence of mind to run to the house of her mother-in-law, to whom she told her story and demanded protection, which was granted.

After this incident Lord Primrose fled abroad and the story goes that his wife, wondering about his whereabouts, consulted a fortune-teller. The mystic led Lady Primrose to a large mirror, in which she perceived the inside of a church and a wedding party. To her astonishment the bridegroom was none other than her errant husband! According to the vision in the mirror the priest was about to pronounce the couple husband and wife when a guest approached the altar, sword drawn, and attacked the groom. In another amazing twist, Lady Primrose recognised her own brother as the assailant. At this point the vision became confused and indistinct, before fading away completely.

A few weeks later, Lady Primrose's brother returned from a visit to Amsterdam and told his sister that while he was in that city he had become acquainted with a rich merchant, whose beautiful young daughter was about to be married to a Scottish nobleman. As his new friend was of course a Scot, the merchant invited him to the wedding. When he got to the church he immediately realised that the groom was his brother-in-law, Lord Primrose, who was about to conduct a bigamous marriage. Lady Primrose's sibling immediately cried foul, stopping the wedding in its tracks. The vision in the mirror had come true.

Lord Primrose died in 1706 at the age of just 26.

Not surprisingly, his widow, though still young, resolved never to marry again, thanks to her terrible experience. Given her singular beauty and distinguished family, she had many suitors, but refused them all. One such was John Dalrymple, 2nd earl of Stair, scion of one of the most powerful families in the land. Dalrymple was building a huge reputation for himself in Britain's wars with the French and would later be honoured with many senior military titles, including vice admiral for Scotland and commander-in-chief for the south of Britain. He was undoubtedly a great catch, but Eleanor turned him down flat.

After many rejections, Lord Stair became desperate. One night he bribed his way into her ladyship's house and in the morning appeared stark naked at the front window. The damage to her reputation was such that Lady Primrose had no alternative but to agree to his marriage proposal and they duly tied the knot. Lady Stair died in 1759, having outlived her second husband by twelve years. The house and the close in which it sits have both borne the Lady Stair title since that time.

Left: Ornamental dragon, Wardrop's Court

Above: Robert Burns plaque, Lady Stair's Close

stretching from John Barbour in the fourteenth century, and Sir David Lyndsay in the sixteenth, to more contemporary writers, such as Gaelic poet Sorley MacLean who died in 1996, and Muriel Spark, whose slab was added in 2008. Sponsors and other interested parties are invited to recommend quotes, so that this living artwork can continue to grow. A makar is similar to a poet laureate although the word *makar* (maker) emphasises the role of a poet or author as skilled worker, a craftsperson of letters.

Turn around and walk across the courtyard, pass the street lamp in the centre and go towards the exit in the right-hand corner. The short tunnel has four ornamental dragons. A plaque on the right-hand wall at the exit of the close informs you that two of them were carved by Patrick Geddes's son while he was under the wing of a master mason.

On exiting the tunnel turn right and head up Lawnmarket.

As you walk, look up to your right and you can see carved heads under the oriel windows that stick out from the tenements; these represent different occupations. The first with tools, the second with cooking and cleaning implements; the final head, a scholar with books and sporting equipment.

Also on the right, above the entrance to Lady Stair's Close, is a plaque in memory of Robert Burns's first visit to the city and his stay in the house previously owned by Lady Stair.

At the entrance to Lady Stair's Close there is a plaque on the left. Amongst many interesting details it briefly describes how in 1717 Sir Richard Steele provided a supper for eccentric beggars. Steele was an Irish politician and co-founder of *The Tatler* magazine, who, while visiting the city, decided to give a feast to the strangest homeless folk he could find, in order to observe their bizarre behaviour.

Next to Lady Stair's Close is Gladstone's Land (477B Lawnmarket), which has been meticulously restored by the National Trust for Scotland and now looks every inch the wealthy merchant's property it was during the seventeenth century. With space then at a premium the Land, or tenement, is only seven-metres wide but six storeys in height. There is much to admire including the stone arches (once common in Scottish towns but now a rarity), winding staircases and the remarkable hand-painted Renaissance interiors. The building dates back to the sixteenth century but it was Thomas Gledstanes, a wealthy merchant, who is responsible for most of what we see today. Gledstanes (an ancestor of British prime minister William Ewart Gladstone) purchased an existing property here in 1617 and greatly extended it in at least two stages. His

Gladstone's Land (*centre*) with the golden hawk

The painted chamber, Gladstone's Land

aim was to provide a home for himself and his family, luxurious accommodation on the upper floors for affluent tenants and to rent out the ground floor as a food and cloth shop (known then as a 'luckenbooth') and the basement as a tavern. There are two other interesting features at the front of Gladstone's Land. The first is the outdoor staircase, which helped keep some distance between the residents of the property and the filth of the street, which meant that the area partly enclosed by the stairs could be used to keep pigs. The other is the golden bird of prey we see above the arches: this is a hawk, which in Scots is a *gled,* a clear link to the Gledstanes family name. Gladstone's Land complements another National Trust for Scotland property: the Georgian House in the New Town, which is kept in the manner of an upper-class residence of the eighteenth century.

Go straight across the road and head into Riddle's Court.

In Riddle's Court we find Bailie John McMorran's courtyard house, c.1590, one of the oldest buildings in Edinburgh after Edinburgh castle and Holyrood palace. Now A-listed, it is of great architectural and historical significance and should not be missed by anyone with an interest in the development of the city. McMorran was said to be the richest merchant in Edinburgh and also served on the council as a bailie (senior councillor). Such was the house's prestige that, in 1598, it hosted a banquet for James VI and his queen, Anne of Denmark, while James himself used it to entertain nobles as part of a successful campaign that led to him being crowned king of both Scotland and England in 1603.

Bailie McMorran was not able to enjoy the comforts of his mansion for long because, in 1595, his life was cut short by one of the most heinous crimes in Edinburgh's history. As a senior member of the town council McMorran was called to the old Edinburgh high school to investigate a protest. The pupils there had barricaded themselves in, along with a stock of weapons, and were refusing to budge until extra school holidays were granted. McMorran arrived at the head of a force of city officers and demanded that the protest be called off. The situation became agitated

Above: Riddle's Court

Right: James ('s) Court

and the authorities broke down a door, panicking the boys. One of their number, William Sinclair, lifted his gun and put a ball through McMorran's head, killing him instantly. The resulting shock calmed the situation and the boys were arrested. Sinclair escaped trial, partly because of his age – he was no more than 13 years old – but also because his father was the powerful chancellor of Caithness, a man with much influence in royal circles.

For the next two hundred years, the court continued to be occupied by the wealthy and well-connected, including Alexander Seton, Chancellor of Scotland. A later resident of Riddle's Court was philosopher David Hume (*see Walk 4 for more on Hume*), who took a flat here in 1751. In a letter he wrote that he lived with 'two inferior members – a maid and a cat'. However, by the mid-nineteenth century, Riddle's Court had become a slum, home to almost 250 people living in wretched conditions. Fortunately, in the 1890s, the visionary town planner, Patrick Geddes, took action: he undertook sensitive renovation using his renowned technique of 'conservative surgery', and in the process created not only a student hall of residence but also a venue for his renowned summer schools.

Today, following extensive works by the Scottish Historic Buildings Trust, costing many millions of pounds, Riddle's Court has been restored to former glories. Although first and foremost a wonderful example of a merchant's house of the sixteenth century the interiors reflect period aesthetics and include a tempera ceiling of the 1590s, plaster ceilings from the seventeenth century and a painted ceiling by the eminent Victorian artist, Thomas Bonnar. Note also the unusual external stairs between the second and third floors. Fittingly, Riddle's Court is now home to the Patrick Geddes Centre for Learning and Conservation and his motto *Vivendo Discimus* (by living we learn) has been chiselled into the archway leading into the inner courtyard.

Susannah Stephen memorial, James Court

Leave Riddle's Court and return across Lawnmarket.

To the left of Gladstone's Land is the east entry to James Court; go down this short close and past the Jolly Judge pub, which has a reconstructed, Renaissance painted ceiling. With Wardrop's Court on your right, turn left into the courtyard of James Court. Alongside the trees in James ('s) Court there is a small statue of a parakeet in a garden trug and some leaves; this is a memorial to the landscape architect and founder of the Scottish Society of Garden Designers, Susannah Alice Stephen (1960–97).

James Court was built between 1725–7 by James Brownhill to provide homes for the wealthy and influential and as one historian points out it 'was for some years regarded as the *quartier* of greatest dignity and importance in Edinburgh'. A massive double tenement, it still impresses today. The newly affluent David Hume bought a flat here and James Boswell was also a resident. In 1783, when Samuel Johnson visited Boswell, he was struck by how spacious and handsome his apartment was. One of the most striking features for Johnson was that due to the sleep slopes of the hill, the ground floor in James Court is four floors above the street on the other side.

The Traverse theatre once occupied a building here that went by many names over the years, including Hell's Kitchen and Kelly's Paradise, and served many different functions, including as cheap lodgings and as a brothel. The sixty-seat, transverse-stage theatre moved to West Bow when the building was condemned in 1969 and then to its current position in Saltire Court.

There are three entrances and exits to James Court, the east entry that we came through, the mid entry, and, at the end of the courtyard, the west entry. Leave via the west entry – a short close that is tight and dark enough to give you an idea of quite how claustrophobic and unpleasant the Old Town must have been.

Victoria Street shops

Exit the close onto the Royal Mile again, this time at the top of Lawnmarket with Edinburgh castle and the Hub to your right. Cross the road, turn right, then left, and head down Upper Bow. On the right there is St Columba's, of the Free Church of Scotland, built in 1846; at the end of this short street there is a set of steps, go down them and you arrive on Victoria Street.

Across the street is the nineteenth century St John's parish church and parish school, now home to bars and clubs. Cross the road, turn right and head down Victoria Street with its fascinating boutique shops, cafés and restaurants. Victoria Street was built in the 1830s to improve access into the Old Town. Eighteenth-century buildings still remain including those at the end of the street where the original name, West Bow, is still used. A good example is Crocket's Land (91 West Bow) of 1705, a merchant's house on five storeys built by the eponymous Thomas Crockett but renovated over time and now with a nineteenth-century doorway. Crocket's Land has survived at least two regeneration schemes and deserves to be seen for its curved gable, Dutch-style architecture, the two oval flight holes for doves and the splendid, well-preserved interior (not generally open to the public).

Follow the road around the corner and enter Grassmarket.

On your right a well stands in the middle of the road. This is the Bow wellhead. This is one of a few original cisterns that were installed in the late-seventeenth century to provide people with water from Comiston loch. On it are interesting carvings and plaques explaining the history of the well.

Continue to follow the road around, moving left, and leave Grassmarket. Cross the road and walk up the hill to the right. Before you do, turn around and you will get a nice view of Grassmarket and the castle.

We are now on Candlemaker Row and as we walk up there is a high wall on the

The West Bow sorcerer

In 1670, the witchcraft panic, which had virtually died out, once again reared its ugly head. Major Thomas Weir, who lived in West Bow with his unmarried sister Grizel, was a fervent Presbyterian, an officer in the town guard, and, immediately recognisable by his dark cloak and the staff he always carried, the picture of respectability. However, he took ill and started to rave incoherently about his involvement in incest, sorcery and murder. This shocked Edinburgh society so much that Weir was put on trial, found guilty and sentenced to be strangled and burnt at the stake. As the flames consumed him, his staff was thrown into the flames. It is said that he refused to ask God's forgiveness, exclaiming, 'I have lived as a beast and I must die as a beast'.

Grizel – who was later hanged – was accused of witchcraft and at her trial did little to help her brother's case. She testified that years earlier a fiery coach had come to their door and a mysterious stranger had invited Major Weir to go with him. Whatever happened in the coach she said that from that day on demonic power was now invested in his staff. Given the superstitions of the time the Weir house on West Bow lay empty for almost a century and reports of the major's ghost appearing circulated widely; in one account he was seen clambering onto a headless horse and galloping off in a whirlwind of fire.

right. This is part of Greyfriars kirkyard. Walls like this were built to deter graverobbers, known as resurrectionists, who would dig up corpses and sell them to anatomists at Edinburgh's medical school. Two infamous characters associated with this trade were the notorious Burke and Hare, although to be precise they were murderers and not graverobbers (*see Walk 10*).

At the top of the street take the sharp left turn at the statue of the famous dog, Greyfriars Bobby (we shall meet him again in Walk 10).

Our walk now goes straight along George IV Bridge.

During the nineteenth century access to the Old Town was improved and George IV Bridge was built to provide a southern approach. Plans for the bridge were formulated by Thomas Hamilton following the 1827 Improvement Act and construction was completed in 1834. The name is in honour of King George IV and reflects the warm feeling surrounding the royal visit of 1822. This was the first visit by a reigning monarch for nearly two centuries and the occasion was brilliantly choreographed by Sir Walter Scott. George IV is also honoured by a statue (Francis Chantrey, 1831) on George Street – the street is named after his father, George III – and as one of the two princes for whom Princes Street is named, the other being his brother Frederick (*Frederick details, Walk 1*).

Amongst the older tenements on the left you can find a converted church and also the Elephant House café, the place where, it is claimed, J. K. Rowling wrote several of her Harry Potter books (*see 'The Harry Potter trail' at the end of this walk*). On the right is the eclectic design of the Augustine United church named after St Augustine of Hippo (AD 354–430) the noted theologian and philosopher. It was created in the late 1850s, a time when many churches were built in the city, but none with the same mix of Romanesque, Renaissance and Classical elements, not least the interesting wedding-cake tower (*see photo overleaf*).

Augustine United church, George IV Bridge

Further along the bridge, on the left, is central library, operated by Edinburgh City Council; it is a lending library and its collections include many books, photographs and papers relating to the city's history. The stylish and confident exterior (G. Washington Browne, 1887) is matched by the outstanding interior which includes a grand staircase and a pilastered reference room with a domed ceiling. From the outside we can see French Renaissance carvings and the coats-of-arms of Edinburgh, Scotland and the United Kingdom. The library was opened in 1890 and the funding, as with many other libraries in Scotland, came from the Dunfermline-born steel magnate, Andrew Carnegie.

Directly across the road we find another large library, the National Library of Scotland, a rather disappointing modern design (Reginald Fairlie, 1936). Building work started in the 1930s but was not finished until 1955 as construction was interrupted by the Second World War. Despite its unprepossessing appearance, the NLS is a major cultural resource, a 'library of deposit', and as such has a statutory right to request a copy of all printed items published in the UK. The numbers are staggering: within its walls there are fifteen million books, seven million manuscripts and two million maps, with five thousand items being added every week.

When walking past central library, look to your left above the door of the next Victorian building. Here you can see a statue of Caledonia with her hands on the heads of two youths, one of whom is wearing a kilt.

Cross over Victoria Street and turn left onto Victoria Terrace.

The modern hotel building we briefly walk under stands on the site of the old medical school. As you walk along the terrace, on your left you can see the attractive architecture of India buildings (David Cousin, 1864), a Scots Baronial and Jacobean-style structure that once housed a branch of the British Linen bank; the gateway on the left was apparently intended for carts. The inscription two floors above it, *Dominus Providebit*, means 'The Lord Will Provide'.

Turn right into Fisher's Close.

Some closes were named after the businesses that were found there and one might expect that this was named after a fish market. However, this street, like many others, was named after the wealthy

India buildings

The libraries on George IV Bridge: central library (*top*); National Library of Scotland (*above*)

resident with the grandest house, in this case Thomas Fisher, the first chamberlain of Edinburgh. Despite having nice houses, these higher-status residents had to live cheek by jowl with the rest of society in the overcrowded closes.

Continue up the close, at the end we arrive back on Lawnmarket. Turn right and walk down Lawnmarket.

On the right we pass the entrance of Brodie's Close. It is named after Francis Brodie, the Deacon of Wrights, and as the painted board erected by the café points out, there are still elements of the seventeenth-century building that remain. However, as you will also find out, the famous Brodie, the one for whom the pub across the street is named, was Francis's infamous son, William (*see Brodie panel, facing page*).

Before you reach the crossroads of Lawnmarket and George IV Bridge you pass an old police box – now painted black – on your left. It was designed by city architect and director of housing Ebenezer MacRae (1881–1951). The design of the boxes, which allowed police constables to communicate with local stations and enjoy a cup of tea, was intended to fit in with Edinburgh's architecture, especially that of the New Town. Some still survive in Edinburgh as venues for businesses. MacRae must be credited with much more than simply the design of telephone boxes; in the eyes of many commentators he did more than anyone to shape modern Edinburgh. While one of his specialisms was in the provision of street furniture – lamp standards, tram shelters, traffic lights, and, of course, police boxes – his greatest legacy was undoubtedly the expansion of the council's housing stock. Thanks to his strong Christian ethos MacRae was driven to help others and he zealously pursued the building of new estates, determined that the working classes should have access to high-quality accommodation. It is a measure of his success that more than twelve thousand new council houses were completed during his tenure.

Continue to walk down Lawnmarket and cross over George IV Bridge at the traffic lights.

On the ground, next to the crossing, on Lawnmarket, are three very small brass plates in an 'I' shape, along with a wall plaque. They mark the location of the last public execution in Edinburgh, that of George Bryce, the Ratho murderer, who was hanged here in 1864. Bryce, who was said to be a simpleton, brutally murdered 22-year-old Jane Seton, a nursery maid, by cutting her throat with a razor. On the day of his execution an angry crowd, thousands strong, turned up to watch, most of them

The double life of Deacon Brodie

Respectable businessman and town councillor by day. Criminal mastermind by night. That summed up William Brodie. That he preyed on respectable merchants, most of whom he knew well, and who considered him a friend, made his misdeeds yet more infamous. He was a source of endless fascination to the public, who turned out in their tens of thousands for his trial and execution. Little wonder then that Brodie was the inspiration for Robert Louis Stevenson's great novel *The Strange Case of Dr Jekyll and Mr Hyde*. But who was William Brodie and why did a man who seemed to have it all go so spectacularly off the rails?

At the foot of Lawnmarket there are many references to the Brodie family. The name adorns pubs and cafés and there is also a Brodie's Close. However, it is not always the same man. One is a respected figure, Francis Brodie, a successful wright and glass grinder, for whom the close is named. The other is his notorious son, Deacon William Brodie (1741–88).

For a time, father and son worked in partnership and the young man acquired a well-deserved reputation as a cabinetmaker and locksmith. The furniture he crafted was of the highest quality and he was patronised by the Edinburgh elite, including Stevenson's father, who bought a number of pieces, some of which can be seen in the writers' museum (*see page 58*). To the outside world, William Brodie was the epitome of bourgeois respectability, a status underlined by his election as deacon of the Incorporation of Wrights. This was not only an important organisation in the commercial world but it also meant he became a member of Edinburgh's town council.

However, the life of a respectable businessman was not exciting enough for Brodie. He was a heavy drinker, an inveterate gambler with a liking for the

Deacon Brodie board

cockfighting pits of Grassmarket and a womaniser with two mistresses and five illegitimate children. These were expensive pursuits and he quickly became mired in debt. After he had squandered a legacy from his father that included a cash sum of £10,000 – a fortune for the time – he urgently needed to raise money.

The solution, as Brodie saw it, was simple. He would use the trust he had built up with his rich customers to steal from them. His modus operandi was simplicity itself: while working in a house or a shop he took impressions of keys in lumps of putty and handed them to an accomplice, George Smith, a blacksmith. Smith made duplicate keys, enabling Brodie and his gang easy access to homes and businesses. The gang targeted jewellery shops, tobacconists and even the premises of tea merchants.

Brodie was emboldened by the success of his nefarious enterprise. So much so, that, in 1788, he planned an armed raid on the biggest prize of them all: the excise office in Canongate. It was the biggest mistake he ever made: burgling shops and private homes was one thing; stealing from the government quite another. The robbery was a disaster. The gang was disturbed and forced to flee, having stolen just £16. In the aftermath, a reward of £150 was posted, and, succumbing to temptation, one of Brodie's partners-in-crime went to the authorities. Seeing the writing on the wall Brodie fled to Amsterdam but was quickly apprehended and brought back to Edinburgh.

The trial of William Brodie captured the public imagination, packing the High Court day after day. Despite having Henry Erskine, one of the leading advocates of the day, as his defence counsel, Brodie and his accomplice Smith were found guilty and sentenced to death. It is said that while he waited in the tolbooth prison for his sentence to be carried out he was in good spirits, receiving visitors and charming them with his wit and humour. Brodie also had a hand in his own execution. The new-fangled drop platform now used on the gallows had been designed by him and while waiting for the hangman to do his worst Brodie inspected his handiwork. Noting the fine workmanship, and with a smile of satisfaction, he nodded his approval. It certainly did the trick. Moments later he was dead.

There is a story that Brodie, by bribing the executioner, was able to wear a steel collar to avoid strangulation and that after the trap opened he was quickly whisked away in order that his friends could revive him. If the story of the steel collar is true, it was to no avail. He perished on the gallows.

Deacon Brodie

enraged by Bryce's brutality. As he was led to the gallows he was roundly jeered and pelted with all manner of missiles, a tumult that only subsided when his head was in the noose. What happened next was truly gruesome: thanks to a miscalculation by the hangman Bryce fell only two feet and instead of instant death he was very slowly strangled. Estimates vary, but some observers calculated that his dance of death lasted between thirty and forty minutes.

Another well, the Lawnmarket well-head, which is similar to the Bow wellhead, is on your right. Few people realise that, as the street signs attest, this small section of street is still part of Lawnmarket.

Cross Lawnmarket, turn left and turn right into Bank Street.

The opulent Bank of Scotland building, a real Edinburgh landmark, perched high up on the edge of the Old Town, is now in front of us. The original structure dates from 1806 but was repeatedly altered, most substantially so by David Bryce in 1863. This was partly for aesthetic reasons but also due to practical considerations, such as the need for more space and because the location, on a steep rubble slope, was not structurally sound. Amongst the many statues and carvings, you can see the Bank of Scotland coat of arms above the main entrance, and, on the domes, Prosperity holding an urn and grapes and Plenty with a sheaf of corn. The golden statue on the central dome is Victory. On the inside the highlight is the magnificent two-storey banking hall.

Turn right onto St Giles' Street, and in the left corner go down the News Steps, which are named after nearby premises owned by local newspaper the *Edinburgh Evening News*. From here you have a view of the New Town, Fife and Calton Hill. At the bottom, we arrive at Market Street with a clear view of the mighty Scott monument,

Top left: Bank of Scotland headquarters

Above: Black Watch statue

Left: Museum on the Mound

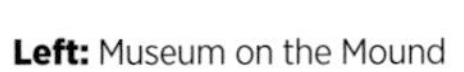

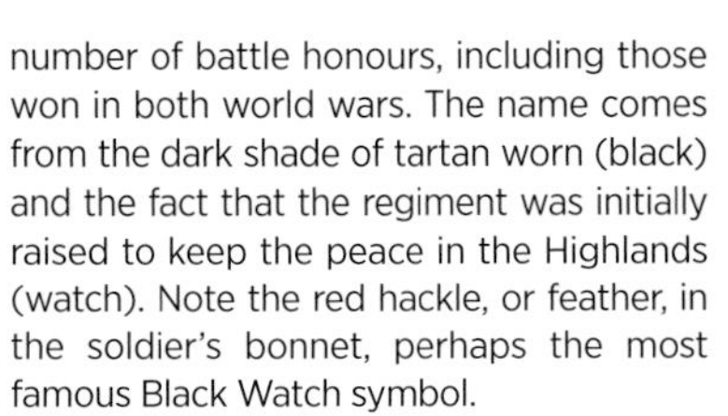

which is over two hundred feet (61 metres) high and the world's tallest monument to a writer. It was completed in 1844 and the design was chosen in a competition that was launched soon after Sir Walter Scott's death in 1832. Visitors are still able to climb the 287 steps to the top and enjoy the wonderful views, however the upper parts of the monument do get rather narrow and somewhat claustrophobic.

Turn left and head up the hill. From here you will notice the giant walls built to shore up the Bank of Scotland building.

At the top of the hill – on ground donated by the Bank of Scotland – is a striking, 11-foot/3.3 metre bronze statue of a Black Watch soldier in Highland dress looking towards the castle. It was designed by W. Birnie Rhind, unveiled in 1910 and has a plaque that lists those soldiers who fell in the Second Boer War. The Black Watch name, which stretches back to 1725, is one of the most revered in Scottish military history and the regiment has an incredible number of battle honours, including those won in both world wars. The name comes from the dark shade of tartan worn (black) and the fact that the regiment was initially raised to keep the peace in the Highlands (watch). Note the red hackle, or feather, in the soldier's bonnet, perhaps the most famous Black Watch symbol.

Turn left past the statue cross over the road at the pedestrian crossing. Turn left and continue up the hill.

Over the road on the left is the Museum on the Mound, which details Scotland's banking history and in which you can see Scotland's oldest banknote. On the right is the entrance to Lady Stair's Close; enter the close and you will recognise the inscriptions of Makars' Court. At the top of the stairs we end our walk back at Wardrop's Court.

Our walk has finished but if you wish to start the next one, leave the courtyard through the top left exit, turn left, and walk down High Street to St Giles cathedral.

IN DEPTH

The Harry Potter trail

Born in the south-west of England, Joanne, or JK, Rowling moved to Edinburgh in 1993, as a hard-up single mother, with ambitions to become a writer. In those early years she spent a lot of time in local cafes, working tirelessly on the stories and characters that would make her name; the result of course was the Harry Potter series. It is estimated that more than five hundred million Potter books have been sold, with several being turned into blockbuster films, amassing Rowling a fortune said to be £600 million (she is a noted philanthropist, who has donated large sums to good causes). While Edinburgh does not explicitly feature in the books, it is highly likely that locations in and around the Old Town fired her imagination.

CREATING A LEGEND

The first stop on the Harry Potter trail has to be the Elephant House, on George IV Bridge. It is said that Rowling wrote much of her first published novel, *Harry Potter and the Philosopher's Stone* (1997), here and in other Old Town cafes. There are many myths about its creation; for example, that she jotted down the plot on napkins because she was so poor that she couldn't afford paper. Yet she was a regular customer in the Elephant House, even if it was more for the coffee and the magnificent view of Edinburgh castle than the free writing materials.

DIGGING UP OLD CHARACTERS

Not far from the Elephant House you will find Greyfriars kirkyard. Some of the most important characters in the Harry Potter books have names that were either taken from, or inspired by, the names Rowling found on headstones as she wandered around the graveyard. Many have noted the similarity between the names of Professor Minerva McGonagall and the Scottish poet, William McGonagall, who is commemorated in the kirkyard by a wall plaque. Yet it was a less famous man, Thomas Riddell, whose grave attracts the most attention; with a slight spelling change, Rowling created Thomas Marvolo Riddle, the original name of Lord Voldemort, the terrifying villain of the books. Riddell died in 1806 and his final resting place in Greyfriars is regularly visited by fans, who leave letters, both pleasant and less so, at the grave of the 'world's worst wizard'.

AN INSPIRATIONAL INSTITUTION

Edinburgh's ancient schools occupy grand buildings and Rowling almost certainly used them to help conjure up an image of Hogwarts, Harry Potter's magical school. Although none are an exact replica, and we are not given a location for the School of Witchcraft and Wizardry, Rowling maintains it was in Scotland. In the Old Town a clear contender has to be George Heriot's, in Lauriston Place; its grounds are right next to Greyfriars kirkyard and the towers and turrets of this magnificent seventeenth-century building are clearly visible over the graveyard walls. While the school is off-limits to visitors, you can get a good view of it from many locations around the Old Town.

RIGHT UP OUR STREET

The incredible success of the books and films has left its mark on Edinburgh.

Shops such as Diagon House on Cockburn Street sell a wide range of Harry Potter goodies, from simple souvenirs to replica wands and broomsticks. Diagon House gets its name from Diagon Alley, the mysterious alley found behind the Leaky Cauldron pub. The real-life version of this cobbled street, with its colourful shops selling a wide range of intriguing goods, is Victoria Street, which connects Grassmarket and George IV Bridge. It may not be as narrow as Rowling's imagined alley, but its curved, steep rise, with Victoria Terrace above, gives it a magical feel. Victoria Street even has a couple of Potter-themed shops for wannabe wizards to explore.

TURNING THE CLOCK BACK

Another touch of Potter can be found in the Balmoral hotel, the impressive building at the junction of North Bridge and Princes Street. With the royalties pouring in, Rowling could now afford a very different location to draft the final volume in the series. It was in what is now known as the JK Rowling suite that *Harry Potter and the Deathly Hallows* (2007) was written. The hotel's luxurious function room includes the writing desk Rowling used, a bust of the Greek god Hermes, signed by Rowling, and a brass owl-shaped door knocker, a link to Harry Potter's magical pet, Hedwig. The Balmoral was previously the North British hotel, which opened in 1902. Its grand clock tower is visible across the Old and New towns of Edinburgh, and, apart from the thirty-first of December when Edinburgh's Hogmanay celebrations are in full-swing, it is always wrong. As any local will tell you, the Balmoral clock is three minutes fast, apparently to ensure that commuters rushing to Waverley station do not miss their train. It is not only Harry Potter and his friends Ron and Hermione who can find themselves moving back and forward through time.

MAGICAL MOMENTS

Whether you are a long-term fan or a newcomer to the Harry Potter world, following the Harry Potter trail is a magical experience, something that Edinburgh has officially acknowledged. In the quadrangle in front of the city chambers on the Royal Mile you will find JK Rowling's handprints.

The Hogwarts express on Glenfinnan viaduct

WALK 4
ST GILES CATHEDRAL AND THE TOP OF HIGH STREET

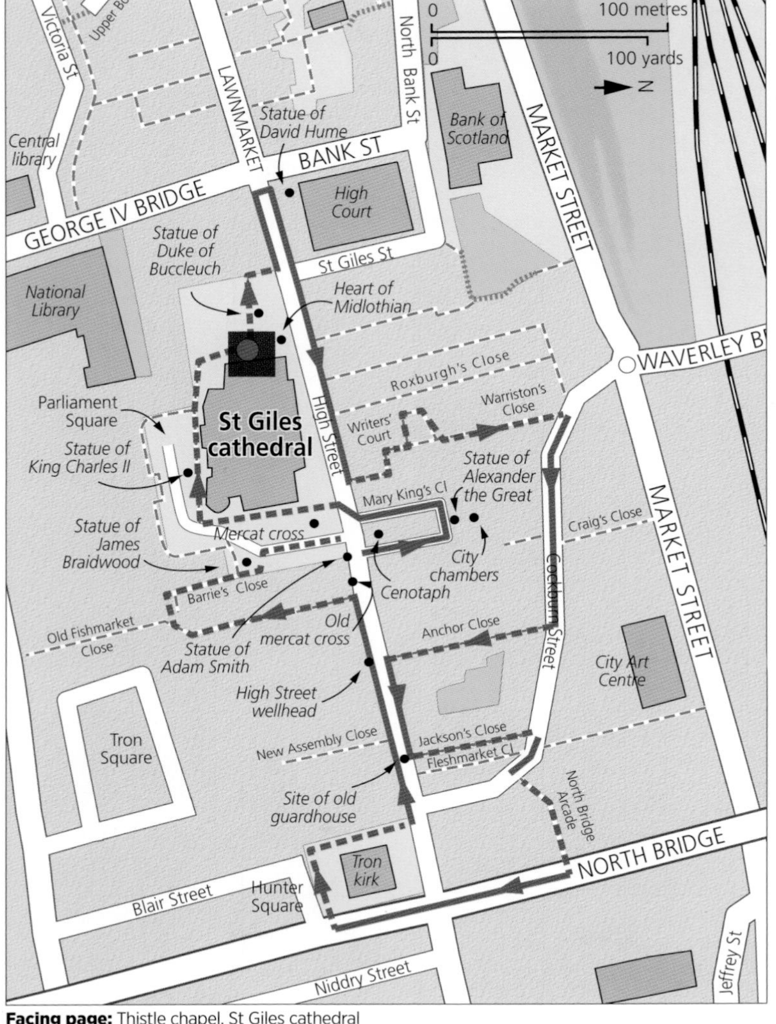

Facing page: Thistle chapel, St Giles cathedral

Start St Giles cathedral (west side), High Street

Summary After experiencing the splendour of St Giles cathedral, we investigate the top of High Street with its impressive buildings, fine statues, varied closes and hidden spaces. We also take in Cockburn Street and the walk finishes in the grandeur of Parliament Square, now the location of Scotland's most important law courts.

Highlights St Giles story • Thistle chapel and St Giles cathedral • Heart of Midlothian • David Hume story • Luckenbooths • Indian Peter • Warriston's Close • Cockburn Street and Lord Cockburn • North Bridge Arcade • Tron kirk * Faculty of Advocates building • Death of Montrose • Mercat cross • Adam Smith statue • Edinburgh city chambers • Statue of Alexander and Bucephalus • Parliament Square • King Charles II statue • John Knox grave • In-depth: Underground city

The Walk

We start outside St Giles cathedral, known also as the High Kirk of Edinburgh, on the west side of the building. Founded in the 1130s, St Giles was for centuries the only parish church in the burgh of Edinburgh, which accounts for its ample size and position at the heart of High Street. It is without question the best-known place of worship in Scotland and has been the stage upon which many important historical events have played out. The term 'cathedral', the official church of a bishop, is a misnomer and applies only to two short Episcopalian periods, 1633–8 and 1661–89. However, given its importance to Christian worship in Scotland the cathedral title has been retained.

At the steps leading to the main entrance, look above the doors and observe the relief of St Giles with a deer. Giles, a seventh-century hermit, lived in woods near Nimes, France, his only companion a deer. One day Flavius, king of the Visigoths, was out hunting and he fired an arrow at the deer, only for the projectile to miss the target and pierce the hand of the hermit, who was saying his prayers. Despite the pain, Giles continued with his devotions and also refused compensation from the King for his injuries. Flavius was deeply impressed by Giles's spirituality and eventually persuaded him to found a monastery near Nimes. One of the most popular figures among Christians of the Middle Ages, Giles is the patron saint of lepers, beggars and those driven into solitude. He is also the patron saint of Edinburgh.

After the Reformation of 1560 St Giles became a Protestant place of worship, with John Knox elected minister. Knox used the power of its pulpit to fulminate against 'popery' in general and Scotland's Roman Catholic monarch – Mary, Queen of Scots – in particular. St Giles also played an important role in the history of the Coven-

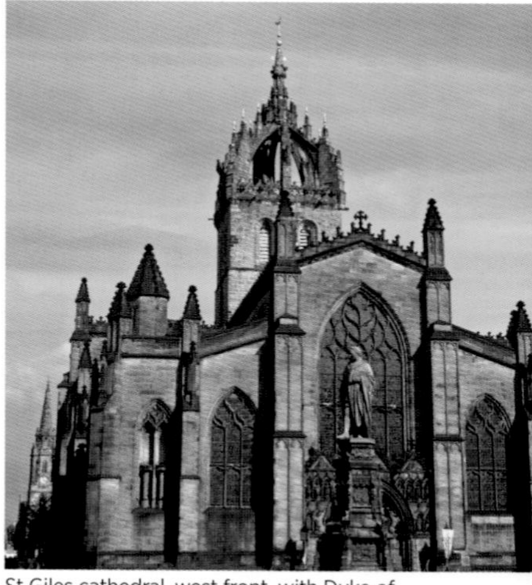

St Giles cathedral, west front, with Duke of Buccleuch statue

anters (*see Walk 10 for more on the Covenanters*). It was here in 1637, according to tradition, that Jenny Geddes stood up during the reading of Archbishop Laud's liturgy on how the church should be governed and made her famous protest. She hurled a stool at the bishop, while proclaiming 'Wha' daur say mass in my lug?' ('Who dares to say mass in my ear?'). The congregation roared its agreement with Geddes and a riot ensued. Many have argued this was the first clear expression of the Covenanting movement and led to the signing of the National Covenant in 1638.

The layout of St Giles has changed markedly over the centuries. There used to be four separate churches, separated by substantial stone walls, one for each of the city's four parishes, but this was gradually reduced to one. Inside, the choir, medieval vault and eastern bay are original, but, on the exterior, only the magnificent crown tower – an Old Town landmark – survived the 1829–33 refacing by William Burn. In the south-east corner of St Giles, we find the exquisite Thistle chapel – dedicated to the venerable Order of the Thistle – designed in the Gothic style by Sir Robert Lorimer in 1909. The chapel is intensely ornate and almost every inch of its surfaces is covered in intricate carvings, most notably the wonderful ceiling. See if you can spot the three carvings of angels playing bagpipes.

On exiting St Giles by the main entrance, look out over West Parliament Square. The large statue is of the 5th duke of Buccleuch (J. Edgar Boehm), unveiled in 1888. Among the scenes from the duke's life are some surprisingly graphic depictions of battle.

Veer to the right and take a few steps towards High Street.

On the ground between the duke's statue and the cathedral there are markers to indicate the location of the old tolbooth, which was a weigh-house for the market but also used as the Scottish Parliament building, a town hall and a prison before it was destroyed in 1817. Look for the plaques with dates on them and the brass-adorned cobbles extending out to your left; the dates record the tolbooth's construction and expansion over the years. Close by is the heart-shaped mosaic, the Heart of Midlothian (named for Sir Walter Scott's novel, *The Heart of Midlothian*), where it is thought the main door to the tolbooth prison was situated. Tradition claims that spitting on the heart brings good luck, although there is not enough evidence to tell us when, or why, this practice came about. It could be that spitting on the heart replaced spitting on the door of the prison, a way of showing distaste for the criminals and sinners, or that locals began spitting in protest at the destruction of such a long-standing local feature.

Heart of Midlothian

Turn left and walk up High Street.

On the left is a metal board that has a lot of information about the various buildings in West Parliament Square.

Continue past the Lawnmarket well-head, turn right and cross the road.

You will now be on Lawnmarket, outside the High Court of Justiciary, which is used for the most serious criminal trials. The building was originally constructed, in 1937, to house Edinburgh Sheriff Court, which has since moved to a large complex on Chambers Street.

In front of the court building is a statue of David Hume, commissioned by the Saltire

David Hume

The importance of David Hume (1711–76) to intellectual history cannot be understated: in his magisterial *A History of Western Philosophy*, Bertrand Russell describes Hume as 'one of the most important among philosophers'; the great German philosopher Immanuel Kant insisted that Hume had awakened him from his 'dogmatic slumber'; the *philosophes* of the French Enlightenment – Diderot and Rousseau among them – lionised him. Yet Hume's talents were not confined to philosophical enquiry: he was a brilliant economist, political scientist and historian and, if all this was not enough, he was in addition a wonderful prose stylist, described by James Boswell, no less, as the finest writer in Britain.

Born in Edinburgh, Hume's father was a minor landowner and lawyer while his mother was the daughter of a senior judge. After an education at Edinburgh University – which he attended from the extraordinarily tender age of 10 – Hume, like his father, seemed destined for the legal profession. However, his passions were philosophy and history, and by the age of 25, after eschewing a legal career and while living in France, he produced his first great work, *A Treatise of Human Nature*. Although it received little attention at the time – Hume himself admitted the book 'fell dead born from the press' – it is recognised today as one of the key philosophical texts. The *Treatise* is firmly rooted in the British empirical tradition and considers how the mind works in acquiring knowledge. In essence, Hume argues, no theory of reality is possible because there can be no knowledge of anything beyond experience. It follows from this that man cannot reason about God, because experience allows no firm knowledge of such a being, a conclusion that would bring Hume into conflict with Christian teaching.

After spells in England, Canada and at the family seat in Ninewells, Berwickshire, Hume returned to Edinburgh in 1751, where he took lodgings in a succession of Old Town houses. He had previously sought the chair of moral philosophy at Edinburgh University but his appointment was vetoed by an influential group of Church of Scotland ministers. He did, however, secure amenable employment in 1752 as keeper of the library of the Faculty of Advocates. With a degree of financial security now guaranteed, Hume was able to play a full part in the intellectual life of the city and he joined a range of philosophical and literary societies. It was at this time that he met Allan Ramsay, the leading British portraitist of the day, who would paint Hume twice (*see facing page*).

Thanks to the huge array of books at the Faculty of Advocates, Hume entered one of his most productive periods. Further philosophical works appeared and he was also able to write the work that would eventually be known as *The History of England*, an immediate best-seller that made him 'not only independent, but opulent'. It allowed him for the first time to buy, rather than rent, a house, a third-storey property in James's Court on Lawnmarket in the heart of the Old Town. At the age of 52, comfortable and respected, Hume appeared happy with a life of leisure. Yet there would be one more adventure.

Flattered by an invitation from an influential French aristocrat, the *comtesse* de Boufflers, that lavished him with praise, Hume travelled to Paris in 1763, where he served as personal secretary to the British ambassador, the earl of Hertford. Hume was widely feted and was even presented at court, where he had many admirers among the French royal family. While in France he agreed to a request from the *comtesse* that he should find refuge in

Portrait of David Hume (1766) by Allan Ramsay

England for the radical philosopher Jean-Jacques Rousseau, who was once again in trouble with the French authorities. Although Hume brought him to London, Rousseau's pride did not allow him to accept what he saw as charity and he soon returned to France.

Back in Edinburgh in 1769, Hume followed the well-trodden path from the Old to the New Town, which was now home to a growing number of the Edinburgh elite. He had a house built in St Andrew Square, with the adjoining street being named St David's (now St David) Street in his honour. But by 1772 his health began to decline and despite many attempts to find a cure, including taking the waters at Bath, David Hume died on 25 August 1776 and was buried in Calton churchyard.

David Hume statue

Society in 1997, which depicts Hume as a classical philosopher. The chair represents the easy chair Hume missed when he was away from his apartment in James's Court. Tourists are told that his big toe is rubbed by students to bring them luck in their exams. It is ironic that a superstition has been created around the statue of a philosopher who believed evidence and empirical facts were the only path to truth.

Facing the Hume statue, turn right and walk down the Royal Mile.

This is the start of High Street and at one time this section would have been occupied by the luckenbooths, or locked booths, which were housed in a four-storey, timber-framed tenement built in the fifteenth century, and joined at the west end to the old tolbooth. The luckenbooths were Edinburgh's first permanent shops, initially providing premises for jewellers and goldsmiths and later for a variety of merchants including bakers, chemists and milliners. Between the luckenbooths and St Giles there was a narrow passageway called the krames (creams), for traders without a permanent home, who sold everything from lollipops to toys. Due to the congestion they caused, both the luckenbooths and the krames had been demolished by 1817.

Byer's Close, on the left, was often home to advocates, lawyers and judges who worked in Parliament Square. Next is Advocate's Close, of 1735, which will afford you an excellent view of the Scott monument. At its mouth there is a plaque

Indian Peter

The luckenbooths had many colourful tenants, none more so than Peter Williamson, or 'Indian Peter' as he was known. Williamson had an extraordinary life. In 1743, at the age of 13, he was snatched from the quayside in his home city of Aberdeen and taken to the American colonies, where he was sold into indentured servitude. Thanks to a humane master he was freed and later bought a farm, only to be captured by the Delaware tribe, who also made him a slave. After escaping Williamson joined the British army and fought the French and their Indian allies, before becoming a prisoner-of-war. On his return to Scotland he rented an Edinburgh luckenbooth, from which he operated the world's first penny-post system as well as publishing a magazine. Later in life he opened a tavern. Remembering his adventures in North America, Williamson often dressed in Native American clothes.

Indian Peter

detailing some of the important figures who resided here. In 2014 the superb restoration of Advocate's Close was recognised by the award of a number of major architectural prizes for the way in which old and new buildings had been brought together.

Next on the left is Roxburgh's Close, which has a plaque dedicated to Gaelic poet Donnchadh Bàn Mac an t-Saoir (1724–1812), Duncan Ban MacIntyre in English, who was born in Glen Orchy, Argyll but died in the Old Town and was buried in Greyfriars kirkyard. The poet memorised all his work as he never learnt to write. His best-known poem was '*Mòladh Beinn Dobhrainn*', 'In Praise of Ben Doran', while another poem, *Òran don Bhriogais*, translates as 'Ode to Trousers' and was inspired by the Dress Act of 1745, which banned the wearing of kilts. Roxburgh's Close was also home to the premises of Chambers, the eminent Edinburgh publishers and printers, owned by siblings William and Robert. The company produced many successful and influential titles, including *Chambers' Edinburgh Journal* and *Chambers' Encyclopaedia*. William Chambers became Lord Provost of Edinburgh in 1865 and used his considerable energies to promote schemes for Old Town improvement and in

Cockburn Street

addition spent £30,000 of his own money on the restoration of St Giles cathedral.

Turn left into Mary King's Close, which leads to Writers' Court and Warriston's Close, the latter named for Sir Archibald Johnstoun of Warriston (1611–63), a leading proponent of the National Covenant of 1638, who had his townhouse here.

Follow signs for Tattoo Office and Mary King's Close.

Directly in front of you is Writers' Court, which is now the entrance to the Real Mary King's Close tourist attraction. Writers' Court has nothing to do with authors but is named for writers to the signet, or senior lawyers. The Signet library was here before moving to Parliament Square.

Turn left, follow Warriston's Close right and then turn left into Roxburgh's Court.

Although only one tree still stands in the left section of Roxburgh's Court, the decorative bases of the missing trees are extant. In the other section of the court, in the area in front of the restaurant, there is a collection of plaques with the Latin names of the trees and the year in which they were discovered or introduced to Britain.

Return to Warriston's Close, turn left and head down the steps.

A plaque on the right recalls that John Knox had his manse here. From this spot you have a good view of the New Town, including, on Princes Street, the Scott monument and Jenner's department store – the so-called Harrod's of Scotland – a prestigious emporium built in the 1890s to replace an earlier shop destroyed by a fire.

Continue down the long flight of stairs. When you reach the bottom, you are on Cockburn Street with its sinuous curve and striking architecture. The street was built in 1859 by the Railway Station Access Company to provide a route from Waverley station to Royal Mile. It is named after Henry, Lord Cockburn (1779–1854), a lawyer, senior judge, leading literary figure and noted conservationist. His name lives on through

Warriston's Close

The highly atmospheric Anchor Close

the Cockburn Association, founded in 1875 to campaign for, and protect, the beauty of Edinburgh.

Turn right and walk up Cockburn Street.

Immediately on the right there is a plaque. It is at the foot of the city chambers' walls and details the building's construction. Three closes were destroyed to create the city chambers: Craig's Close, Allan's Close and Old Post Office Close where, in 1713, there was only one postman to service the entire Old Town.

If you're sharp-eyed as you go up Cockburn Street, you will notice that, across the road on your left, a window has nineteenth-century corbelling, incorporating a jester underneath. On the right are the remnants of Craig's Close and a plaque near the bottom of the stairs describes how poet Robert Fergusson frequented the Cape Club in the Isle of Man tavern that once stood here. He was not the only famous patron: the Isle of Man attracted the celebrated, such as portrait painter Henry Raeburn, as well as the vilified, such as Deacon Brodie. Craig's Close was also home to the first offices of *The Scotsman* newspaper in 1816.

Next right is Anchor Close. Go up it and head to High Street.

Anchor Close is named after the Anchor tavern. At the end of the close a plaque gives information about the close's history. Sir Walter Scott's parents lived here but Anchor Close is best known as the home of *Encyclopaedia Britannica*. The great work was produced here in 1768 in the print works owned by William Smellie (1740–95), an autodidact, who is also credited with being the editor of the first edition.

Turn left and head down the Royal Mile.

Geddes ('s) Entry and North Foulis Close on the left are blocked. James Gillespie, famous for an Edinburgh school founded by his philanthropic donation, had a snuff shop in North Foulis Close and was known for travelling around the town in a grand yellow coach.

Old Stamp Office Close had Royal Bank of Scotland offices in the eighteenth century as well as the government stamp office. The plaque inside the close mentions some famous residents, including Flora MacDonald, who helped Bonnie Prince Charlie escape after the Battle of Culloden in 1746, and attended a boarding school here.

Also on the left, if you look up above the shop fronts you will see a plaque dedicated to Elsie Inglis (1864–1917), a pioneering Edinburgh doctor, suffragette and founder of the Scottish Women's Hospitals for Foreign Service organisation. At the start of

Anchor Close plaque

Dr Elsie Inglis

the First World War, Inglis offered her services to the War Office and the Red Cross but was rejected by both. Undaunted she raised substantial amounts of money, which she used to set up ambulance units and field hospitals for soldiers wounded on the front line, mainly in France and Serbia. In 1915, Dr Inglis went to Serbia to work in one of the hospitals and was later taken prisoner by Austrian troops, before being released in 1916. She went right back to her war work with the Serbian troops, but, a sick woman following a cancer diagnosis, she was forced to return to Britain, where she died in November 1917.

Pass Lyon's Close and Jackson's Close and you will find yourself outside the entrance to Fleshmarket Close.

Look to your right and find the brass plaques among the cobbles of High Street. They mark out the old city guardhouse, described by Sir Walter Scott as a low, long, ugly building. As well as being home to the guard it was used to punish those found guilty of petty crimes, often in painful and humiliating ways.

Turn left into Fleshmarket Close and head down to Cockburn Street. Cross the street, where Fleshmarket Close, the lower section, continues.

Fleshmarket Close gets its name from the meat market that was on the right-hand side at the bottom of the close steps. Today it serves as a short-cut to Waverley station and two pubs halfway down will quench your thirst before you finish climbing or descending the stairs.

Don't enter the lower part of Fleshmarket Close. Instead turn right on Cockburn Street, passing two shops, and when you get to a stone archway turn left into the covered street of North Bridge Arcade. (The arcade's entrance is invariably covered by clothes and souvenir items and is therefore easy to miss.) It was built in 1900 and is one of five remaining Victorian arcades in Scotland. It still has the original bowed-glass shop-fronts and an impressive stained-glass dome.

Exit the arcade onto North Bridge and turn right. Walk up the bridge whilst appreciating the nineteenth-century architecture and interesting carvings on the buildings until you return to High Street/Royal Mile.

Cross the Royal Mile to the entrance of Tron kirk.

The kirk was built by John Mylne jun. and John Scott in 1636–47 to cater for a congregation displaced when St Giles became a cathedral. Much altered, not least by the construction of South Bridge in the 1780s, which meant the loss of its south aisle, and also by the great fire of 1824, which led to the 1828 insertion of a new and much larger steeple. Note the original hammerbeam roof and the stained-glass windows. In the 1970s, archaeological work on the floor of the church unearthed cobbles of the sixteenth-century street, Marlin's Wynd. Today the Tron houses a flea market and café.

Continue along the street with the Tron on your right. This is now South Bridge. After

Above: Dome, North Bridge Arcade

Right: Tron kirk

the church and the public toilets turn right into Hunter Square.

Hunter Square and the nearby Blair Street were named after James Hunter Blair, Lord Provost in 1784, who was responsible for the building of South Bridge. In the square is a golden pillar box, one of more than a hundred that were painted to celebrate British gold-medal winners at the 2012 Olympics. This one is dedicated to Edinburgh-born cyclist Sir Chris Hoy, who won a total of six Olympic gold medals.

At the post box turn right and leave Hunter Square by climbing the three steps.

Walking up the steps you will notice sculptures of fruit baskets and granite seats, with inscriptions of quotes about different food items, unveiled in the late 1990s. As you leave the square you pass a fountain in the shape of a basket made by coiling forms, which represents Edinburgh's volcanic geography.

When you reach the Royal Mile turn left.

Pass Stevenlaw's Close and next left is New Assembly Close (142 High Street), which leads to the Lord Reid building, now home to the Faculty of Advocates, and open during office hours. The classical structure

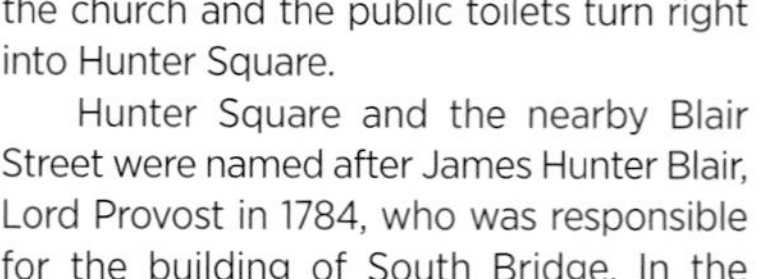

Sir Chris Hoy post box

of 1814 (James Gillespie Graham), with its fine Ionic columns and pedimented entrance replaced the eighteenth-century assembly rooms, which held balls and receptions. This building was home to the Commercial Bank and later the NSPCC. New Assembly Close was also home to the Edinburgh wax museum until it closed in 1989 and a plaque at the entrance recalls Charles Cameron

Faculty of Advocates building

(1927–2001), an exponent of 'bizarre magick', astrology and the supernatural. He was the museum curator and performed shows here.

Further up the High Street, past Bell's Wynd, Burnet's Close and Covenant Close, is the High Street wellhead. If you read the plaque you will learn about how the original was damaged by a horse-drawn fire-engine. On the other sides of the plaque there are the theatrical masks of comedy and tragedy. This is because it stands in front of Old Assembly Close, where dances and balls were held.

We continue up Royal Mile, pass Borthwick's Close, until we are outside the entrance to Old Fishmarket Close with the metal fish around its sign.

Before you enter the close, look at the ground to your right. The octagonal, cobbled area marked out is the site of the original mercat cross. First mentioned in 1305, it was a site for public proclamations and executions (*including the Marquis of Montrose; see overleaf*). During the Enlightenment, when Edinburgh was an intellectual hothouse, George II's chemist remarked that he could stand at the mercat cross and within a few minutes 'take fifty men of genius by the hand'.

Turn left into Old Fishmarket Close and walk down the hill.

This close was home to George Heriot (1563–1624), made famous as 'Jingling Geordie' by Sir Walter Scott. Heriot made his fortune as a goldsmith and it is said that

Site of old mercat cross

James VI's queen, Anne of Denmark, bought £50,000-worth of jewellery from him, equivalent to tens of millions today. With his wealth, Heriot helped to finance the royal court and one story claims he showed off his wealth to King James by heating his house with burning banknotes. Old Fishmarket Close also had the house of the city hangman, which meant he was able to quickly get to and from Parliament Square, one of the major execution spots, without too much aggravation from the citizenry.

Halfway down Old Fishmarket Close, turn right up the short flight of steps and turn right again into Barrie's Close. Climb the stairs and you arrive in East Parliament Square. At the top of the steps, turn right and walk towards High Street.

The statue on the left is of James Braidwood. He created the world's first municipal fire-brigade in 1824, and, although it was unable to prevent the great fire in

James Braidwood statue

The death of Montrose

Marquis of Montrose

James Graham, Marquis of Montrose, soldier and poet, is one of the most romantic figures in Scottish history. During the turbulent 1640s, as wars in England, Ireland and Scotland raged, Montrose defended the interests of Charles I in Scotland against the Covenanter forces led by the Marquis of Argyll. His initial campaign of 1644, in which he won six battles, was brilliant, but after a defeat at Philiphaugh, in 1645, he was forced to flee to Norway. In 1649, enraged by the execution of Charles, he returned to Scotland, swearing revenge, but his small force was routed at Carbisdale in 1650. Montrose, now on the run, took refuge in Ardvreck castle with Neil MacLeod of Assynt. It was a fatal error: MacLeod betrayed him to the authorities for the reward money, the then huge sum of £25,000. Taken to Edinburgh, Montrose was summoned before Parliament and sentenced to death without the inconvenience of a trial.

On 21 May 1650, at two in the afternoon, Montrose was taken from his cell in the tolbooth prison and marched up High Street to the mercat cross. With his long hair carefully combed and dressed in his finest scarlet and black, with white gloves, silk stockings, ribboned shoes and hat in hand, one spectator was prompted to observe that he looked more like a bridegroom than a traitor about to die. At the cross the stage had been set: a gallows thirty-feet high was sitting on a platform covered with black cloth. The crowd had been encouraged to shower him with abuse but Montrose's quiet dignity stunned them into silence. After he gave the hangman a gold coin, his arms were tied and he ascended the ladder to the noose. It is said his last words were 'God have mercy on this afflicted land.'

After hanging for three hours his body was taken down and dismembered. His head was stuck on a spike at the tolbooth, where it remained for eleven years, while his limbs were sent to four Scottish towns to be put on display. As fate would have it, his great adversary, Argyll, would suffer the same fate eleven years later. Having fallen foul of Charles II, he too was hanged at the mercat cross and dismembered, with his head impaled on the same tolbooth spike occupied by Montrose.

Adam Smith statue

Mercat cross, with the city chambers in the background

November of that year, Braidwood and his men became very popular. He died in 1861 and thousands attended his funeral.

On the left you will also find the mercat cross, built in 1885 to replace the earlier iteration (*described above*), which dated from the fourteenth century but was destroyed in 1756. The cross-house we see today, completed in 1885 to designs by Sydney Mitchell, is a copy of that original and incorporates some elements from the older structure. With an octagonal shape and complemented by a unicorn finial, it is decorated with British and Irish coats of arms as well as those of Edinburgh, Leith and Canongate. The Latin inscription praises Sir Walter Scott, for lamenting the demise of the old cross, and Prime Minister William Gladstone, who as MP for Midlothian helped find the money for reconstruction.

On High Street the statue of father-of-economics Adam Smith (1723–90) is on your right. The statue faces Kirkcaldy, where he was born, and the plaque details his connection to Edinburgh, while the plough on the statue represents the agrarian economy that existed before his ideas (*for more on Smith, see Walk 6*).

Cross High Street.

We are now standing outside Edinburgh city chambers (253 High Street). Originally built for the city's merchants in 1761 as the Royal Exchange, the original design – later modified – was by the eminent Scottish architects, siblings Robert and John Adam, and is now the only eighteenth-century public building still extant on the Royal Mile. Never a success as an exchange, it was taken over by the city council in the nineteenth century and later expanded. It houses the council's debating chamber.

Before you enter the three-sided courtyard of the city chambers, you can look at the cenotaph memorial to the fallen in the centre of the arcade. Erected in 1927 it is a simple granite block that reads, 'Their name liveth for evermore'.

Enter the courtyard by the right-hand entrance.

Alexander and Bucephalus statue

Mary, Queen of Scots plaque

On the wall, to your right, is a plaque detailing the history of the city chambers and at your feet as you enter the square there is a memorial to the late president of South Africa, Nelson Mandela, and one of the charities he established, 46664, which was his prison number.

In the centre of the square is a bronze statue *Alexander & Bucephalus* (John Steell 1883), which depicts Alexander the Great wrestling his horse Bucephalus. It was modelled fifty years before it was cast and originally located in St Andrew Square. An old Edinburgh story is that because the money ran out before the statue was finished the sculptor gave the horse a pig's ears. Early models show the ears were certainly altered, so perhaps the story is true.

Walk across to the other side of the courtyard.

Among the paving slabs, you can find the handprints and names of the Edinburgh Award winners. Started in 2007 the competition honours Edinburgh natives, or residents, who have made an outstanding contribution to the city. Past winners include author J. K. Rowling, businessman Sir Tom Farmer and world champion boxer Ken Buchanan.

Turn left and leave the courtyard. On the wall as you exit is another plaque. This recalls the last night of Mary, Queen of Scots in the city before her detention in Loch Leven castle.

Cross High Street one more time. Walk across Parliament Square with the mercat cross on your left and St Giles on your right. When you pass the church, turn right.

The grand buildings that form three sides of this square are now solely used by the Scottish higher courts but originally this was Parliament house, built in the 1630s as the permanent seat of Scottish government. Although the exterior was much altered in the nineteenth century, the magnificent Parliament hall, where the Scottish Parliament once met, has survived. The hall is 123 feet long, 42 feet wide and 40 feet high and is crowned by an impressive hammerbeam roof of 1639, made of oak imported from Denmark. Another striking feature of the hall is the great window on the south wall, installed in 1868, which has 8,000 pieces of stained glass covering 390 square feet; it celebrates the founding of the Court of Session in 1532 by King James V. Parliament hall is open to the public during normal office hours and is well worth a visit.

Parliament house also contains one of the most beautiful spaces in Scotland, the

King Charles II statue in Parliament Square

Parliament hall, in a nineteenth-century drawing

Signet library (William Stark, 1813). Arranged on two floors, it is the upper library that takes the breath away. Described by one architectural historian as a 'classical cathedral', at 136 feet it runs the entire length of the building and is supported by magnificent Corinthian columns, with the ornate semi-elliptical ceiling and the roof-lit dome adding to the Georgian ambience. The lower library has a tea salon.

In the centre of the square is a lead statue of King Charles II, the oldest statue in Edinburgh and perhaps the oldest lead equestrian statue in the United Kingdom. It was made in the seventeenth century during the King's lifetime (perhaps by Dutch sculptor Grinling Gibbons) and has him dressed as Julius Caesar. The statue was originally intended to be of Lord Protector Oliver Cromwell, who ordered Charles I's execution and abolished the monarchy. However, Cromwell died in 1658 and Charles II was crowned before the statue was finished so the plans were altered.

Walk across the square with St Giles on your right.

Above one of the windows on the right is a small crown; in line with this, there are plaques on the ground that mark the grave of John Knox, one of which indicates that

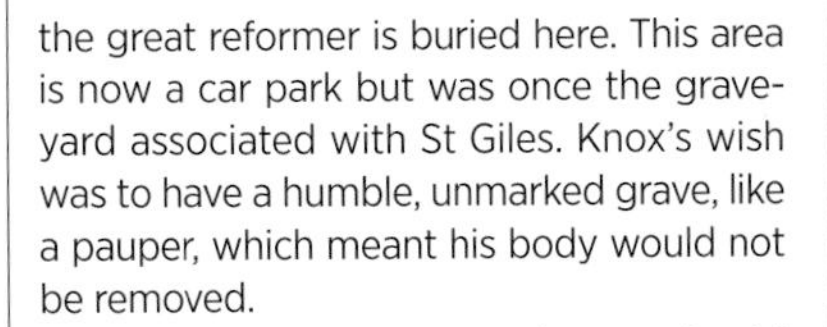

the great reformer is buried here. This area is now a car park but was once the graveyard associated with St Giles. Knox's wish was to have a humble, unmarked grave, like a pauper, which meant his body would not be removed.

Leave the square and you should recognise West Parliament Square. On your left is the entrance to the Signet Library Colonnades tea salon, which occupies the lower floor of the library. Pop in to appreciate the grand elegance of its interior.

We have reached the end of this walk. If you want to start the next one, return to the High Street, turn left, cross over the crossroads and go down to John Knox house.

Plaque marking John Knox grave

IN DEPTH

Underground city

Many visitors to Edinburgh hear tales of an 'underground city'. Stories about secret tunnels under the Royal Mile and whole streets underneath the buildings and closes of the Old Town pique your curiosity and capture your imagination. However, like many tales of the Old Town the true picture is not exactly what the stories lead you to believe but can often be more interesting than the fiction.

THE GROWING CITY

Until the eighteenth century, when Edinburgh began properly to expand beyond its city walls, space was at a premium. People were squashed into the narrow closes and the city was built upwards in a rather haphazard fashion. Over time these buildings were repeatedly enlarged, rebuilt and replaced. The foundations and interiors of many of the buildings on the Royal Mile are much older than the frontages. Spaces, cellars and even whole streets are buried under the modern city, occasionally acting as time capsules, preserving Edinburgh as it once was.

HIDDEN SPACES

Many of the forgotten streets are covered with rubble and inaccessible, part of the foundations of more recent buildings. Tron kirk was revealed to be built over Marlin's Wynd, a street that was destroyed during the construction of South Bridge. Others are inaccessible, something that can cause problems for the modern city. When a large fire took hold in Cowgate in 2002 the fire brigade struggled fully to extinguish the blaze as these tight, forgotten spaces continued to burn but access to them was almost impossible.

There are, of course, many underground areas that are explorable. Many of them have been converted into storage for shops or themed pubs and restaurants. The low, arched ceilings give a claustrophobic feel and bring to mind the ghost stories that Edinburgh has conjured up over the centuries, which some businesses have been keen to exploit, declaring their bars to be the most haunted in the country. However true this might be the close air and eerie cool do give these spaces a disconcerting atmosphere.

THE VAULTS

The bridges built to improve access to the Old Town created most of the accessible spaces. The largest archways of George IV Bridge have for many years been used as theatre space during the Edinburgh Festival Fringe and as nightclubs for the rest of the year. Being underground not only facilitates loud music but also adds to the alternative, experimental nature of the acts that perform at the Fringe.

For those who want to step in to the past the best areas to visit are the vaults under South Bridge. Before the current buildings closed off access to the arches of the bridge, these spaces were occupied and some remnants can still be found. On the north side of the bridge visitors are taken through the vaults and tunnels by walking tours. Here they are told of the cobblers and taverns that legitimately traded in the area but also of the illegal activities that took place once the area was closed off.

On the south side of South Bridge the vaults were expanded into the other streets and squares that existed before the bridge was built. One former building was an illicit whisky distillery that was raided by the authorities in 1815. Newspapers at the time detail how ingenious the subterfuge was: the original door was plastered over and a fireplace in another room was covered by a grate, which, when opened, led to a passage that gave access to a trapdoor into an upper floor where the stills were located. Secret pipes ensured running water and an exhaust for the smoke.

Mary King's Close

MARY KING'S CLOSE

By far the most intriguing underground space in Edinburgh is Mary King's Close, which is now a visitor attraction. Once home to hundreds of people, the close was afflicted by an outbreak of bubonic plague in 1645, in which many residents perished. Although the town council employed a local doctor, Rae, to assist the plague victims, local tradition says otherwise, painting officialdom as the villain of the piece. One story has it that the council tried to contain the plague by bricking up the close, trapping the unfortunate inhabitants in their houses. Although this is almost certainly untrue, the close acquired a sinister reputation, leading many to conclude it was cursed and haunted. In consequence, many vacant properties were never reoccupied, leading to access being obstructed. Although some locals had access, and converted rooms into cellars, and the lower buildings were used as foundations for the Royal Exchange – now the city chambers – for most of Edinburgh Mary King's Close was largely forgotten for more than two hundred years.

Today Mary King's Close is fully accessible and a successful visitor attraction (fee payable). Walking through the preserved buildings, it is unmistakeably an old Edinburgh street and you can see the traditional interiors with original plaster ceilings and prints on the walls. Yet the feeling of being underground is never forgotten. There are stories of the ghost of a small girl said to walk the old street and for whom visitors often leave toys.

Mary King is said to have been a successful businesswoman, a merchant burgess and the daughter of Alexander King, an advocate, but like so many elements of old Edinburgh, this is hard to prove. Other documents give alternative names for the close so more research is required. Perhaps that will uncover more of lost Edinburgh.

John Knox house, High Street

WALK 5
THE BOTTOM OF HIGH STREET

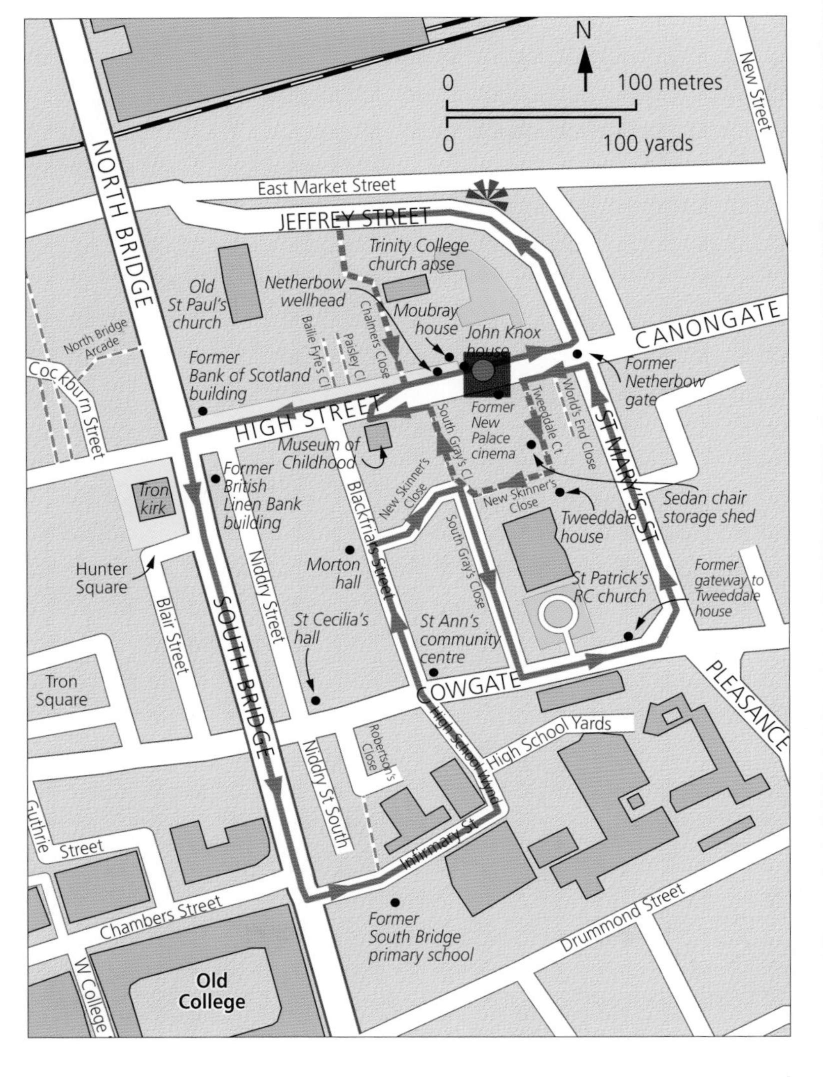

Start John Knox house, 43–45 High Street

Summary From the Knox house we discover the history of this part of High Street, get a striking view of Calton Hill, take in the area around South Bridge and finish with part of Cowgate and its environs.

Highlights John Knox house • John Knox story • Moubray house • Calton Hill view • Trinity College apse • Heave awa' disaster • Old St Paul's church • St Cecilia's hall • Cardinal Beaton story • Regent Morton's house • St Patrick's church and the Venerable Margaret Sinclair story • World's End • the Begbie outrage • In-depth: Festival city

The Walk

Whether or not John Knox ever lived in the wonderful house that bears his name is a question that divides historians. There was no Knox family connection to the property, nor did he ever own it. All that we can be certain of is that if he did reside there, it was for a very short period at the end of his life, and even that is debatable. It may well be that the name 'John Knox house' owes more to legend and wishful thinking than to historical fact.

The house was built in 1470 (close to the Netherbow port, or gate, the main entrance into Edinburgh) as a two-storey dwelling but the structure we see today is largely the result of the substantial extensions made in the 1560s by the wealthy goldsmith, James Mossman, and his heiress wife, Mariota Arres, whose family had owned the house for decades. Mossman was a close ally of Mary, Queen of Scots, supplying her with several pieces of jewellery. She was quick to recognise his service: in 1561, Mary appointed him master of the royal mint, knighting him in 1565. After her forced abdication in 1567, Mossman stayed loyal, and was one of the occupiers of Edinburgh castle during the 'lang' siege when the Queen's men defended the great redoubt against her enemies. It was, however, a losing battle, and, in April 1572, Mossman was captured by Mary's enemies, found guilty of treason and later hanged at the mercat cross.

The house would not have been empty during the long years of the siege: it is likely that the Mossman family continued to live there, as would the distinguished goldsmith himself, albeit intermittently, during the many truces that were agreed. Due to the fighting in Edinburgh, John Knox had decamped to St Andrews in May 1571 and did not return until 31 July 1572. Given that he died on 24 November 1572 this narrows the period of his possible occupation of the 'House in the Netherbow' to between three and four months. The problem is that no conclusive documentary evidence exists, even for such a short stay.

In fact, it was only in the late eighteenth century – two hundred years after the death of the great reformer – that the property became known as John Knox's house. Many reasons are advanced for naming it thus: nearby Trunk's Close was once known as Knox's Close, although it was named after another John Knox; there was a sculpted figure on the wall, which many took to be Knox; the house was very old and he had previously lived in the vicinity, so it was theoretically possible. The most likely explanation, however, was that as interest in Scottish history grew it seemed to many people entirely appropriate that the 'Apostle of the Scots' should have lived in such a fine property.

We should be thankful that the house was linked so strongly to John Knox, for otherwise it would have been lost. Down the centuries the properties in this part of the

Old Town fell into disrepair. In 1839, part of the adjoining tenement split off and collapsed, apparently exposing the occupants in the remaining half eating their breakfast. But for the intervention of the Free Church of Scotland and the Society of Antiquaries, supported by many of Edinburgh's prominent citizens, it is likely that the whole area, the Knox house included, would have been cleared. Instead a substantial refurbishment programme was put in place, one writer describing it as the result of Scotland's first conservation campaign.

The questions about Knox's occupancy should not deter you from making a stop here; this is one of the oldest houses in Edinburgh, providing a marvellous insight into life in the capital during the late-medieval period. While the major portion dates from the Mossman family ownership in the mid-sixteenth century, there are parts that stretch back to 1470. The exterior, with its projecting timber galleries and forestairs is striking, leading Pevsner, our leading architectural historian, to describe it as 'improbably picturesque'. At the corner, between the ground and first floors, you can see a statue of Moses kneeling on a sundial; above it, on the left, are the names of God in English, Greek and Latin. Note also the Scots quote around the building, which instructs the reader to 'Love God above all and your neighbour as yourself'.

Yet it is perhaps the interior of the Knox house that is most memorable: the massive walls, a metre thick; the stone turnpike staircase; the huge tiled fireplaces. Then the pièce de résistance: the oak room on the third floor, with its oak panelling and splendid painted ceiling, on which you should look for the hidden figure of the Devil. The house is open to the public and now incorporates the Scottish Storytelling Centre, an arts venue, which is on the ground floor. The centre has a variety of attractions, including an interactive story-wall as well as the remnants of the 'luckenbooths' (locked booths), an early type of shopping centre. It also hosts a variety of events, including live storytelling, exhibitions, music and theatre.

To the left of the Knox house, and attached to it, is Moubray house (53 High Street), with four storeys, attic, outside stairs

Above: Moses and the sundial, John Knox house

Right: Moubray house

John Knox

There is no doubt that John Knox (1514–72) is one of the most influential figures in the history of Scotland and certainly its most significant clergyman. His writings and sermons were the inspiration for the Protestant Reformation that swept away Roman Catholicism in the 1550s. He was an important social reformer, insisting that every kirk in the land should have a teacher to instruct children and that the church had a duty to care for the poor. Knox was also a brilliant historian whose writings provide valuable insights into a crucial period. Yet there is still a degree of controversy about his legacy: he was seen even by some allies as too uncompromising, while his fulminations against women alienated many, including, for a time at least, Queen Elizabeth I of England.

Knox was born in the East Lothian town of Haddington and after attending St Andrews University he was ordained as a Catholic priest in the late 1530s. However, he was attracted to the fledgling Protestant movement, a particular influence being George Wishart, a fiery preacher who did much to spread the new religion. When Wishart was hanged and burnt at the stake in 1546 it set off a chain of events that led to the worst two years of Knox's life. The man who had ordered the execution of Wishart, Cardinal Beaton, was himself assassinated, throwing Scotland into turmoil and prompting Mary of Guise – regent on behalf of her 5-year-old daughter, Mary, Queen of Scots – to turn to her native France for help. In 1547, a French fleet duly arrived in St Andrews and took many Protestants into custody. Knox was one of those captured and he was sentenced to serve as a galley slave on one of the ships. It would be nineteen long months of unspeakable hardship before Knox was released from captivity.

Much of the next decade was spent in first, England, and latterly, in Geneva, where he was profoundly influenced by Calvin, the great Protestant philosopher. Knox loved Geneva, which he described as the 'maist perfyt schoole of Chryst', and it gave him time to think and write. It was during this period that his infamous tract, *The First Blast of the Trumpet Against the Monstrous Regiment of Women*, was published, in which he argued that for a woman to exercise sovereign power went against the laws of nature. While his main target was the Catholic queen of England, Mary Tudor, it also offended her Protestant successor, Elizabeth I, who ascended to the throne in 1558.

The exile of John Knox ended in 1559. With the Lords of the Congregation, Protestant nobles, now in open revolt against Mary of Guise he came home to support them. He started by preaching a provocative sermon against Catholicism and 'idolatry' in Perth, provoking a riot, and then travelled widely, rousing both the common people and the Protestant armies with his fire-and-brimstone speeches. Before long the insurgents were in the ascendancy and when Mary of Guise died in June 1560, the last obstacle to the creation of a Protestant state was removed. By August of that year, the Reformation Parliament abolished papal jurisdiction over Scotland and enshrined the new religion. Knox's dream had come true.

There was, however, a cloud on the horizon. In August 1561, Mary, Queen of Scots, the daughter of James V and Mary of Guise, and the rightful heir, arrived in Edinburgh to claim her throne. Although a staunch Roman Catholic, Mary gave official recognition to the reformed religion, the quid pro quo being that she could attend mass and practise her religion, as long as her observance was done in private. This was too much for John Knox. In his eyes, 'one mass was more dangerous than ten thousand armed enemies'; he would brook no compromise of any kind with Roman Catholicism, even if his sovereign was an adherent of that faith.

John Knox preaching to the Lords of the Congregation, 1559 (Sir David Wilkie)

As the minister of St Giles, Knox occupied the most influential pulpit in the land and from 1561–5 he used his sermons to rail against Mary and her faith, whom he described as 'that wretched woman, the mother of all misery'. This did not go down well with those Protestant aristocrats who had accepted positions in the Queen's government, but Knox was unmoved. He also met Mary four times, and, while the interviews ended amicably, Knox stuck firmly to his view that all Catholic queens were Jezebels intent on persecuting God's people. He even turned down the opportunity to be Mary's spiritual adviser, fearing it was a ploy to encourage him to water down his sermons.

It would be Mary's own poor judgement and not Knox's preaching that would lead to her being removed from the throne in 1567 and her subsequent exile in England. The reason was that just three months after the murder of her first husband, Lord Darnley, (*see Walk 9*) she married the main suspect, the earl of Bothwell, turning the nobles and most of the country against her.

Even with Mary gone Edinburgh was a dangerous place. Her supporters fought on, occupying Edinburgh castle during the 'lang' siege of 1571–3. For most of this time Knox found it safer to be in St Andrews, where he found an adoring audience among the many students in that most academic of towns. In the summer of 1572, with the armed conflict now at an end, he returned to Edinburgh, preaching once again at St Giles despite his rapidly deteriorating health. His last sermon was given on 9 November and he died two weeks later.

The legacy of John Knox lives on to this day and he continues to be an inspiration to Presbyterians in Scotland and in many other countries. Almost all Protestant groups have at one time or another laid claim to his memory, the most heated debate taking place during the Disruption of 1843, when dissenters in the Church of Scotland left to form the Free Church of Scotland, claiming they were following Knox's principles. His writings have also proved to be highly influential, in particular his great work, *History of the Reformation in Scotland*, which was first published in 1587 and provides invaluable source material for this most crucial period in the nation's past.

Patrick Geddes statue, Trunk's Close

Netherbow wellhead

and an eccentric window layout. The foundations of the building date from the 1470s, and, although the façade is seventeenth century, Moubray house is one of the most ancient buildings in the Old Town (not currently open to the public). It has been home to many fascinating people, including novelist Daniel Defoe, who wrote *Robinson Crusoe*, and Archibald Constable, publisher of the *Edinburgh Review*, one of the nineteenth century's most influential periodicals. The interior is highly atmospheric, with painted ceilings from the seventeenth century.

Just to the left of Moubray house is Trunk's Close. Go down the close, turn right and you will find one of the keyhole gardens designed by Sir Patrick Geddes, as well as a sculpture of the great man. This little green oasis with its circular lawn is the ideal place to stop, have a seat and recharge the batteries. If you turn left instead of right at the bottom of the close, you will have an excellent view of Trinity College apse, which is covered in more detail later in this walk.

Leave Trunk's Close the same way you came in. You are now back on High Street, facing Moubray house.

Before we start the rest of our walk look behind you and you will see the Netherbow wellhead. It has been moved from its original position outside the entrance to Fountain Close and you can see a large dent where buckets were hastily filled by locals.

Turn to face John Knox house and walk past it down the hill.

As we walk down the street, immediately on the right, you can see the carved signage on a building indicating that it was once the New Palace cinema. It was built in the 1920s, converted into a nightclub and was then derelict before renovation.

Passing John Knox house, on your left, you can see a stylised version of the wooden sign that marked the entrance to the Netherbow port, or gate. This was one of the six city gates and we will see it later. 'BEATI PACIFIC' means Blessed are the Peace-

Netherbow port sign

Scottish Storytelling Centre

makers, I R 6 stands for James VI and 1606 was the year the entrance was remodelled.

Behind John Knox house, and attached to it, is the Scottish Storytelling Centre, an arts venue. Inside they have the 1621 old port bell, which hung over the Netherbow, as well as a plaque from 1606.

When you pass Baron Maule's Close look up and find a carving of how the Netherbow would have looked with its curved towers and a square clock tower above the gate. The carving also details when the Netherbow was demolished because it was slowing traffic into the Old Town.

When you reach the crossroads (Jeffrey and St Mary's streets) look for the brass plaques on the road, which indicate the

Netherbow port carving, Baron Maule's Close

Brass plaques indicating Netherbow port site

Calton Hill view

original location of the Netherbow port. This was the end of the Old Town. Beyond here lay Canongate and land owned by the Crown.

Turn left onto Jeffrey Street.

This road was built in the nineteenth century to attach High Street to the train station and built over Leith Wynd, the original route to Leith and the docks. If you look at the tops of the buildings on the right you can see interesting carvings, including grouse.

Follow the road as it curves to the right and appreciate the view of Calton Hill.

Of the monuments you can see the most striking are the Parthenon-style columns of the national monument, designed by William H. Playfair and C. R. Cockerell and promoted by, among others, Sir Walter Scott and Lord Cockburn. This attempt to build a replica of the Parthenon in honour of those who fell during the Napoleonic Wars ran out of money by 1829, so only twelve pillars were completed. It was considered an embarrassment and called 'Edinburgh's disgrace'.

The tower that resembles an upside-down telescope to the left of the national monument is the Nelson monument (Robert Burn, 1807) in honour of the British naval hero. A time ball at the top of the tower was used alongside the one o' clock gun to aid ships in setting their clocks accurately. It has been restored and the ball can be seen rising and falling at exactly 1 p.m.

St Andrew's house is the large 1930s building in front of Calton Hill. Before devolution it was the British government's Scottish Office and is now the headquarters of the Scottish government. It was built on the site of the notorious Calton jail and the older building to the left of St Andrew's house is the only remaining prison building, the governor's house.

The final two monuments are the 1830s Athenian temple-style monument to philosopher Dugald Stewart (William H. Playfair, 1831), which is behind the left wing of St Andrew's House, and the tall obelisk of the martyrs' monument. The latter was built in the late-nineteenth century and stands in the Old Calton burial ground as a memorial to those arrested and deported for advocating universal suffrage in the late

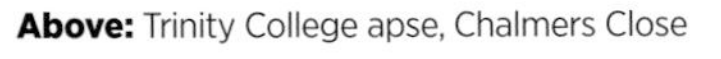

Left: North Bridge and the Balmoral hotel

Above: Trinity College apse, Chalmers Close

eighteenth century. Old Calton also houses David Hume's mausoleum and a monument to those Scots who died in the American Civil War.

Follow Jeffrey Street round to the left.

Look up and you will see North Bridge, built in 1896 to replace the eighteenth-century bridge that had already collapsed once before. The Balmoral hotel, the grand building with a clock tower located to the left of the bridge, was built around this time whilst the General Post Office building across from it was a little earlier. The GPO was situated next to Waverley station, which glass roof you can see.

Stop outside the Jury's Inn hotel. Our next close is unmarked and accessed through the car park of the hotel. This involves a short walk, with the hotel on either side of you. From the car park there is a small set of stairs; this is the foot of Chalmers Close, where our walk continues.

On the left, as you walk up, is Trinity College apse, the only surviving remnant of a great medieval foundation, built in 1460 by Mary of Gueldres, in memory of her late husband, King James II. Trinity College included a hospital and manse, as well as a church, and was situated in a valley below Calton Hill. However, in 1848, Waverley station needed to be expanded and the town council sold out to the North British Railway Company, which then demolished the church and its associated buildings. A condition of the sale was that the church had to be rebuilt elsewhere and every stone from the old structure was carefully numbered and stored. However, it took until the 1870s for the work to be completed, by which time many of the original stones had disappeared.

The rebuilt Trinity church was itself largely demolished in 1964, leaving only the apse, which can be seen to best advantage from nearby Trunk's Close. Note the painted numbers on some of the apse stones, a reminder of the demolition process, and also the sign in the small garden, which explains the features worth looking for, such as gargoyles and green men. Many people today still bemoan the destruction of Trinity, the oldest Gothic structure in the city, and a wonderful example of a medieval church. It certainly caused huge controversy at the time, with the venerable Lord Cockburn

Above: The 'heave awa' memorial, Paisley Close

Right: Old St Paul's church, Carruber's Close

describing it as a 'scandalous desecration'.

Continue up the close and return to High Street. At the top turn right and walk up the hill.

On our right as we walk up is Paisley Close. The carving above the entrance depicts a young lad and the words 'Heave awa' chaps I'm no dead yet', a memorial to the so-called Heave Awa' disaster, in which thirty-five people died after a tenement collapsed here in 1861. This is the image of 12-year-old Joseph McIvor and the words he shouted as rescuers sifted through the rubble. An investigation by Dr (later Sir) Henry Littlejohn, the medical officer of health, into housing conditions in the Old Town started soon after and led eventually to the Improvement Act of 1867. Promoted by William Chambers, the lord provost, it brought safer buildings, cleaner streets and more lighting. However, no indoor toilets were provided as the locals were not trusted to keep them clean!

Also, on the right, you can see a seventeenth-century heraldic panel, surrounded by carved shamrocks, above the entrance to Bailie Fyfe's Close and a carved lintel above a window on the second floor.

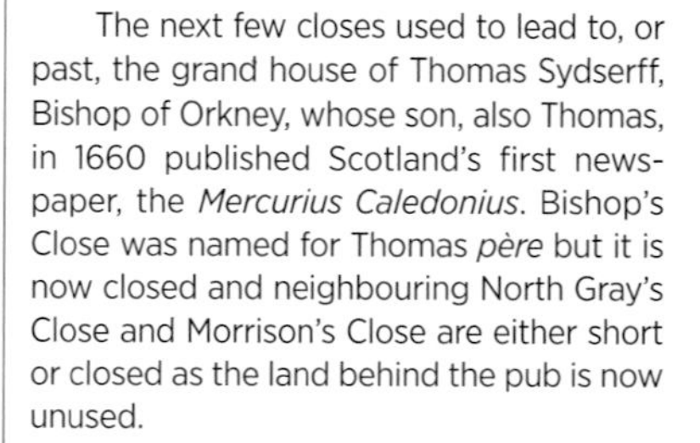

The next few closes used to lead to, or past, the grand house of Thomas Sydserff, Bishop of Orkney, whose son, also Thomas, in 1660 published Scotland's first newspaper, the *Mercurius Caledonius*. Bishop's Close was named for Thomas *père* but it is now closed and neighbouring North Gray's Close and Morrison's Close are either short or closed as the land behind the pub is now unused.

On the left side of High Street is the Radisson Blu hotel, which has incorporated three closes: Melrose, Cant's and Dickson's. The hotel was built in the late 1980s in the Scots Baronial style and kept the street names better to fit in with High Street.

At the end of this section of High Street, just before the nineteenth-century former Royal Bank of Scotland building (now partly the Hilton hotel) on the right-hand side, is the entrance to Carrubber's Close, which leads to the distinctive Old St Paul's church, the front entrance of which is at the bottom of the close, in Jeffrey Street. Established in 1689 as a breakaway group from St Giles cathedral, the congregation – the oldest Episcopal congregation in Scotland – at first conducted its services in a wool store in

Carruber's Close. Due to their strong associations with the Jacobite cause many members of Old St Paul's took up arms in the risings of 1715 and 1745 and for decades thereafter were persecuted. However, more than three hundred years after its formation it is still actively serving the Old Town.

The current Old St Paul's building dates from 1880 (Hay and Henderson), and is well worth visiting. It straddles a narrow, steep slope and when you see the number of interior steps you will understand how difficult the construction process must have been. Its richly furnished Gothic interior includes a carved-oak high altar, elaborate reredos and many fine stained-glass windows. In the memorial chapel you will find a wonderful modern painting, *Still* (2004) by Alison Watt. *Still* is twelve feet high and is made up of four panels depicting hanging fabrics, with a cross-like effect where the panels meet. Perhaps because of the dim light in the chapel the painting seems to glow.

Facing Carruber's Close, turn left and cross High Street at the pedestrian crossing.

The building in front of us was a branch of the British Linen Bank, and dates from 1923. The street to its left side is Niddry Street, which had to be moved when South Bridge was built.

Walk down South Bridge with the hotel on your left.

As buildings cover eighteen of the nineteen spans of South Bridge it is difficult to appreciate that this is actually a bridge. It was built between 1785 and 1788 and many of its spans are now vaults used for storage, as pubs or as spooky tourist attractions.

Two thirds of the way along the bridge, you reach a set of railings, which offer a view out across Cowgate. On the right, the modern buildings replaced historic buildings destroyed in a fire of 2002. On the left, if you look down, you can see the edge of St Cecilia's hall (on Niddry Street), named after the patron saint of music. Designed by Robert Mylne and built for the Edinburgh

St Cecilia's hall

Musical Society in 1763, it was extended in 1812, and is the oldest purpose-built concert hall in Scotland. Following extensive renovations St Cecilia's has been restored to former glories by its owner, the University of Edinburgh, and its oval concert room, with dome, is a delight. With seating for two hundred, it is still a music venue, hosting concerts and recitals all year round, including performances during the Edinburgh International Festival. There is also a music museum, which holds the university's collection of old musical instruments, including its world-famous harpsichords.

Continue to the end of the bridge and turn left onto Infirmary Street.

Infirmary Street is named after the eighteenth-century hospital, the first in Edinburgh. This hospital was destroyed during the construction of South Bridge, by which time a larger complex had replaced it. Many eminent doctors operated here, such as Sir James Simpson (1811–70), who discovered the anaesthetic properties of chloroform. In the nineteenth century the grander hospital on Lauriston Place made these newer buildings obsolete.

On the right of Infirmary Street, you can see the old South Bridge primary school and the nineteenth-century swimming baths and, on the left, the former Lady Yester's church of 1805, now offices.

The assassination of Cardinal Beaton

At the end of the street turn left down High School Wynd onto Cowgate.

Opposite us is Blackfriars Street, named after a thirteenth century Dominican monastery. The monastery was a powerful and wealthy institution that received benefactions from several Scottish kings, but it was looted, and then destroyed in the wake of the Reformation.

Cross over Cowgate and head up Blackfriars Street.

The building on the right corner is St Ann's community centre, which was originally a 'ragged school', providing free education for destitute children. The plaque explains that Cardinal David Beaton (1494–1546), the last cardinal in Scotland before the Reformation, had a house here (built by his uncle, Archbishop James Beaton). With its distinctive hexagonal turret, Beaton's house, or palace, was one of the finest properties on Cowgate, befitting a man who was not only the most powerful clergyman in the country but also a trusted adviser to James V and later Chancellor of Scotland. During the Reformation, Beaton zealously persecuted those he saw as heretics, his most infamous act being the execution of George Wishart, a Protestant preacher who was burnt at the stake. Beaton – already unpopular thanks to his string of mistresses and many illegitimate children – provoked a savage reaction: in May 1546 a band of Protestant lairds entered St Andrews castle in Fife, dragged him from his bedchamber and stabbed him to death before mutilating his body and hanging it from a castle window.

On the right as you walk up the street you can see a sign for George McKay Bowling Green Bowl Maker, the last maker of wooden bowls in Scotland, which closed as recently as 2008 after more than two hundred years of trading. Note also, at 63 Blackfriars Street, the carved entrance to the Lodge of Journeymen Masons, which organisation has been in existence for more than three hundred years.

Halfway up the street, at the entrance to New Skinner's Close, look to the left, where you will see an early-sixteenth-century townhouse, with distinctive semi-octagonal staircase (8 Blackfriars Street).

Regent Morton's house

This is Regent Morton's house, now a hostel, and named after James Douglas, 4th earl of Morton (1516–81). He was a prime mover in the overthrow of Mary, Queen of Scots, becoming fourth regent to the infant James VI in 1572. An inveterate intriguer, Morton was heavily implicated in the murders of David Rizzio, musician and courtier to Mary, in 1566, and of Lord Darnley, Mary's husband, in 1567. It was for the latter crime that Morton, in 1581, was beheaded by the 'maiden', an early form of guillotine, his severed head stuck on a spike on the tolbooth gaol.

From the Morton house, go back down Blackfriars Street and turn left into New Skinner's Close.

This close was named after the headquarters of the Incorporation of Skinners in the seventeenth century and as we walk down it we pass Coinyie House Close, named after the royal mint, which operated here from 1574–1709. On your right is a gate that is very rarely locked; if you wish you can go through it and into the attractive gardens of Coinyie House Close, however, this walk continues along New Skinner's Close.

Follow the bend in the road along New Skinner's Close, which ends in a crossroads.

New Skinner's Close ends at a crossroads. Turn right down South Gray's Close, passing the presbytery of St Patrick's church and the church itself on the left.

At the bottom of the close turn left.

St Patrick's RC church (façade on Cowgate), on the left, was significantly expanded in the nineteenth and twentieth centuries but dates from 1774, when it was an Episcopal chapel. The church was acquired for £4,000 by Bishop James Gillis in 1856 to cater for the growing Irish Catholic population in the city. It is the spiritual home of Hibernian, one of the city's two great football clubs (the other being Heart of Midlothian). Canon Edward Hannan, a priest here, formed the Catholic Young Men's Society in 1869, which, six years later, became Hibernian FC, or Hibs.

St Patrick's church, Cowgate

Venerable Margaret Sinclair

St Patrick's is also renowned as the parish church of the Venerable Margaret Sinclair (1900–25), who lived with her father, a council dustman, her mother and five siblings in Blackfriars Street, overlooking the church. After working in a biscuit factory, she moved to London in 1923 taking holy orders with the Order of the Poor Clares, where she

St Mary's Street

was named Sister Mary of the Five Wounds. Although she died just two years later, Margaret Sinclair had become widely known for her deep Christian values and in particular her dedication to helping the poor, so much so that devotion to her memory grew strongly among Catholics. In 1942, the first steps towards canonisation were proposed by Pope Pius XII, and in 1978 Pope Paul VI awarded her the title of Venerable. It is hoped by Scottish Catholics that one day she will be canonised, becoming St Margaret. There is a shrine to her in St Patrick's and a small area with more information on her life.

Near the end of Cowgate we can see an old wall and archway on our left. This was the gateway to Tweeddale house stables but some believe it was originally part of the sixteenth century King's wall, which ran along where the Cowgate is today.

At the end of the Cowgate turn left up St Mary's Street.

St Mary's Street is named after the chapel, hospital and almshouse for poor women that was established here in the fifteenth century. This was destroyed in the Reformation to prevent it offering shelter to Catholic fugitives and most of the buildings are nineteenth-century tenements.

At the top of St Mary's Street turn left.

We are reminded that we have now re-entered where the Netherbow once stood by the name of the first close we pass, World's End Close, and the pub named after it. In the seventeenth century the colonel of Oliver Cromwell's army was housed here whilst Scotland was occupied. The World's End pub was also where, in 1977, two young girls, Christine Eadie and Helen Scott, both 17, were last seen before being abducted, raped and murdered. Despite the best efforts of the police this heinous crime remained unsolved for decades until DNA evidence led them to serial killer Angus Sinclair. Tried for the World's End offences in 2007 Sinclair was acquitted but thanks to a change in the double-jeopardy law, he was re-tried in 2014 and found guilty. His sentence of thirty-seven years was the longest ever handed down by a Scottish court.

The next close on our left is artistically carved and leads to Tweeddale Court. Go down it.

Quite soon on the left, behind an iron

gate, is a fountain that symbolises the herbal tradition in Edinburgh, with inscriptions in Scots, Gaelic and Latin. As the court opens up, on the right-hand side are some large walls, believed to be part of the original King's wall before it was replaced by the much larger Flodden wall and some sheds. These housed sedan chairs, the preferred method of travel by Edinburgh's elite, carrying them about town without stepping on the dirty streets.

Tweeddale house at the end of the close was built in the early seventeenth century and later remodelled by siblings John and Robert Adam, 1752–3, becoming the headquarters of the British Linen Bank. When the bank moved to the New Town, Oliver and Boyd, publishers and printers, took over the premises and traded here for over a century. Their name is still above the door and a hoist for lifting paper can be seen on an adjoining house.

In 1806 Tweeddale Court was the scene of a notorious crime. A bank porter, William Begbie, was stabbed to death in the passageway and the £4,000 he was carrying was taken. Edinburgh was outraged and the authorities made a huge effort to catch the perpetrators, with every known criminal in the city being questioned. Although, a year later, £3,000 from the robbery was recovered from a hole in the wall in a Leith garden, the identity of the killer, or killers, remains a mystery to this day.

Turn right past Tweeddale house and continue up the road.

The closes we are walking past include Fountain Close, where the first bible printed in Scotland was made in 1574, and Hyndford's Close, where the Duchess of Gordon was regularly visited by Robert Burns.

Continue past the barrier onto South Gray's Close again. At this point turn right and head up to High Street.

Turn left and on our left is the Museum of Childhood, which contains a history of toys. It was opened in the 1950s and

Tweeddale Court

extended in the 1980s. Exhibits range from many historical periods and from the familiar to the creepy and bizarre.

Walk up High Street.

Todrick's Wynd, on the left, was the boundary of the town guard in the eighteenth century. It is also said to be where Mary, Queen of Scots bumped into her future husband the earl of Bothwell and the assassins with explosives who were on their way to kill Lord Darnley, Mary's first husband.

At this point cross over the road and turn right to head back to where we began. The final close to notice is on your left and this is Monteith's Close, which, in the sixteenth century, housed the royal tennis court.

When you reach the Netherbow wellhead our walk has finished. To begin the next walk, continue down the High Street, crossing over the crossroads to Canongate. Walk until you reach Canongate kirk on the left-hand side.

IN DEPTH

Festival city

Although the playhouse left Old Playhouse Close a long time ago the Old Town is still an area strongly associated with theatre and performance, especially in August. Thanks to a plethora of festivals, Edinburgh is a city transformed: the population more than doubles, the streets are filled with performers and there are hundreds of different venues ranging from large theatres to small rooms above pubs.

SEASONAL FESTIVITIES

Most large cities have street parties to celebrate the moment a new year begins, but few go to the lengths Edinburgh does for its Hogmanay. The New Town plays host to the Christmas market, outdoor ice rink and many other seasonal attractions but the Old Town is also involved. On the 'night afore' a giant torchlit procession down the Royal Mile recalls the Viking influence on Scotland and on Hogmanay itself a major concert is held at the castle before spectacular fireworks are set off to usher in the New Year.

Since the 1980s two reimagined festivals have joined Hogmanay in signalling the changing seasons. Beltane and Samhuinn were traditional Celtic celebrations of the beginning and end of summer; today they involve performers in costumes and body paint dancing, fire-wielding and behaving wildly in processions down the Royal Mile often ending up in West Parliament Square around a bonfire. Beltane is the best known and its popularity grows each year while Samhuinn occurs at Halloween and the fire, creepy costumes and erratic dances enhance the spooky atmosphere.

ART AND CULTURE

For three weeks in August the Edinburgh International Festival (EIF) hosts the finest dance, opera, music and theatre from across the world. It was the first major festival in Edinburgh, a response to the destruction caused by the Second World War. The inaugural EIF opened on 24 August 1947 aiming to use art and culture to help the world recover from conflict. Its line-up was more focused on music than the current incarnation but other features have remained. The EIF is still three weeks long and aims to showcase Scottish culture to the world while at the same time presenting Scotland with culture from around the world. The main base of the International Festival is the Hub, the converted church at the base of Castlehill, with events held all over the city.

In addition to the EIF, Edinburgh has other, more specific, festivals. For example, in July there is the Jazz and Blues festival, which centres around Grassmarket and attracts the finest international musicians. Another significant event is the Edinburgh International Film Festival, which has not only premiered many important films but also hosted their stars. Interestingly, the organisers chose to move the festival to June to prevent a clash with other summer festivals. However, August is still the busiest time with the television and book festivals complementing the EIF and the Fringe.

FRINGE PERFORMERS

It is ironic that the world's largest arts festival is described as a 'fringe'. When eight theatre groups decided to perform in Edinburgh at the same time as the International Festival, despite not being invited, they called

A group of performers from South Korea promoting their Edinburgh Fringe comedy show, Royal Mile, 2017

themselves the 'Fringe' as they were on the outside of the main event. However, as the years passed the Fringe outgrew the official festival, becoming an arts behemoth. The statistics are quite staggering: in 2017, there were 53,232 performances of 3,398 shows in 300 venues.

Whereas many EIF acts are funded by government grants of one kind or another, the Fringe's acts are self-financing and the alternative nature of the comedy, theatre, dance and music comes not only from the artistic spirit of the performers but also from a strong sense of independence. It is a very democratic festival – anyone can put on a show, if they can find a venue – but inevitably a much more raucous affair with so many acts competing for an audience.

MILITARY PRECISION

One event stands out in the August festival calendar: the Edinburgh Military Tattoo. Every summer, over a three-week period, more than two hundred thousand people arrive at the castle esplanade to watch this celebration of military heritage and music. It started in 1950 and has run every year since, its proud boast that despite the Scottish weather it has never cancelled a performance. As well as Scottish regiments the Tattoo hosts military bands from around the world. There are popular recurring elements, which include a lone piper on the castle battlements and a flyover by military aircraft.

MUCH MORE BESIDES

It would take too long to mention the myriad of other festivals Edinburgh hosts annually as well as the one-off celebrations that are held in the Old Town. These can be niche events, known only to those who participate in a particular subculture, to giant events such as The Gathering of 2014, in which tens of thousands of people from around the world came to Holyrood park to celebrate their Scottish ancestry. Despite the competition the many Edinburgh festivals continue to thrive, so it is likely that the Old Town will be part of the festival city for many years to come.

IN 1688 KING JAMES VII
ORDAINED THAT THE MORTIFICATION
OF THOS. MOODIE GRANTED IN 1649 TO
BUILD A CHURCH SHOULD BE APPLIED
TO THE ERECTION OF THIS STRUCTURE

WALK 6
THE TOP OF CANONGATE

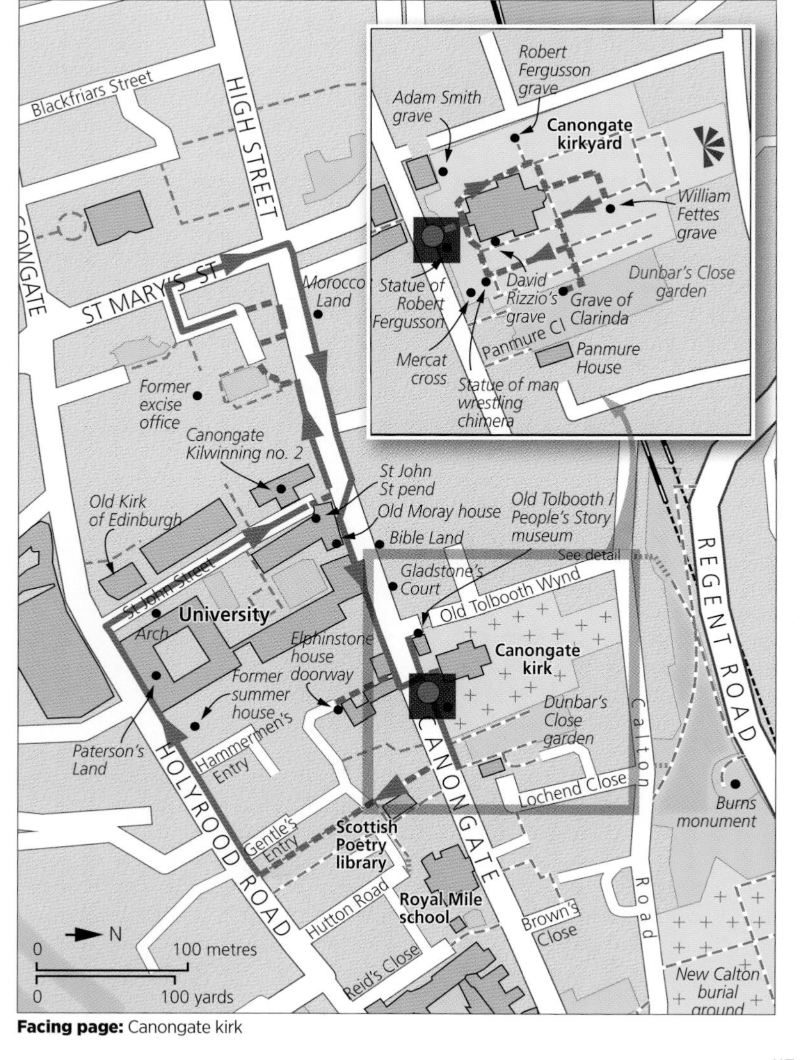

Facing page: Canongate kirk

Start Canongate kirk, 153 Canongate

Summary We begin with a walk around historic Canongate kirk and its kirkyard, which houses the graves of some of Scotland's most interesting and influential people. This is followed by a tour of the top of Canongate, once a burgh in its own right, discovering many historic buildings and closes.

Highlights Canongate kirk and kirkyard graves • Robert Fergusson story • Canongate's mercat cross • Dunbar's Close gardens • Adam Smith story • Scottish Poetry library • Union of Scotland and England • Morocco Land • Moray house • Museum of Edinburgh and Huntly house • Bakehouse Close and Acheson house • Canongate tolbooth and the People's Story museum • In-depth: the Edinburgh Enlightenment

The Walk

Canongate kirk was built 1688–91 to accommodate those worshippers displaced when James VII converted the nave of Holyrood from the parish church of the burgh of Canongate into a chapel for the Order of the Thistle. James then ordered that a legacy left by merchant Thomas Moodie should be used to construct a new church and the result was the wonderful building we see today. The exterior is a striking design in the Dutch style by James Smith with – perhaps incongruously – a Roman Doric portico at the entrance, while the interior is in the shape of a Latin cross, with nave, transept, chancel and apse. The chancel and apse do not conform to the Presbyterian form of worship and some have speculated that it was a deliberate attempt to make the church adaptable for Roman Catholic use.

The initial impression of the interior is its simplicity and lack of ostentation. Yet there is much of interest and the first thing that catches the eyes are the flags, which include regimental colours, the standards of former governors of Edinburgh castle and a banner celebrating the Royal British Legion. These are reminders of the Canongate church's military connections, which led it to be designated as the regimental kirk of the Royal Regiment of Scotland. The royal connections are equally strong; the front pew on the east side is the royal pew, with the coats of arms of the Queen, duke of Edinburgh (both of whom have worshipped here) and the Prince of Wales, or duke of Rothesay as he is designated while in Scotland. In addition, there is a plethora of artefacts including paintings, photographs and memorials, as well as fascinating pieces of church furniture.

We start outside the entrance to the

Robert Fergusson statue

church grounds with the statue of Robert Fergusson on our right. This was unveiled in 2004 and has the poet hurrying along the street with his words inscribed by his feet. His grave in the kirkyard was originally unmarked as he died penniless but later, Robert Burns, a Fergusson admirer, paid for a grander memorial and when this fell into disrepair, another writer, Robert Louis Stevenson, was going to pay for its restoration but died before the work could go ahead. Instead, the Saltire Society erected a plaque in front of the grave with Stevenson's intended words.

Enter the grounds of the church.

On the ground, a few feet from the entrance, you will notice a tiny plaque hinting at one of the more famous residents of the kirkyard, Adam Smith (*see Smith panel on page 119*).

Turn left and walk around the church. If you wish to find Smith's final resting place it

Adam Smith grave

Robert Fergusson: Edinburgh's poet

If Robert Burns was the bard of rural Scotland, then Robert Fergusson (1750–74) was his urban equivalent. Born in Edinburgh he attended St Andrews University but was forced to abandon his studies after the death of his father. To support his mother and sister, Fergusson took a post as a clerk in the civil service, writing poetry in his leisure hours. His work was highly praised, leading many to view him as the heir to Edinburgh's leading literary figure, Allan Ramsay. Fergusson's best-known work is the long poem, *Auld Reekie*, first published in 1773, a brilliant evocation of Edinburgh and its people.

However, by the time *Auld Reekie* appeared, the young poet's life was in disarray. He was a heavy drinker and a regular client of Edinburgh's many prostitutes, habits that caused his health to deteriorate sharply. He lost his job, and, in a state close to manic depression, retreated to his room, where he read the Bible compulsively. In July 1774, he fell down a flight of stairs, injuring his head. Now in a state of physical and mental collapse, he was taken away to the Bedlam, the city's asylum, where he died just three weeks later at the age of 24.

Robert Burns was a great admirer, so much so that thirteen years after the tragic death of the young poet, he paid for a headstone commemorating his life and work, writing that Fergusson was 'my elder brother in misfortune, but far my elder brother in muse'.

Robert Fergusson grave

is in the top corner (west side) of the kirkyard, facing away from the road, surrounded by railings and backing onto a wall. There is no path, but it can be reached without too much difficulty.

Continue walking past the church.

The small path on the left leads to Robert Fergusson's grave, with an inscription by Robert Burns, and the plaque at the foot of the memorial with the words chosen by Robert Louis Stevenson.

When you circle around the back of the church you get a good view of Calton Hill and its monuments and an excellent one of the Royal High School of Edinburgh, one of the city's architectural gems.

With your back to the middle of the church, walk along the path, down a few steps, turn sharp right and down another couple of steps. You are now in the eastern half of the kirkyard.

In front of you is the mausoleum of Sir William Fettes (1750–1836), who was lord provost of Edinburgh but is best known for founding Fettes college, the so-called 'Eton of Scotland'. In the bottom left you will also see a small plaque that remembers Sir Walter Scott's friend and publisher John

Grave of Agnes Craig, 'Clarinda'

Ballantyne, who died in poverty.

Turn right and walk up the path in the direction of the church until you find a crossroads. Turn left and head to the far wall. Turn right and as you walk along the path look for the grave of Agnes Craig (1759–1841). It has a bronze plaque of a woman in profile. This is the famous 'Clarinda', who corresponded with Robert Burns and inspired his love poems, such as 'Ae Fond Kiss'.

Turn back and retrace your steps to the crossroad. Turn left and walk towards the gates, with the church on your right.

The last grave on your right, next to the wall of the church and lying flat on the ground, is said to be that of the musician and friend of Mary, Queen of Scots, David Rizzio. Rizzio, spelt Riccio on the plaque, was rumoured to be an agent of the papacy and was hated by Mary's second husband, Lord Darnley. In 1566, Darnley was a lead conspirator in his murder despite the fact it was Rizzio who had organised Darnley's marriage to the Queen.

As you pass the church turn left and you will be presented with a very odd statue. A man wrestling a chimera, an animal with a

David Rizzio grave

Canongate mercat cross

lion's head, the head of a goat and with a snake for a tail. This artwork, *The Last Chimera* by Josefina de Vasconcellos, is from 1950 and represents truth and purity overcoming threats to the Christian church.

On our right, twenty feet away, is the mercat (market) cross of the Canongate. In 1128 the Canongate was given burghal status. A burgh had rights, including a market, of which the mercat cross was the centre. Originally it stood in the middle of the street but was moved in the eighteenth century and finally placed here in 1953. The cross is ornamented with a plaque describing its restoration in 1888, and the Canongate coat of arms.

Retrace your steps away from the cross, past the chimera, continue past the front of the church and turn left to leave Canongate kirkyard.

The first entry on your left is Dunbar's Close (137 Canongate). Go down the close

Gardens, Dunbar's Close

Panmure house

and through the gates into the gardens.

These gardens are open to the public but are not well known, which is a pity because this is a welcoming and tranquil green lung just a few steps from the bustle of Royal Mile. In the 1970s this was a building site, which could easily have ended up as a car park. However, along came Scottish charity the Mushroom Trust, which, in 1976, purchased the land and engaged landscape architect Seamus Filor to create a garden. Filor's simple, yet elegant, design harks back to the seventeenth century and features elegant parterres of clipped shrubs and a canopy of trees. An inscription on the wall to the left and on the notice board behind you give information about their history.

If you walk a short distance into the gardens and turn right the eighteenth-century building in front of you is Panmure house, where the great economist Adam Smith lived.

The gardens can be enjoyed by walking in a simple circle and leaving the way we came in.

When you leave Dunbar's Close turn left.

Panmure Close, first on the left, is decorated with red poppies in memory of Lady Haig's poppy factory, which operated in the area from 1931–65. Further down the close you get another view of Panmure house and the plaques around the entrance of the close give more information about its famous residents. Panmure house (which can best be accessed from nearby Lochend Close) was built in the late seventeenth century and was the grand townhouse of the earls of Panmure. It is an L-shaped, crow-stepped property and is best known today as the house in which Adam Smith lived for the last twelve years of his life, 1778–90. The house was bought by Edinburgh Business School in 2008, and after substantial refurbishment (ongoing at the time of writing) EBS intends to reopen it as a learning centre, specialising in economics and the social sciences.

From the front of Panmure Close cross the road and head down Crichton's Close.

Crichton's Close has a number of modern developments, including the Scottish Poetry library, which moved here in 1999, and is said to be the only purpose-built public poetry library in Europe. Designed by Malcolm Fraser Architects, the library won

Scottish Poetry library

Adam Smith and *The Wealth of Nations*

Adam Smith is one of those geniuses associated with Edinburgh during the period known as the Scottish Enlightenment. Yet he was not a native of the city. He was born in Kirkcaldy in 1723 and went to school in that town before studying at Glasgow University and then Balliol College, Oxford. Following a brilliant series of public lectures in Edinburgh, he was appointed professor of logic at Glasgow University in 1751, and while at that institution he published his acclaimed philosophical work, *The Theory of Moral Sentiments*. Leaving Glasgow in 1764, Smith became tutor to the family of the duke of Buccleuch and on their tours of the Continent he got to know many of the leading philosophers. From 1766, he lived in Kirkcaldy with his mother, where he worked on the book that led to him being described with some justification as the 'father of economics'. Its full title is *An Inquiry into the Nature and Causes of the Wealth of Nations*, published in 1776. Two years later he moved to Edinburgh after being appointed commissioner of customs, and from then until his death in 1790 he resided at Panmure house in Canongate.

What are the ideas that make *The Wealth of Nations* so influential? Smith begins by examining the doctrine of mercantilism, which held sway in many countries, including Britain. Mercantilism holds that the key to a country's prosperity is its stock of gold and silver and that everything possible must be done to maintain its value. Therefore, to mercantilists, importing goods was bad because it meant giving up precious metals to pay for them while exporting was good because it meant the precious metals came back. Another harmful effect of mercantilism was that in attempting to maintain the stock of gold and silver severe restrictions on business and trade were imposed.

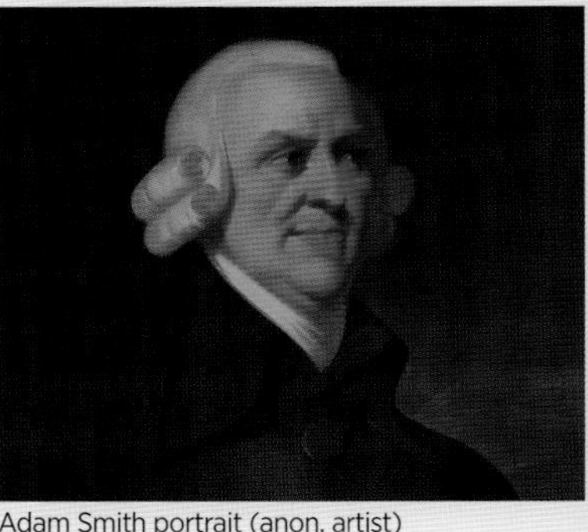

Adam Smith portrait (anon. artist)

However, Smith's view is that free trade is beneficial to all; both buyers and sellers can profit from a transaction. What counts is not hoarding gold and silver but the totality of a country's commercial transactions, what we would term today as gross national product. Smith also points out that if economic efficiency is to be maximised, controls on business must be swept away and replaced by free markets and open competition. Many of his contemporaries were afraid that chaos would result, but Smith was unconcerned. Free markets, he argues, are guided by an 'invisible hand', which acts to balance supply and demand, ensuring that resources are effectively allocated.

Smith's ideas had a significant influence on economic policy, providing the underpinning for the great free-trade explosion of the nineteenth century. The United States was particularly receptive: Thomas Jefferson, third president and chief author of the Declaration of Independence, described *The Wealth of Nations* as the 'best book to be read on money and commerce' and he would quote extensively from it in his speeches. Even today, it is doubtful if any other economist is studied or debated to the same degree.

Summer house, Moray house complex

Moray house complex, Holyrood Road

several awards for the modern, yet contextual, design. It houses around 45,000 items, its core of Scottish holdings complemented by collections from around the world. At the bottom of Crichton's Close, where it meets Holyrood Road, look to your feet and you will find metal plates including one inscribed with a poem by Stewart Conn about the history of the area.

When you reach Holyrood Road turn right.

Holyrood Road today consists of many new buildings. Historically this area was mostly open space. In the early nineteenth century, apart from a brewery, it was fields and an open sewer ran along where we now walk.

One of the most historically interesting buildings in this area is quite hard to find. After the modern developments end, there is a two-storey building adjacent to a goods entrance that services an Edinburgh University complex (it faces a bus stop across the road). If you look through the iron gates of the goods entrance, there is a small, locked building to the right. This is the old summer-house located in the gardens of Moray house (the main entrance to Moray house is on Canongate, see below). It is often speculated this is where the Treaty of Union between Scotland and England was signed, an issue that is discussed in the panel on the facing page.

The next building on the right-hand side has interesting fruit, nut and a gold bird details on its iron gates. This is Paterson's Land (37 Holyrood Road), part of the Moray house school of education and sport at the University of Edinburgh. It was built as a teacher-training college in 1914 and is named for Dr Maurice Paterson, rector of the Free Church of Scotland training college at Moray house from 1864–1905.

After you pass Paterson's Land turn right up St John Street.

On this street first look left at the Old (or Great) kirk of Edinburgh and its church

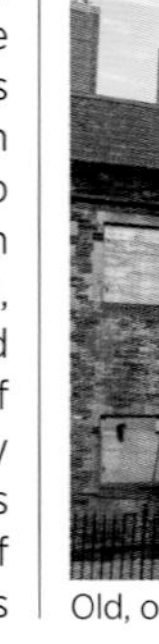

Old, or Great, kirk of Edinburgh

The Act of Union, 1707

During the seventeenth century there were various attempts to engineer a political union between Scotland and England. For some people this had a certain logic; after all, the two countries already shared a monarch, thanks to the Union of the Crowns in 1603. None of these initiatives were successful but matters came to a head around 1700, following the collapse of the Darien expedition, Scotland's disastrous attempt to establish a colony in the New World. Darien not only impoverished a huge number of influential Scots but also highlighted the need for Scotland to have access to markets in England's growing colonies. After much political skulduggery, including threats from Westminster to impose tariffs on Scottish exports to England, the Scottish parliament voted for the Treaty of Union in January 1707 by 110 votes to 67. Scotland's time as an independent, self-governing nation had come to an end.

Many in Scotland were outraged by what they saw as betrayal. Ordinary people believed their political masters had been bribed, or, as Robert Burns would later put it, 'bought and sold for English gold'. There were regular anti-Union riots in Edinburgh, with those seen as leading lights in the process needing round-the-clock protection. James Ogilvie, 1st earl of Seafield (1644–1730), needed protection more than most: as lord chancellor of Scotland, his astute management of the Scottish parliament had been a key factor in the treaty's approval. People were also enraged by the flippant comment he made when parliament was dissolved; 'there goes the end of ane auld sang [song],' he declared.

Seafield's Edinburgh residence was Moray house. The story goes that because of a fear of violent disorder the Act of Union was signed in the summer house in his garden, with Seafield and his aristocratic friends out of sight of the mob. This seems unlikely. The Scots parliament had already approved the measure, meaning there was no legal requirement for it to be signed by anyone. However, it may well have been that Seafield met with his allies in the summer house, even after the parliamentary process had been completed. The Act of Union did not take effect until 1 May 1707 and Edinburgh would have been a dangerous place for men of his political persuasion in those months. A secret meeting place may have been a necessity.

hall (it is on the corner with Holyrood Road) built in 1882, but which was also part of the Moray house teacher-training college in the early twentieth century. Then, halfway up the street and through the railings, you will see, amongst the trees, an old arch that gave entry into the gardens of Moray house, which predated the teaching college. Next on the right is the purpose-built nursery school, a small white building in the neo-Georgian style (Frank Wood, 1932). It is now an administrative facility for the Moray house complex and a plaque by the doorway gives more information.

Near the end of St John Street, on the left, is Lodge Canongate Kilwinning No. 2 (23 St John Street), one of the most influential masonic institutions in Scotland and active to this day. The main block dates from 1737 and incorporates a wing from the late seventeenth century. Its most famous member was Robert Burns, who visited the lodge in February 1787 and was duly 'assumed' after a unanimous vote.

Lodge Canongate Kilwinning No. 2

At the top of the street before you go through the pend, look up. A carved sign tells you that the writer Tobias Smollett (1721–71) resided here. Smollett, born in Dunbartonshire, took a medical degree at Glasgow University and practised as a surgeon but his main passion was literature. Although he is little read today his work was critically acclaimed during his lifetime and he counted Samuel Johnson and Oliver Goldsmith among his friends. His best-known book is the novel, *The Expedition of Humphrey Clinker*.

Go through the pend to Canongate

Plaques on either side of the pend describe the connection with the Knights of St John, Tobias Smollett and educationalist Sir Godfrey Hilton Thomson.

Turn left and head up Canongate.

On the road as you walk up you will notice the St John's cross laid out in a mosaic. This marks the historic west boundary of Canongate. A plaque on the wall to your left gives more information.

Tobias Smollett sign

St John's cross mosaic

Chessel's buildings

Old Playhouse Close on the left was named after the Playhouse theatre (or the Canongate theatre as it is sometimes known). Opened in 1747 by actor John Ryan it faced constant opposition from the Church of Scotland, many of whose clergy had a visceral dislike of theatricals. It is therefore ironic that the most successful play performed there, *Douglas*, was written by ordained minister John Home (1722–1808). Its first performance in 1756 was greeted with great enthusiasm, prompting one member of the audience to exclaim, 'Whaur's yer Wullie Shakespeare noo?' The church authorities instigated proceedings against Home, which eventually led to his resignation from the ministry, but *Douglas* successfully transferred to the London stage, where it was performed by the great David Garrick. The theatre in Old Playhouse Close closed in 1769, as a plaque indicates.

Continue up Canongate. On the left another plaque remembers George Chalmers, whose money helped build a hospital on Lauriston Place.

When you reach the arches of an arcade, the entrance to Chessel's Court, go under the arches into the courtyard and gardens.

The structure on the south side here – three storeys, with basement, and sometimes known as Chessel's buildings – dates from c.1745 and is a wonderful example of an eighteenth-century mansion-style tenement. Archibald Chesil, who designed the block, was a master carpenter, whose development was aimed at the more affluent citizens of the Old Town. By 1765 Chessel's Court was also home to the excise office (now demolished), and this is where the notorious Deacon Brodie gang carried out its last, fateful robbery in March 1788 (*see Walk 3 for more on Brodie*).

Turn right and exit the court, take the first right through Pirrie's Close and you will arrive back on Canongate.

Turn left and head up the hill. We pass Gibb's Close, which exists now only as a business entrance. The next left is Gullan's Close; go down it.

Walk straight ahead and at the end of the close turn right onto Boyd's Entry. Just before the end of the street look to your left and you will see a plaque describing the

1867 Improvement Act sign

Morocco Land statue

renovation of the area and nineteenth-century corbelling of a bull underneath the window.

At the end of the road turn right and walk up St Mary's Street.

Just before the crossroads look to your right and you will see a stone sign that tells you this was the first building erected under the 1867 Improvement Act. The older, less well-made buildings were torn down and larger, better-built tenements were constructed.

At the crossroads, cross over, and turn right, looking down Canongate.

The name Canongate comes from 'canon gait', the walk the Augustinian canons made to the abbey until the Reformation in the sixteenth century.

Walk down Canongate. When you come to the first street on the left you will have a great view of Calton Hill and the former governor's building of the old Calton jail. If you wish to explore further, head down this street a short way and you'll notice it bears left. On your left are a number of newly opened, though often temporary, shops, bars, cafes and restaurants, part of a new development known as The Arches. If you do investigate this area, simply return to Canongate to continue the walk.

Continue down Canongate, past the nineteenth century Presbyterian church, which is now a language school, and you arrive outside the entrance to Mid Common Close.

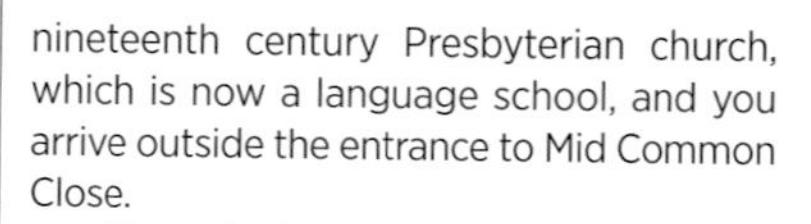

If you look up from here, on the left, between the first and second storeys, there is a protruding stone statue. Complete with turban and necklace, it is reputed to be a likeness of an Emperor of Morocco from the early eighteenth century. The building is known as Morocco Land (265 Canongate), and there are two explanations for the name. The first is that it was owned by a merchant who made a fortune trading in North Africa, his sister marrying the Emperor of Morocco, hence the name and carving. The second story concerns one Andrew Gray, an Edinburgh man who was tried and sentenced to death for his part in a riot. Fleeing the city before the sentence could be carried out he was captured by Moorish pirates and made a slave. However, Gray somehow found favour with the Emperor of Morocco, becoming a rich man in that country. Years later, in 1645, a Moorish ship dropped anchor in Leith harbour at a time when Edinburgh was rife with plague and thus defenceless. Although the Moors originally demanded a ransom, they took pity on the stricken people of the city, so much so that their leader even cured the

Moray house, west face

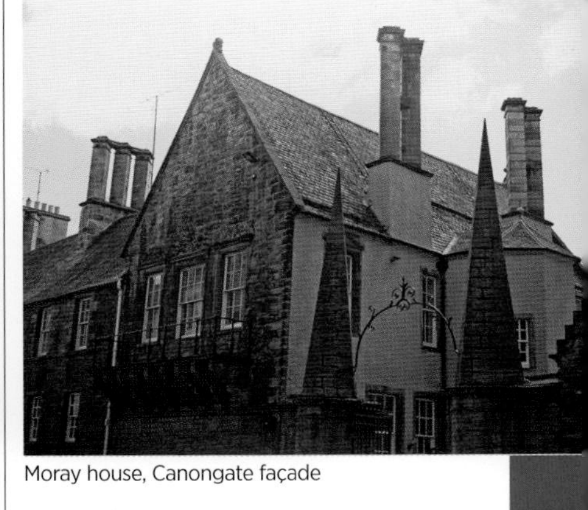

Moray house, Canongate façade

daughter of the Lord Provost. The healer promptly revealed himself as the fugitive, Andrew Gray, and, as in all the best stories, he married the young woman he had saved. The happy couple then set up home in Canongate, adorning their house with an effigy of the Emperor of Morocco.

Keep walking down Canongate, crossing over New Street until you reach the pedestrian crossing. On the right, a new development has opened up the area to our left. As well as new retail and office space the regeneration includes a few open-air popup bars and restaurants.

Cross at the pedestrian crossing and turn left past the entrance to St John Street we came out of earlier.

After St John Street, the next interesting thing on the right is a gated entrance with two steep pyramids on either side. This is the entrance to the highly distinctive (Old) Moray House (174 Canongate), built c.1625 by Mary, the dowager Countess of Home, but later named for the Moray family after her daughter Margaret married the earl of Moray. It is the finest surviving aristocratic mansion in the Old Town, described by Daniel Defoe as 'very magnificent, large and princely'. Oliver Cromwell was impressed enough to lodge here on his first visit to Edinburgh in 1648, meeting his political allies in the elegant reception rooms. On the exterior, note the wonderful Renaissance gable on the west side, the pyramid-shaped gate piers and the balcony overlooking Canongate. Today the house is in the ownership of Edinburgh University and is used as administration offices for its education department.

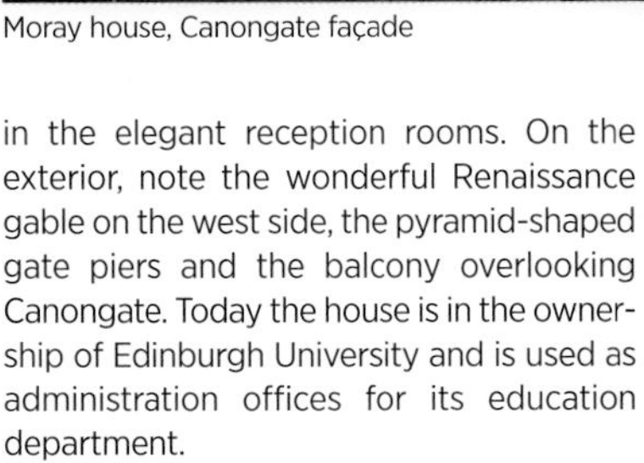

It was from the balcony of Moray house, in May 1650, that James Graham, Marquis of Montrose, was ritually to be abused by guests of Archibald Campbell, Marquis of Argyll, whose son was being married in Moray house. Montrose and Argyll had fought on opposite sides during the wars of the 1640s and when Montrose was finally captured he was conveyed up the Canongate in a cart, headed for the tolbooth prison where he would await his execution two days later. On the way, in what was a stage-managed ploy, the cart stopped outside Moray house, where the wedding guests stepped onto the balcony. However, despite being in considerable pain from recently inflicted war wounds, Montrose impressed everyone with his natural dignity and noble demeanour. Everyone that is apart from Argyll's wife, who, clearly unable to forget the past, spat on Montrose (*for more on Montrose's execution, see Walk 4*).

Keep walking down Canongate

'Bible Land'

On the other side of the street, to your left, you can see a fine example of a restored seventeenth-century tenement (185 Canongate), built by the Incorporation of Cordiners (the Cordiners were artisans who used leather from Cordova in Spain). Above the front door is a carving of the period that proclaims psalm 133, which gave the building the nickname 'Bible Land', as well as symbols connected to the leather trade. Close by is Shoemakers' Land (195 Canongate), also associated with the Cordiners.

Also, across the street, under the arcades on the left, is the entrance to Gladstone's Court, named after British prime minister and Midlothian MP William Ewart Gladstone. This area once housed a Magdalene asylum for 'fallen women'.

Continue walking down Canongate.

The first close on the right is Sugarhouse Close (160 Canongate). If you walk under the pend you can see the whitewashed eighteenth-century sugar refinery, which sits alongside contemporary buildings.

On the right you pass three houses that are now combined as the Museum of Edinburgh (142–146 Canongate). It is remarkable to think that in the nineteenth century more than three hundred people were squashed into these properties. The

Museum of Edinburgh/
Huntly house

Bakehouse Close

final building of the three, painted yellow and dark red, is Huntly house, a sixteenth-century house loosely connected to the aristocratic Gordons of Huntly.

Enter Bakehouse Close, which runs under the museum building.

Bakehouse Close is named after the bakehouse and other property owned here by the Incorporation of Bakers in the Canongate. It is one of the best-preserved closes in the Old Town and gives you a great insight into what life was like in eighteenth-century Edinburgh. There is also another view of Huntly house, as well as an eighteenth-century bakery. Down the close on the left is a gate, with a sign indicating that the doorway was taken from Elphinstone house, which stood on the Cowgate where St Patrick's church is now.

Hidden by a walled courtyard in Bakehouse Close, we find the front of historic Acheson house – the wall facing Canongate is actually the side of the house – started in 1633 by Sir Archibald Acheson (1583–1634), secretary of state for Scotland under Charles I. Developed at a time when Canongate was home to many of Scotland's elite, it must be regarded one of the Old Town's most notable structures. There is a fascinating carving above the front door on the left: it features the Acheson family crest of a cock standing on a trumpet, the date

Acheson house

1633 and the initials of Acheson and his wife, Margaret. After falling into disrepair, Acheson house was bought by the Marquis of Bute in 1935 and extensively restored by him. It is now home to Edinburgh World Heritage.

Leave Bakehouse Close by retracing your steps and exit via the pend.

Before you exit, on your left, you might be able to access the garden of the Museum of Edinburgh. This gate is not always open so if you wish to visit the sculpture garden you need to enter the museum. Visible from the gate is the polyhedral sundial with dials on each face.

When you leave Bakehouse Close turn round and look up at the front wall of the Museum of Edinburgh. You will see why the building is often known as the 'Speaking house': there are five Latin inscriptions, including four from the sixteenth century:

> *SPES ALTERA VITAE* – There is another hope of life.
>
> *CONSTANTIPECRORI RES MORTALIVM VMBRA* – Mortal affairs are a shadow to a steadfast heart.
>
> *VT TV LINGVAE SIC EGO MEAR(VM) AVRIM(M) DOMINVS SVM* – As thou art (master) of my tongue, so I am master of my ears.
>
> *HODIE MIHI CRAS TIBI CVR IGITVR CVRAS 1570* – Today to me, tomorrow to thee; why therefore takest thou thought.
>
> The last inscription was inserted in the early twentieth century when the building was restored and reads, *ANTIQUA TAMEN JVVENESCO* – I am old but renew my youth.

Walk further down Canongate until you reach the entrance of the Museum of Edinburgh, so that you can fully appreciate Huntly house. The Museum of Edinburgh contains many fascinating and historically important exhibits, among them the National Covenant of 1638, the collar and bowl of Greyfriars Bobby and beautiful examples of early Scottish glass and jewellery.

Turn around and cross the road so you are nearly back at our start and finish point. However, before we finish, turn left and head up to the Canongate tolbooth, which is home to the People's Story museum (163 Canongate).

The People's Story (companion to the Museum of Edinburgh, above) details working-class life in Edinburgh from the eighteenth century to the present day. For example, on the wall, you can see a plaque to those from the Canongate who fell

Canongate tolbooth

fighting in the First World War and above it a large plaque with the Canongate coat of arms. There is a strong emphasis in the displays on using the words of ordinary people to tell stories, whether they are about work, home life, wartime hardship or crime and punishment.

The tolbooth is not only one of the most distinctive buildings in Canongate but also its oldest, dating from 1591. There was in fact an earlier tolbooth here, of 1477, for which the current structure was a direct replacement. As the name suggests, tolls were collected here but in addition it incorporated the council chamber of the former burgh of Canongate, which was reached by the external staircase. Its other uses have included a police court and it was even a prison until 1818, when Calton jail replaced it. Under the tolbooth is the entrance to Tolbooth Wynd, which housed a workhouse until the twentieth century and if you look up you can see the much-photographed clock, which was added in 1884.

Latin inscription, Museum of Edinburgh

Retrace your steps down the Canongate to arrive at the end of our walk. To begin the next one, walk to the end of the Canongate and turn right to the front of the Scottish Parliament building.

IN DEPTH

The Edinburgh Enlightenment

Between 1730 and 1832, the year in which Sir Walter Scott died, Edinburgh was an intellectual powerhouse and it was an Englishman who best summed-up a century of achievement in the arts and sciences. Visiting the city in 1750, Mr Amyat, chemist to King George II, remarked that, 'Here I stand at what is called the cross of Edinburgh and can, in a few minutes, take fifty men of genius by the hand.' He was not exaggerating. The Scottish Enlightenment, with Edinburgh at its heart, changed the way we look at the world, prompting Voltaire, the great French philosopher, to observe that, 'We look to Scotland for our ideas of civilisation.'

PHILOSOPHY

David Hume, Edinburgh born and educated, is perhaps the most influential philosopher Britain has ever produced. (*see Walk 4*)

Adam Smith, the 'father of economics', made his name with a series of public lectures in Edinburgh and later in life became an Old Town resident. (*see Walk 6*)

LITERATURE

Sir Walter Scott was the world's best-selling writer for much of the nineteenth century. Born and educated in the Old Town, Scott was an advocate who practised in Edinburgh's courts. (*See Walk 9*)

James Boswell, biographer par excellence, was born in the Old Town, and lived in a spacious flat in James's Court, off Lawnmarket. (*See Walk 2*)

Allan Ramsay, poet, playwright and impresario, opened the world's first circulating library in the Old Town. (*see Walk 2*)

Francis Jeffrey, a lawyer who became both an MP and a judge in the Court of Session, was also a prominent literary figure, achievements that saw the Old Town's Jeffrey Street named for him. In 1802, in his third-floor flat at 18 Buccleuch Place, which is close to the university, he co-founded *The Edinburgh Review*, a quarterly publication that would set new standards in literary and political criticism. The *Review*'s stellar list of contributors included Scott, essayist William Hazlitt, historian Thomas Babington Macaulay and educator Thomas Arnold.

Henry Cockburn, a lifelong friend of Francis Jeffrey, was another who combined the law and literature. He rose to the top of the legal profession as solicitor-general and Court of Session judge but is best remembered today as the author of several memorable books on Edinburgh's social history. There is a Cockburn Street in the Old Town that commemorates him, and, as someone who had a deep interest in conserving the city's old buildings, he is deservedly remembered in the eponymous Cockburn Association, Edinburgh's premier conservation organisation.

William Robertson, another Edinburgh polymath, was an ordained minister, moderator of the general assembly of the Church of Scotland, a brilliant historian, and, from 1762, principal of Edinburgh University. He was a leading figure in the Enlightenment, expanding the university campus and appointing a slew of brilliant dons.

ART AND ARCHITECTURE

Robert Adam was the oldest, and most eminent, of four siblings, all of whom made significant contributions to architecture. He was born in Fife but educated in

James Boswell

Edinburgh, mixing with the likes of David Hume and Adam Smith. He was appointed architect of the King's Works in 1761 and for a twenty-year period was the most fashionable architect in England. Following the failure of his ambitious Adelphi scheme he moved back to Edinburgh for the last decade of his life, producing notable designs for city landmarks such as Old College, Charlotte Square and Register house.

James Craig, Edinburgh born and bred, was just 26 when, in 1766, he submitted an entry for an architectural competition aimed at expanding the city to the north of the Old Town. His plan was simplicity itself; a gridiron based on three streets running in parallel: Princes Street, George Street and Queen Street. The result was the glorious New Town, perhaps the finest example of urban planning anywhere in Europe, and now, like the Old Town, a World Heritage Site.

Sir Henry Raeburn was born in Edinburgh, in 1756, and educated at George Heriot's school before being apprenticed to a city jeweller. His artistic endeavours began with miniatures and as his exceptional talent emerged so too did commissions from many aristocratic patrons. Now recognised as Scotland's greatest portrait painter, Raeburn's work includes the best-known representation of Sir Walter Scott and of course his iconic masterpiece, *Reverend Robert Walker Skating on Duddingston Loch* (Scottish National Gallery).

SCIENCE AND MEDICINE

James Hutton, the 'father of geology', was born in Edinburgh and studied at Edinburgh University. His most important research was done in his house overlooking Salisbury Crags. (*see Walk 7*)

Joseph Black was one of the great chemistry researchers, the scientist who first identified carbon dioxide and in addition greatly advanced our knowledge of thermodynamics. He also helped to develop the talents of James Watt. Born in Bordeaux in 1728, Black studied at both Glasgow and Edinburgh universities, at which latter institution he became an esteemed professor. Gregarious and sociable, he was a friend of Hume, Smith and Hutton, with whom he regularly dined, and the host to influential visitors to Edinburgh, one of whom was Benjamin Franklin, the great American polymath and politician.

William Cullen became a ship's surgeon at the age of just 19 and after periods spent in medical practice in Scotland he was drawn to the world of academia. An assiduous medical researcher and a noted author of medical textbooks he was, however, best known for his inspirational teaching, particularly at Edinburgh University, where he was appointed a professor of medicine in 1755. Lecturing in English rather than Latin, Cullen drew students to Edinburgh from across the world, many of whom would become important figures in science and medicine.

Scottish Parliament building, Horse Wynd facade

WALK 7
SCOTTISH PARLIAMENT AND THE FOOT OF CANONGATE

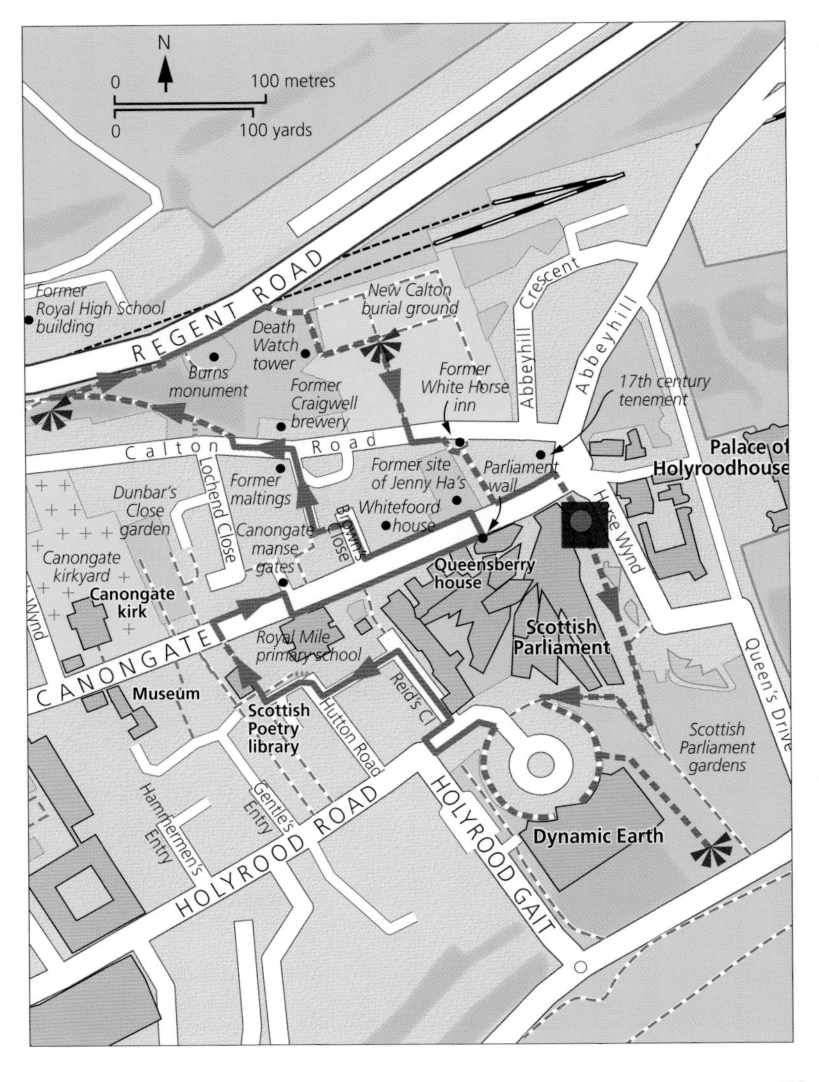

Start Facing Scottish Parliament, Horse Wynd, at the foot of the Royal Mile

Summary We discover the Scottish Parliament building, and then take in Our Dynamic Earth. This is followed by a walk along the bottom end of Canongate and a stroll along Regent Road, where we find the wonderful Royal High School of Edinburgh.

Highlights Scottish Parliament: history, design, functions • Our Dynamic Earth • James Hutton story • Canongate • Queensberry house • Duke of Queensberry • Jenny Ha's • Whitefoord house • Royal High School of Edinburgh • Burns monument • New Calton burial ground • White Horse Close • In-depth: How the Scottish Parliament works

The Walk

With the Palace of Holyroodhouse behind us, we start by facing the Scottish Parliament. While we will consider its design below, it is necessary to begin with a short history of how the parliament came to be built. Almost everything about it proved to be controversial: the site; the chosen architect and his radical ideas; the management of the project; the cost, which escalated tenfold from planning to completion. It is therefore hardly surprising that the political debate around the entire process was so fierce.

The creation of a new parliament building was deemed necessary following the historic referendum of 1997, in which 74 per cent of those who voted backed the devolution of a range of political powers from Westminster to Scotland. The first elections to the parliament were held in 1999, and, as we saw in Walk 2, the new body used the assembly hall on The Mound (owned by the Church of Scotland) as a temporary home. During this period the issue of a permanent home was discussed, with several options being considered, including the former Royal High School building on Calton Hill. However, it was decided that the most suitable place was facing Holyrood palace, on the site of a former brewery at the foot of the Royal Mile.

The next requirement was to find an architect and a competition was launched in 1998, with the Scottish public invited to view, and comment on, the plans submitted by five teams of architects. Although the concept produced by Uruguayan architect Rafael Viñoly was the most popular with the public, a committee chaired by first minister Donald Dewar (with strong representation from the architectural profession) opted for a design by Enric Miralles, a Catalan. Miralles was known for his abstract, modernistic style, which some lauded, but others found chaotic and hard to understand.

Construction began in 1999 and the new Scottish Parliament building was opened in 2004, three years behind schedule. Originally estimated by Donald Dewar to cost between £10 and £40 million, spending spiralled out of control during the construction phase, resulting in a quite incredible final bill of £414 million. Reasons given for the overspend included the additional office space demanded by elected members (MSPs), the expensive materials used, poor project management and the complexity of the architect's design. Neither Donald Dewar nor Enric Miralles were around to defend themselves; both died during the construction period.

The big idea behind Miralles's design for the parliament was that it should complement its immediate environment: the old town houses of Canongate as well as the rugged natural features of Holyrood park and Salisbury Crags, both of which overlook

Scottish Parliament, with Queensberry house (centre) and Calton Hill (background)

the site. He would reflect wider Scottish themes and landscapes – for example, the flower paintings of Charles Rennie Mackintosh, and, most commented on, roof structures in the shape of upturned boats on the shore – to create a building 'growing out of the land'.

On the walls there is a clear timber-and-granite motif around the windows, which has been compared to an anvil or hair-dryer but is supposed to represent curtains being pulled open to reveal what is happening inside and out. On the outside you will also see references to Scotland's history and geography, complemented by paving slabs with quotes from Scottish writers, and later we will see a wall covered in inscriptions and with many types of Scottish stone inset. From here we can see the ponds, which represent lochs, and, to our left, the garden with many Scottish plant species. As well as reflecting nature, the building is designed to be environmentally friendly and sustainable, powered entirely from renewable sources.

While the Miralles design was acclaimed by many architects and in academia, and has since won a number of awards, it mystified many Scots.

Turn left and walk alongside the parliament. Follow the path up the slight incline with the gardens to your left. An information board on the left of the path tells you more about the natural aspects of the parliament's design.

On your right, there is an opening in the wall. Go up the ten stairs and veer to the right. This semi-covered walkway opens up, and, when it does, walk up the stairs on the left.

The marquee-like structure at the top of the stairs is the visitor attraction, Our Dynamic Earth (on Holyrood Road), which tells the story of how our planet was created, along with information on its oceans, forests, ice caps, volcanoes and many other natural features. Aptly, this was the site where James Hutton made his great discoveries about the formation of the earth. The marquee is the top of the two-storey building, surrounding it is an old stone wall from the brewery that once occupied the site.

As we walk up the stairs of the amphitheatre-like entrance, the board on your right gives information about the different rocks, designs and scientific exhibits inside. An identical board is located on the other side. Next on the right, near the top of the stairs, is a metal sculpture of two fulmars. The plaque at the base reveals it was commissioned in memory of a more recent brewer, Sir Alick Rankin of Scottish and Newcastle, who died in 1999.

At the top of the steps turn left and walk around the entrance forecourt to reach the back wall.

Here we have a great view of Salisbury Crags, with an information board that

Our Dynamic Earth

details James Hutton's life, the geology of the area and how much it has changed (*see Hutton panel on facing page*).

Retrace your steps until you are back in front of the entrance and continue around the amphitheatre.

From the top of the amphitheatre you can appreciate the odd shape of the Scottish Parliament. It is supposed to represent upturned boats, with the sterns facing us.

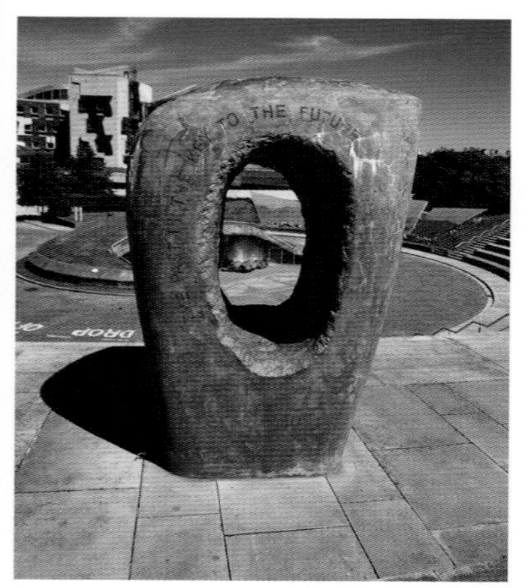
Salisbury Crags

Continue around, descend using the ramp that curves around this side of the amphitheatre.

As we start to descend you can see a stone artwork with the words 'the past is the key to the future' and if you look through the hole you can see the 'earth's core'.

The inscriptions on the floor of the ramp detail when different types of stone found in Scotland were formed and on the right

Stone artwork, Our Dynamic Earth

James Hutton, the founder of geology

It took James Hutton some time and several false starts before he fully turned his attention to geology, the subject he not only loved, but also, according to many scientists, founded. He was born in Edinburgh in 1726, the son of a wealthy merchant and farmer, and entered the university at the age of fourteen to study mathematics and philosophy. After he graduated, he was apprenticed to a lawyer in the city but had little interest in a legal career, preferring to carry out chemistry experiments for the amusement of his fellow clerks. Seeking a change in direction, he left to take a degree in medicine at Leiden University, in Holland, graduating in 1749. Hutton never practised as a doctor, instead turning to farming, and it was during this period that his interest in geology took hold. In 1750, with his friend James Davie, he set up a factory in Edinburgh to produce sal ammoniac (a chemical used in welding metal) from coal soot, a process that he and Davie had discovered while they were students. The business proved to be highly lucrative.

The success of his agricultural and industrial ventures made Hutton a wealthy man, enabling him to give up farming and devote his life to geological research, which he carried out from his home at St John's Hill, overlooking Salisbury Crags. He travelled extensively, examining rock formations and landscapes, the characteristics of which he would painstakingly record. The result was his influential theory of uniformitarianism, which holds that the processes that created geological phenomena can be explained in terms of observable processes and that those processes have operated in a uniform manner for immensely long periods of time. For the age this was a radical departure: based on a literal interpretation of the book of Genesis, there was still a widespread belief that the

James Hutton (1776) by Sir Henry Raeburn

earth was only six thousand years old. It should also be noted that a mere seventy or so years before Hutton, Britain's greatest scientist, Sir Isaac Newton, had tried to fit the earth's creation into a Biblical timescale.

The ideas proposed by Hutton were outlined in lectures given for the Royal Society of Edinburgh in 1785, which formed the basis for his book, *Theory of the Earth*, published posthumously in 1795. Despite the hostility from some quarters, especially from religious conservatives, this was a major turning point in the history of science. It was at this point that geology became a scientific discipline in its own right, based on the principle of uniformitarianism. Hutton also influenced thinking in a wide range of other fields, including biology and evolutionary studies, and was an inspiration to Charles Darwin.

James Hutton did not conform to the stereotype of the solitary, other-worldly scientist. Edinburgh at the time was a fast-growing commercial centre, as well as an intellectual hub, and he played a full part in the life of the city. His circle of friends included the great chemist, Joseph Black, father-of-economics Adam Smith, the pioneering engineer James Watt and the eminent philosopher, David Hume. They met regularly, in what became known as the Oyster Club, to discuss the issues of the day while wolfing down platefuls of oysters and draughts of wine and whisky.

are representative boulders. Each stone has a plaque that details the formation and where Scotland was located in the world at the time. These go from volcanic Scotland, 1.8 million years ago, to samples of Lewisian Gneisses, which are some of the oldest rocks in the world and were formed 2.8 billion years ago.

At the end of the slope you have the option to further explore the amphitheatre. Here you can see more Scottish rocks and where they are found.

From the end of the ramp. Turn left, walk along Holyrood Road until you reach the corner. On your left is a metal sculpture of the world, a sign of Our Dynamic Earth.

Turn right, cross over the pedestrian crossing, turn right, then left and walk up Reid's Close (there is no street sign for Reid's Close).

Reid's Close was named after a successful brewer and offers another view of the Scottish Parliament. Behind the protective wall is the building occupied by Members of the Scottish Parliament. These are offices, and the bay windows are said to have been styled as 'contemplation spaces'.

Halfway up, turn left around the modern building and with an old stone wall on your right. This is the back of Royal Mile primary school. When this road joins up with the end of Hutton Road there is a set of stairs on the right. Go up these stairs.

The redbrick building in front of you was originally one of the many breweries that were built in this area.

Turn right and head up Bull's Close onto Canongate.

When you exit the close turn around and look over the entrance. The weathered stone inscription contains a heraldic shield and the left side reads 'AVXILI' and 'MY HELP'. This was from the older building and reincorporated into the entrance after redevelopment in the early twentieth century.

Cross over Canongate and turn right.

On your left are Lochend Close, Little Lochend Close and the entrance to Reid's Court and Canongate manse.

The iron gates of Canongate manse (Reid's Court, 95 Canongate) have heraldic shields with a bishop's crozier, halberds and a quaich, a Celtic drinking vessel, between two crosses. The white mansion house dates from 1690. It was a coaching inn for a time, as well as the manse for Canongate kirk (*see Walk 6*), but the court's name comes from

Left: MSP offices, with 'contemplation spaces', Reid's Close

Above: Canongate manse

Queensberry house

the Edinburgh brewer and magistrate, Andrew Reid, who resided here in the eighteenth century.

Cross over Canongate at the pedestrian crossing, turn left and keep walking down the hill.

The Royal Mile primary school (86 Canongate) on your right was built in 1888. It was previously known as Milton House school and the original building designed by John Adam is located at the back of the current building. If you look up at the top of the building there is a carving of a woman sitting teaching a boy.

Continue down the Canongate until on your right is the bright, and very grand, Queensberry house (64 Canongate).

The original building dates from the 1660s and was acquired in 1680 by Charles Maitland, Lord Hatton, brother of the Duke of Lauderdale, before being sold to William Douglas, 1st Duke of Queensberry, in 1686. It has been much altered since: in the eighteenth century it was converted to flats, and then, in 1808, it became a barracks, at which time a storey was added. During the twentieth century it became a centre for social welfare, with separate infirmaries for men and women, a night shelter for the homeless and a soup kitchen. While still impressive today it was in its original state a great mansion – 'magnificent, large and princely', one writer called it – with fifty-two rooms, a French roof and windows in the style of Versailles. In 1997, it was acquired by the government and extensively renovated, including returning it to the original height. Queensberry house has now been integrated into the Scottish Parliament complex and provides office accommodation for the presiding officer, the chief executive and other staff.

Queensberry rules

James Douglas, 2nd duke of Queensberry

The Douglas family is one of the most influential and enduring in Scottish history. Indeed the 2nd Duke of Queensberry, James Douglas (1662–1711), played the leading role in the most consequential issue ever to face this country: the union with England. With his aristocratic background, easy charm and political nous, Queensberry was appointed commissioner to the Scottish parliament in 1705, tasked with the job of pushing through the articles of union. He did this with consummate skill, helped in no small measure, his enemies maintain, by the liberal sprinkling of bribes. Thanks largely to the 'union duke', as he became known, the end result was the Act of Union of 1707, with Scotland losing its status as an independent nation (even if it did retain control of its legal system, church and schools). Whether or not the allegations of corruption are true, Queensberry's detractors point to the lavish rewards showered on him after 1707: these included a huge pension, the dukedom of Dover, a marquisate and an earldom.

It is ironic that at the hour of his greatest triumph, the duke would be brought down to earth by a shocking event in his palatial home. His son, Lord Drumlanrig, also James, was a deeply disturbed young man, afflicted by gigantism. In fact, he was so disturbed that he had to be locked in a sealed apartment of Queensberry house, the windows boarded up. On the night that the Act of Union was approved by the parliament, the Duke and his entire household had gone out. According to some accounts it was to celebrate, while others believe he was hiding from the Edinburgh mob, enraged by what they viewed as his betrayal of Scotland. Whatever the explanation for his absence, in the great house there remained only his son and a little kitchen boy. Young Drumlanrig noted how quiet the house was and somehow managed to escape confinement. He was a noted glutton and as he wandered around the house, the savoury odour of roasting meat led him to the kitchens, where the young servant was sitting quietly by the fire, turning a spit. The demented nobleman killed the young lad, discarded the half-cooked meat and put the spit through his victim. After roasting the boy's body over the fire, he began to devour it and it was at this point that the Duke, his father, and entourage, walked in on the terrible scene.

Although the Duke tried to hush up what had happened it leaked out, causing a huge scandal. The 'cannibal earl' was never seen in public again and was later secreted out of Scotland to a discreet location in England. When the Duke died, the title and his estates passed to his second son, Charles. For their part, the ordinary people of Edinburgh believed Queensberry had got his just desserts: to them he had been judged by God for his nefarious tactics in parliament.

Carved wall

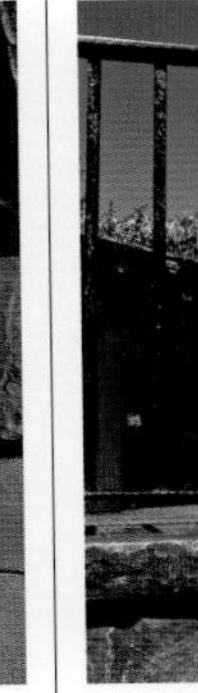

James Balfour railings

Further down Canongate is the artistically carved wall containing stones from all over Scotland, along with quotations. After investigating this, turn left and cross over the road to a covered bus stop.

Behind the bus stop there are iron railings depicting the accountant, James Balfour. In one he is sitting at his desk surrounded by money, in the other dancing and drinking. This is because the site was the location of a tavern run by Janet Hall (Jenny Ha') that dates back to the seventeenth century. 'Jenny Ha's' was famous for claret being drunk from the butt, or barrel. Important artistic and historic visitors were said to frequent the tavern, including playwright John Gay (1685–1732), whose patron was the 3rd Duke of Queensberry and had come to Edinburgh at his lordship's invitation. Gay was not invited to lodge at the grand Queensberry house but was instead found an attic in an old tenement across the street, in which humble accommodation he is said to have written (or at least revised) his comic masterpiece, *The Beggar's Opera*.

Above the small flight of stairs is a relief in memory of the centenary of the buildings in this area being used as veterans' residences. This started in 1910, when 240 war veterans were housed here.

Turn left and head up Canongate.

On the right is Galloway's Entry and just after this there is a plaque detailing part of the history of Whitefoord house and how Walter Scott mentioned the building in his work.

Further up we pass an iron gate that is the entrance to Forsyth's Close and Gloucester gate, access is solely for the veterans who reside in the area.

The next interesting building on the right is Whitefoord house (53 Canongate), designed by Robert Mylne and built in 1769 for Sir John Whitefoord of Ballochmyle (1734–1803), Ayrshire landowner, friend and

Veterans' memorial

Whitefoord house

patron of Robert Burns. The simple structure we see today is operated by the charity, Scottish Veterans Residences, and provides accommodation to former servicemen and women. However, the site was once occupied by a much grander property – the magnificent townhouse of the Seton family, earls of Winton, a powerful dynasty that found itself on the losing side during the Jacobite uprisings, forcing the fifth earl to flee to Rome. A plaque on the wall of the building on the right gives more information.

Next to Whitefoord house is the entrance to Brown's Close but before we venture up there, look at the plaques on the building to the left of the close. They include a coat of arms and information about Bailie John Paterson and his apparent golfing relationship with the Duke of York, the future James VII.

Bailie John Paterson plaque

Go up Brown's Close and at the end turn left; go through the passage on the left. The buildings above you are from the 1960s but were designed to be a more modern interpretation of the traditional style of Edinburgh tenements.

Enter the courtyard and in the centre is a free-standing drinking fountain from the nineteenth century.

Turn right and go down the narrow close to reach Calton Road.

At the end of the path we have the old maltings on our left and across the road the grand entrance of the former Craigwell brewery, which has been converted into houses.

Cross the road, turn left and when you pass the end of the old brewery, on the right there is a small entrance into a wooded area; take this path up the hill.

The path reaches a crossroad, which is a good moment to stop, turn around and

Royal High School of Edinburgh

look out over Canongate. There are views of the Scottish Parliament, Arthur's Seat, Salisbury Crags and the rest of the Old Town.

Take the sharp right that leads up the hill and out onto Regent Road.

Opposite us, on the left, is the old Royal High School of Edinburgh, designed in the Greek Revival-style by Thomas Hamilton and completed in 1829. It is one of the finest neoclassical buildings in Europe and a major factor in Edinburgh being described as the 'Athens of the North'. The school itself can trace its history back to 1128, making it one of the oldest in the world, and before moving here it operated in a variety of Old Town locations. The school closed in 1968, with the pupils relocated, and for a time the building was used as council offices. Then, in the 1970s, as the first proposals for devolving political power to Scotland were formulated, the great hall was converted to a debating chamber for the proposed legislative assembly.

However, the 1979 referendum did not produce a sufficient majority for devolution and it would it would be another two decades before the idea of using the Royal High School as a legislature came back onto the agenda. A second referendum of 1997 approved the setting up of a parliament and Scotland's first minister Donald Dewar, the first person to hold that office, gave serious consideration to using the former school as the venue for the parliament, before opting for a new building at Holyrood, Sadly, Hamilton's masterpiece currently lies unoccupied and while there have been many proposals to develop the site most have been highly controversial and none have yet been approved by the city council.

Turn right and head down Regent Road.

On the right is the Greek temple-style Burns monument (Thomas Hamilton, 1830) with a plaque that goes into detail about the building's features.

After the Burns monument go through

Burns monument

the gate on the right and follow the path through another gate. This is New Calton burial ground.

Turn right and head the short distance along the path until, on your right, there is a two-storey tower.

This is a death-watch tower constructed in the nineteenth century to house guards that protected the cemetery from grave-robbers who stole the freshest dead bodies and sold them to the surgeons and anatomists of the city. As graveyards and burial grounds became better protected, the infamous Burke and Hare kept the business going by resorting to more sinister methods.

Turn left, then right, and head down the hill towards the exit onto Calton Road. We also have a nice view of the city, including Holyrood palace.

As you leave the burial ground, cross over the road and turn left. When the pavement ends take the entrance on the

Death-watch tower

White Horse Close

right (next to the metal railings). Head through the narrow passage, turn left and we arrive in White Horse Close (31 Canongate).

The close is thought to be named after the white horse favoured by Mary, Queen of Scots, which was stabled in its mews. It was also home to the White Horse inn, built in 1623, and, from 1652, to the London coach, which started its two-week journey to the English capital from here. While White Horse Close, with its crow-stepped gables and forestairs, is undoubtedly picturesque and much-photographed, its appearance owes more to modern redevelopment than to the seventeenth century.

Turn right and walk through the close. On your right is a plaque detailing that the founder of Edinburgh University's veterinary school, William Dick, lived here.

As we leave the close we arrive again on Canongate. Turn left and head down the road.

At the end of Canongate, on your left, is a seventeenth-century tenement, which has connections to Sir Patrick Geddes. Above the door the date 1697 can be seen and to the left there is a plaque giving information about the building's preservation and restoration.

Turn right, cross Canongate and arrive outside the front of the Scottish Parliament building. This is the end of our walk. If you want to start our next walk simply cross over to Holyrood palace.

IN DEPTH

How the Scottish Parliament works

POWERS

The Scottish Parliament (usually referred to as Holyrood) has control of a wide range of domestic issues, known as devolved powers; these include education, health, law and order, local government, farming and fishing. The Parliament also has powers on some aspects of income tax as well as the right to vary specified welfare benefits. The Westminster parliament in London retains control over UK-wide and international issues such as foreign policy, defence, immigration, the constitution and most taxes; these are known as reserved matters. In terms of its structure, Holyrood is a unicameral legislature, meaning that there is no upper house or senate.

ELECTIONS

The Holyrood parliament consists of 129 MSPs (Members of the Scottish Parliament), who are elected through a combination of traditional first-past-the-post contests and a form of proportional representation known as the additional-member system. In practice, 73 MSPs are elected through the constituency route by first-past-the-post while 56 come from Scotland's 8 regions, with each region having 7 MSPs. The 56 regional MSPs are elected by the additional-member system.

The electoral system was designed in this way so that smaller parties, which traditionally do not fare well at first-past-the-post elections, could be represented in parliament. It has meant that representatives from parties as diverse as the Scottish Senior Citizens Unity Party, the Scottish Socialists and the Scottish Green Party have won seats, as well as a healthy quota of independents. The voting system also works against a single party having dominance in parliament, and so, of the five elections to date (1999, 2003, 2007, 2011 and 2016), only one has led to a government with an overall majority – the Scottish National Party in 2011.

THE SCOTTISH GOVERNMENT

The government is led by a first minister, who appoints colleagues to a range of portfolios, the most senior of whom serve in the cabinet. Since the setting up of the parliament in 1999, Scotland has had five first ministers: Donald Dewar, Henry McLeish and Jack McConnell (Labour Party); Alex Salmond and Nicola Sturgeon (Scottish National Party). The first minister's official residence is Bute house, an elegant Georgian house in Charlotte Square, which sits in the heart of Edinburgh's fashionable New Town.

INSIDE HOLYROOD

The main focus in the parliament building is the debating chamber, an impressive space finished in oak, steel and glass. The roof structure is particularly noteworthy, its reinforced steel and oak-laminated beams allowing the chamber to span thirty metres without any supporting columns. Another highlight is the west wall, which has more than a thousand square metres of laminated glass panels. Each panel has a sycamore veneer featuring cut-out shapes of people, which was an attempt by the architect to give the building a human dimension.

The shape of the chamber is semi-circular. It was thought this would help to encourage

Debating chamber, Scottish Parliament

consensus and avoid the supposed adversarial style of the House of Commons, where government and opposition parties face each other. In a similar vein the MSPs sit at individual desks and vote quietly via a computer console, another contrast with Westminster where representatives crowd onto communal benches and march, often noisily, through one of two rooms (known as the 'lobby') to vote when a division is called.

There is much else of interest in the parliament building, including the main hall, the committee rooms, the MSP building with its unique windows and contemplation spaces and the garden lobby, a light, open space for informal meetings.

DEBATES AND MAKING LAWS

The debating chamber is where MSPs meet to discuss topical issues, to question the first minister and the cabinet secretaries and to make new laws. Proceedings are supervised by the presiding officer, or by one of two deputy presiding officers, who are themselves sitting MSPs elected by other members and therefore, in theory, politically impartial. In normal circumstances, meetings of the full Parliament take place on Tuesday, Wednesday and Thursday, mostly in the afternoon. It is possible for the public to attend debates but they must first obtain a ticket from the parliamentary authorities.

The Scotland Act 1998 gave Holyrood the power to make laws on most domestic issues and the scope of these powers was significantly extended by the Scotland Act 2012. For a measure to become law it is first necessary to introduce a bill, which can be done by individual MSPs, by one of Holyrood's committees, or, in most cases, by the government of the day.

Every bill has to go through a three-stage process: firstly, the general principles are discussed by a committee and the chamber as a whole; secondly, a parliamentary committee scrutinises the bill in detail; finally, the parliament as whole decides whether to approve or reject the bill. If it is approved the bill becomes an act and part of the law of Scotland.

WALK 8
HOLYROOD: PALACE AND PARK

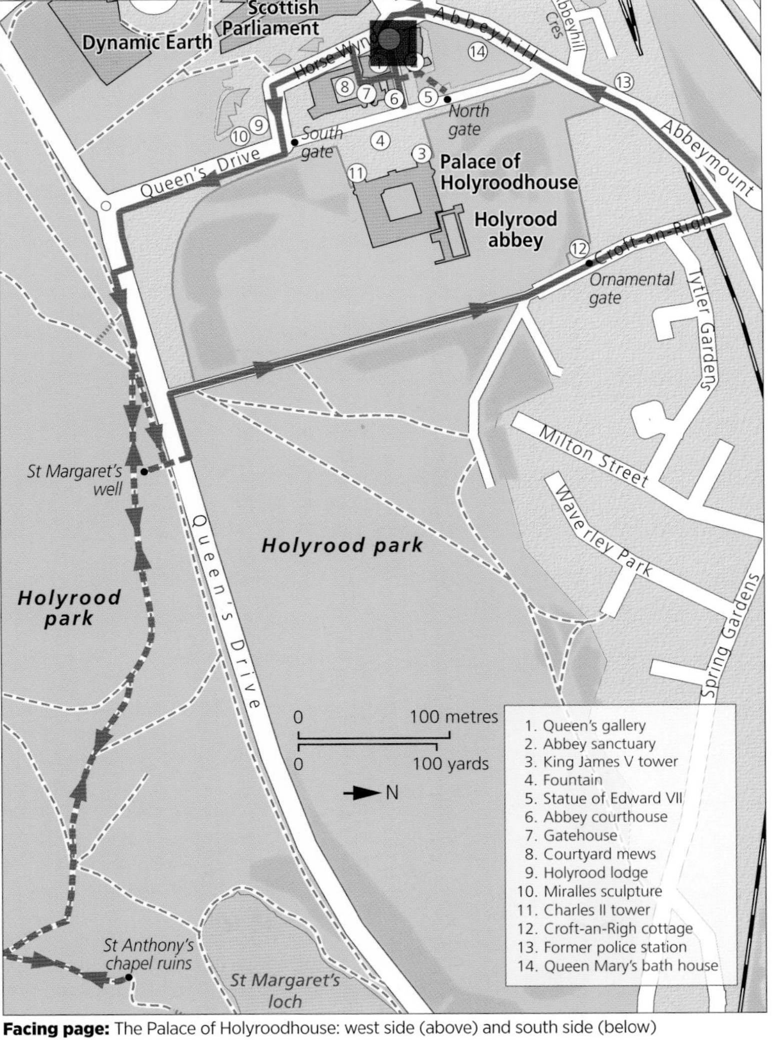

Facing page: The Palace of Holyroodhouse: west side (above) and south side (below)

Start Queen's gallery, corner of Horse Wynd/Abbey Strand

Summary A walk around the Palace of Holyroodhouse, including the Abbey Strand and the Queen's gallery. Part of the route also diverts us through Holyrood park and up the hill to St Anthony's chapel. The walk finishes by going past the east side of the palace and into Croft-an-Righ.

Highlights Queen's gallery • Holyrood palace • Abbey Strand and sanctuary • Holyrood Park • Radical Road • St Anthony's chapel • St Margaret's well • Holyrood abbey • Croft-an-Righ • Queen Mary's bathhouse • In-depth: the Holyrood story

The Walk

We start our walk standing outside the grand doorway of the Queen's gallery. The building (by John Henderson) was constructed in the 1850s for the Free Church of Scotland in the Gothic style and its use has changed over the years. In the 1990s it was extensively renovated, and, like certain other royal residences throughout Britain, it now exhibits works from the royal collection.

The arch in front of us and the ornate door date from this most recent period of construction. The red lion holding the sword and sceptre is based on a design from the tomb of Mary, Queen of Scots and the carvings around the doorway are thistles and daisies. On the door itself we can see the leaves of native plants represented in the upper hinges and the relief of Arthur's Seat and Salisbury Crags on the left, lower hinge, with the Old Town skyline on the right. At your feet there are lights set into the pavement, which reflect the shape of the arch.

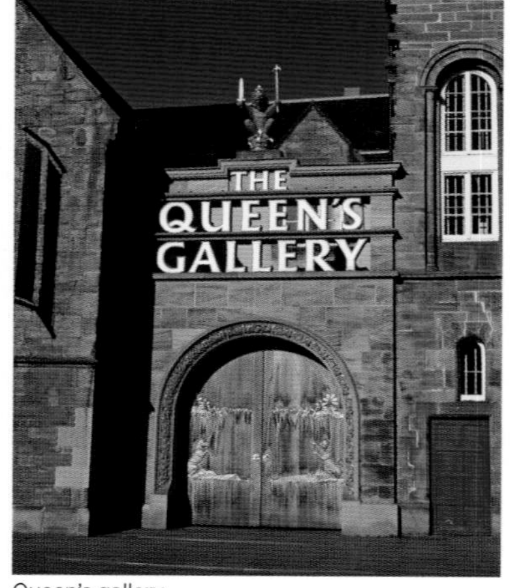

Queen's gallery

The royal collection runs to one million objects, making it one of the largest and most important art collections in the world. Oliver Cromwell sold many royal possessions following the execution of Charles I in 1649 so most of the pieces in today's collection have been accumulated since the restoration of the monarchy in 1660. The Queen as an individual does not own the royal collection; it is held in trust by her as sovereign for her successors and the nation.

Turn to your left and walk past the front of the gallery then turn right into Abbey Strand.

Abbey Strand – the name comes from a stream that ran through the area – has a long and colourful history. The oldest section was built around 1490 and was connected with Holyrood abbey, with some historians suggesting it may have been the abbot's residence. However, Abbey Strand's main use during the medieval period was as an alms-house for the poor and as a hospital.

During the reigns of Mary, Queen of Scots and her son James VI, the royal court grew to around six hundred people and Abbey Strand was extended to provide

Abbey Strand

accommodation for them, as well as for foreign ambassadors and other important visitors. When, after the Union of Crowns in 1603, the court moved to London, the area around Holyrood palace became popular with Edinburgh citizens escaping the city's crowded streets. It was at this time that Abbey Strand became a place to eat and to drink, with a brewery and several taverns opening for business. The area, however, declined markedly in the late eighteenth century as the New Town was developed; the rich and powerful left and Abbey Strand, like many other parts of the Old Town, became an overcrowded slum.

Another of Abbey Strand's ancient functions was as a sanctuary for debtors. Until imprisonment for debt was abolished in 1880, debtors (or 'abbey lairds' as they were known) could evade their creditors by living within a five-mile circumference of Holyrood abbey. On weekdays they were required to stay within the sanctuary but on Sundays could venture freely, without fear of arrest, across the city provided they returned to the designated area by midnight. The line of brass 'S' shapes on the ground marks the border of the sanctuary. On the left of Abbey Strand is the sixteenth-century abbey sanctuary, which, at one time, was one of many buildings that provided accommodation for debtors. After multiple restorations in the twentieth century the building is now a gift-shop.

The buildings of Abbey Strand are currently being redeveloped as a learning centre for Holyrood palace.

Pass the sanctuary on your left and turn left onto the small footpath, follow it round and at the end turn right and walk towards the palace's north gate.

The ornamental gate is identical to the south gate, which we will see later. There are many symbols of Scotland and Britain, such as the lion carrying the English flag atop one column being matched by the unicorn with a saltire on the other. On the metal gates you can find roses, thistles, shields and St Andrew's crosses.

Looking through the gates (to the left of the palace complex) you get a view of the north-west tower, known as James V's

North gate, Holyrood palace

Octagonal fountain, forecourt

tower. Mary, Queen of Scots had her private rooms here, on the second floor, and this is where her friend and adviser David Rizzio was brutally murdered; it is claimed that his bloodstains are still visible (*see 'The Holyrood story' on pages 158–63*).

We can also see the forecourt with the octagonal fountain (Robert Matheson, 1859) in the centre, a replica of one at Linlithgow palace. The fountain is highly ornate and amongst the many crowns, flowers, grotesque faces and heraldic beasts there are representations of Queen Mary, David Rizzio and Queen Margaret.

To the right as you look through the gate is a bronze statue of King Edward VII by Montrose-born sculptor H. S. Gamley. It was paid for with money raised from all over Scotland and unveiled in 1922 as part of the palace renovations, which included the north and south gates and the outer courtyard.

Turn around and retrace your steps along the path to Abbey Strand.

On our left is another set of gates, topped by a stag with a crucifix between its antlers. This is the symbol of Holyrood abbey and also features on the coat of arms of Canongate. How the abbey acquired the stag symbol goes back to the twelfth century and involves a hunting expedition in which the life of King David I was saved following divine intervention (*see 'The Holyrood story'*).

This gate replaced the Abbey Pend, which was demolished in the mid-eighteenth century. If we turn to the right you can see one part of this building, the sixteenth-century abbey courthouse, which survived the redevelopment. On the wall is a heraldic panel, with unicorn, which originally stood above the gatehouse, the letters 'I R 5' stand for James V.

Turn right, walk past the courthouse and turn left under the arch into the abbey courtyard.

On your left is a ticket booth as well as the back of the seventeenth-century guard-

Statue of Edward VII

Heraldic panel, abbey courthouse

house. As we walk further, there is also the main entrance and gatehouse. The rest of Abbey Court consists of eighteenth- and nineteenth-century buildings, which make up the courtyard mews.

In 1861 the gatehouse was built to replace the one at Abbey Pend and was part of the many changes to Holyrood undertaken at the request of Queen Victoria and Prince Albert. Often these were to enhance privacy, allow for easier access and to landscape the area. If you look up you can see the tops of the two towers, which mirror those of the palace.

Through the gatehouse, you can also see the fountain and behind it the main entrance to the quadrangle, with the grand heraldic carving and the clock tower. Previously an array of other buildings occupied the site; many were part of the monastery complex, needed for accommodation and other services.

Leave the courtyard by walking away from the gatehouse, through the main entrance with the Queen's gallery on your right.

Turn left and walk along Horse Wynd.

Follow the road round to the left.

On your right, you can see the artistic bike-stands of the Scottish Parliament complex. Their odd designs, when viewed side-on, combine to form the shape of a bicycle. Next to them is Holyrood lodge, built in 1857 to control entrance to Holyrood park. Today it is an information centre.

Before the road turns right, on our left is Holyrood's south gate. Through the gate, we have another view of the palace. From here you can see the south-western Charles II tower, which repeats the design of the

Holyrood lodge

Holyrood park

King James V tower on the north-west side of the palace.

Follow the road right with the outer walls of the palace complex on your left.

On the right-hand side of the road is a wavy sculpture designed by Enric Miralles, the architect behind the Scottish Parliament. It reflects the local geography but is also supposed to be shaped perfectly for people to sit and lie on whilst the texture of the stone is comfortable against the skin.

Keep on this path when at the end of Horse Wynd it turns left into Queen's Drive and continue along until you reach a pedestrian crossing.

The majestic landscape of Arthur's Seat and Salisbury Crags in front of it are on your right, the south side of Holyrood palace is on the left. The south-facing rooms include the throne room and other apartments in which the Queen holds audiences with Scotland's first minister, visiting dignitaries and to bestow honours.

An information board in front of us explains about Holyrood park and places worth exploring such as Dunsapie Crag, where the remains of iron-age settlements have been found, and St Margaret's and Dunsapie lochs, which were created during the great landscaping of Holyrood park by Queen Victoria in 1844. Many parts of the land round here were cultivated, with crops being grown as late as the 1540s and sheep grazing long after.

Turn right, go over the pedestrian crossing and turn left.

The path that leads up towards the crags, then turns to follow the bottom of the cliffs, is the Radical Road, a public-works scheme devised by Sir Walter Scott to create jobs for unemployed weavers in the 1820s. There was also a great deal of quarrying done here until the 1830s and evidence of that has been found by archaeologists working in the grounds of Holyrood palace.

Walk along the path until you come to a fork.

Our walk will now traverse rougher pathways to reach St Anthony's chapel. This ten-minute walk may not be for everyone and if you would rather not do this, or want to leave it for another day, take the left fork and head for St Margaret's well, skipping three paragraphs. (The well is close to the pedestrian crossing and on the same level as Queen's Drive.)

Take the right fork and follow the path leading up the hill. As you climb you will get great views of Holyrood park, the rest of Edinburgh and also St Margaret's loch, a popular spot for feeding ducks and swans.

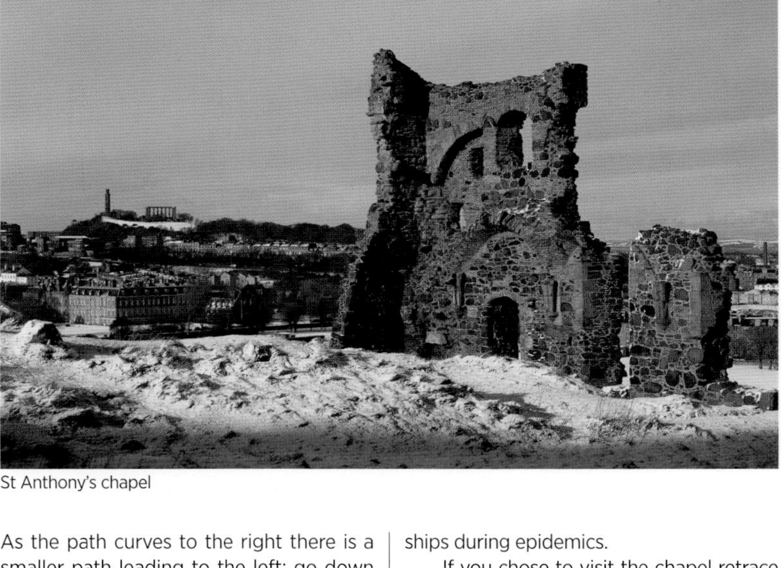
St Anthony's chapel

As the path curves to the right there is a smaller path leading to the left; go down that path. If at any point you wish to climb Arthur's Seat, you would keep on the main path. This is perhaps the longest, but gentlest, ascent.

Following our walk, after taking the smaller path off to the left, there are stone steps; climb these and follow the path round to the right. As the hill levels out, it appears to meet another path. Turn left, almost turning back on yourself and follow this smaller path. If you stay on this path you will find the ruins of St Anthony's chapel.

There is only one of the chapel's walls, the north, still standing, along with a hermitage, which was probably a store room, close by. No one is quite sure when St Anthony's was built but as there is a record of money being spent repairing it in 1426 it must be around six hundred years old. As to its purpose that is equally unclear: one theory is that it was a hospital for infectious diseases while another explanation is that it was a shining beacon on a hill for sailors returning to Edinburgh. A board on your left gives more information. The views are spectacular: if you look out you can see Leith, the port of Edinburgh, while over the water there are the hills of Fife and the island of Inchkeith, which was used to quarantine ships during epidemics.

If you chose to visit the chapel retrace your steps to the fork at the bottom of the hill. We will now take the left fork, following the path that runs next to the road. After a short distance, there is a very short path leading off to the right; this takes you to St Margaret's well.

Set into the hillside and utilising a natural spring, and behind a stone façade, the central arch and carved face of the well

St Margaret's well

Nave, church of Holyrood abbey

are hard to see. It dates from the fifteenth century and was originally located in the village of Restalrig but was moved here in 1859. The plaque above details the history of the well and when it was moved to this natural spring.

Turn around, cross over Queen's Drive and turn left.

Holyrood park on our right was used as fields but also as a mass grave. Under the ground there are in the region of eight thousand corpses; people who perished during the great plague of 1645. This is one of a few plague pits, which were once outside the Edinburgh city walls but are now parks and areas of grassland.

Croft-an-Righ

As the path meets the car park turn right.

We will now walk behind Holyrood palace. If you step up onto the grass of Holyrood park you can get a view of the back of the palace and also see the ruins of Holyrood abbey, which today amount to no more than the church nave.

Originally this area had many more abbey buildings – such as the cloisters, dormitories, chapter house and infirmary – but over the years these were removed to make way for the royal palace. Havoc was also wreaked by invading forces and the Edinburgh mob, the last such event occurring in 1688. By this time all that remained was the nave, which dates from the early thirteenth century, but even that was seriously damaged when its roof collapsed in 1768.

Continue along the path with Holyrood palace on your left until you reach the narrow entrance to the street known as Croft-an-Righ (on your left).

As you walk down this lane on the right is an elaborately carved gateway with flower and cross motifs. It previously sat further south, as an entrance to the grounds of the cottage on the other side of the lane. Croft-an-Righ means 'king's field' and it is unclear why the Gaelic name has been used, but maps as old as the eighteenth century are clearly using this name. The building on the left, Croft-an-Righ cottage, was built in the sixteenth century but remodelled in the seventeenth, perhaps after a serious fire.

The Croft-an-Righ area was the site of St Ann's brewery, established in the eighteenth century. Land around Holyrood was popular for brewing because it was less developed than the rest of the Old Town and because the clean waters of the streams were ideal for beer.

At the end of the lane go under the bridge, turn left. Go under the next bridge and continue along the road.

On the right-hand side of the road is a nineteenth century red-sandstone building with gargoyles, which was once a police station. Later it became an Armenian community centre and in recent years it was said to be a secretive restaurant where booking was essential, with even locals surprised to hear that the building was not abandoned.

Queen Mary's bath house

The area should now start to be familiar. Cross over the road that leads to the north gate and continue along towards a distinctive small building with a pyramid roof.

This sixteenth-century building, on the left, is known as Queen Mary's bath house, but, as the plaque attached to the railings notes, it was more of a summer house or pavilion. Originally there were gardens reached by a wooden bridge, tennis courts, other buildings and a wall but these were demolished in the nineteenth century. The queen referred to is Mary, Queen of Scots.

Follow the road round to Abbey Strand and we are now at the end of our walk. Our next walk starts at Surgeon's hall on Nicolson Street.

IN DEPTH

The Holyrood story

The Palace of Holyroodhouse has been a royal residence for more than five hundred years and is one of the most historically significant places in Scotland. The building we see today has been modified many times throughout the centuries by its royal owners, most notably James V and Charles II. Its location could hardly be more spectacular: it sits at the foot of the historic Royal Mile, overlooked by the dramatic Salisbury Crags and by Arthur's Seat, an extinct volcano that rises to 822 feet/251 metres. Both natural features are part of Holyrood park, which was once a royal hunting ground, but is now a welcoming green lung for the people of Edinburgh.

THE LEGEND OF HOLYROOD ABBEY

The origins of the palace can be traced to the foundation, in 1128, of an Augustinian abbey by King David I. The story goes that David, out hunting in the forest surrounding Holyrood, came upon a magnificent white stag, which charged him. He was thrown from his horse, and, now defenceless, he expected to be gored by the great beast. But as he lay

The symbol of Holyroodhouse

there a silver cloud appeared, from which a hand emerged. The hand delivered a shining cross to David, terrifying the stag, which ran off. That night the king a had a dream, in which St Andrew, patron saint of Scotland, urged him to found an abbey at the very spot on which he had been miraculously saved. The abbey was dedicated to the holy cross, or rood, hence the name Holyroodhouse, and the story also explains the coat of arms of the former burgh of Canongate, a distinctive stag's head and cross.

In the centuries that followed, Holyrood abbey flourished and it became the richest religious foundation in Scotland, so wealthy that in 1189 it was able to grant King William the Lion a large sum of money to redeem Scotland's onerous treaty obligations to the English. The abbey grew in size, adding cloisters, a chapter house, a refectory, a large church and guest houses, including one for royal visitors.

THE ROYAL PALACE

By the fifteenth century Edinburgh had become the de facto capital of Scotland, and while successive kings had the option of residing in the great castle most found it too cold, windy and bleak, thanks mainly to its exposed, and very rocky, summit. They much preferred Holyrood, with its pleasant gardens and hunting park, with the result that many important royal events took place here, including the birth of James II in 1430 and the marriage of James III in 1469. In consequence the royal lodgings increased in size and scope and would eventually eclipse the abbey.

It was King James IV, monarch from 1488, who took the decisive step. He was about to marry Margaret Tudor, daughter of Henry VII of England, and needed a prestigious residence for his new bride. Work started on a palace,

King James V tower

arranged around a quadrangle, which, in fact, was very close to the current palace buildings. Significant development continued during the reign of James V, and in 1528 work began on what became known as James V's tower at the north-west corner of the palace; it is the only part of the original palace that survives today. Interestingly, although the tower was designed primarily as a residence it was also in those dangerous times a defensive bulwark, being equipped with a drawbridge and moat.

MARY, QUEEN OF SCOTS

Mary's husband, Francis II, king of France, died in 1560 and with her prospects now severely limited in her adopted land she returned to her native Scotland in 1561 as the rightful sovereign. Mary took up residence in Holyrood palace, in the north-west tower developed by her father, James V, and imbued the place with her undoubted *joie de vivre*. An educated, Renaissance woman who came to maturity in the sophisticated French court, the Queen was a lover of poetry, music, song and, especially, of dance, the latter predilection particularly infuriating the great Protestant reformer, John Knox, who saw dancing as one of the devil's wiles. Indeed, she employed a group of musicians, whom she would often accompany, either in song or on the lute, which she played to a high standard.

Her taste in clothes and jewellery was also refined and on state occasions she was always beautifully attired. According to one biographer, Antonia Fraser, an inventory of her dresses from 1562 had 131 entries, including gowns made of cloth of gold and silver, velvet, satin and silk. The list of her jewels was equally impressive; as well as adornments shaped from gold and diamonds she had many pieces in her two favoured materials of pearls and rubies. While her love of life delighted many Scots it infuriated Knox and his ilk, leading to a number of heated interviews at Holyrood

Mary, Queen of Scots

David Rizzio

between the reformer and his sovereign.

In her private life Mary found a soulmate in her cousin, Henry Stewart (or Stuart), Lord Darnley – a man with strong claims to both the crowns of Scotland and England – whom she married in 1565. Darnley was given a set of rooms directly below hers in the King James V tower and, initially at least, the union was a happy one (*see Walk 9 for the background to the marriage and Darnley's murder*).

It was in many ways an idyllic existence, but it did not last. The charming and sophisticated atmosphere Mary brought to Holyrood was shattered by one of the most savage murders in Scotland's history. The cause of the crime was not her penchant for the high life, nor her expensive tastes, but her Roman Catholicism. This, it must be remembered, was a turbulent time in Scottish history; following the Reformation of 1560, the country was now officially Protestant, yet Mary was a committed Catholic who continued to practise that religion despite the opposition of many of her fellow Scots, most notably Knox, the most influential clergyman in the land. Many people also felt that she was unduly influenced by her advisers, who were predominantly Roman Catholic.

If one person in her inner circle epitomised everything that Protestants hated it was the Italian, David Rizzio (or Riccio). Short, fat, unprepossessing and arrogant, Rizzio was an accomplished musician and linguist who became Mary's French secretary and one of her closest confidants. He undoubtedly encouraged the Queen to adhere to her religious principles, and this, combined with proposed legal action against certain Protestant nobles, created a poisonous atmosphere at court. It was Rizzio who would pay, with his life.

Mary's living quarters were connected to Darnley's by a spiral staircase. On the night of 9 March 1566, she was eating in her supper room when Darnley appeared, followed shortly thereafter by Lord Ruthven and other nobles. Mouthing curses against Rizzio, the assassins took hold of the little Italian and dragged him into an outer chamber. Rizzio clung on to the Queen's skirts, pleading '*Sauvez moi, sauvez moi*,' but it was to no avail. In an orgy of blood lust, he was stabbed fifty-six times before his body was thrown down the stairs. While all this was going on, Mary, despite being six months pregnant, had a pistol held to her head, in what must have been a terrifying ordeal.

While Darnley may not have wielded the knife, it is clear he was up to his neck in the conspiracy. He had been made promises by Mary with regard to the succession, which had not been kept, and he had become increasingly angered by Mary's closeness to Rizzio. For such an insecure and arrogant man it would have been too much to bear.

Mary's apartments are still largely intact and can be seen by anyone who visits the palace; there is even a portrait of Rizzio and a plaque commemorating him. As for Mary the murder of her secretary set off a chain of events that would result in her abdication (in favour of her infant son, James VI), imprisonment and execution.

CHARLES II

At the restoration of the monarchy in 1660, Charles II, a Stuart, came to the throne and set about rebuilding Holyrood. Plans were drawn up by Scottish architect Sir William Bruce, which included a south-west tower that matched the King James V tower to the north-west, giving the front of the palace a symmetrical look. He also retained the inner-quadrangle concept, modifying it with a cloister-like design that emphasised the palace's monastic heritage. Much of what we see today can be attributed to Bruce.

While Charles never visited Holyrood, his brother James, Duke of York (who later became James VII of Scotland and II of England) and his wife Mary of Modena, a devout Roman Catholic, took up residence in 1679 and again from 1681–2. James had the palace adapted for Catholic worship but when he was replaced as king by the Protestant William of Orange, a mob ransacked the abbey, destroying all vestiges of Catholicism.

BONNIE PRINCE CHARLIE

In the decades after the Stuart dynasty had been deposed, Holyrood was used as grace-and-favour apartments for the Scottish nobility. In September 1745, however, it once again became a royal palace. Prince Charles Edward Stuart, the Young Pretender, in a quest to regain the throne of his ancestors, swept through Scotland at the head of a Highland army and seized control of Edinburgh. Holyroodhouse became his power base, the place where during the day he conducted official business, lunched in public view and then in the afternoon rode out to inspect his soldiers. In the evenings, there were balls and receptions in the palace's great gallery.

The five or so weeks spent at Holyrood must have been the most

Bonnie Prince Charlie

satisfying of the Prince's life, and perhaps the high-water mark of the Jacobite cause. His first appearance in the capital was designed to impress and impress he did. Riding confidently towards the palace, at the head of his army, the thousands who turned out to greet him saw a tall, slim and very handsome 25-year-old. His clothes had been very carefully chosen: blue bonnet with gold lace, tartan coat, red velvet trousers, military boots and with the star of the Order of St Andrew affixed to his chest. Dazzled by his glamour the reception from the crowd was adulatory, especially from women and the so-called common people. It was on this day that people started to use the name by which he is now almost universally known: Bonnie Prince Charlie.

The Jacobites did not get it all their own way in Edinburgh. The mighty castle – just a mile from Holyrood and looming over the city – was controlled by Hanoverian troops, who would rain down cannon and musket fire on any Highland soldier they spotted, causing considerable damage to the Old Town and injuring or killing many civilians. Nevertheless, there were some remarkable triumphs for Charles. On 18 September at the mercat cross, his father, James Francis Edward Stuart, the Old Pretender, was proclaimed James VIII of Scotland, with Charles as his regent. Three days later, the Prince's army, under the command of Lord George Murray, routed the Hanoverian forces of Sir John Cope at the battle of Prestonpans, returning to Edinburgh the next day as conquering heroes. To cap it all, there was support from the French, who sent the Prince some 2,500 muskets and a number of field guns, as well as £5,000 in gold, which was undoubtedly an important statement of intent from the French king, Louis XV.

On 30 October, perhaps emboldened by this run of good fortune, Charles and his advisers took the fateful decision to invade England and seize the crown for the House of Stuart. He rode out, never to return, his dreams crushed at the Battle of Culloden in 1746 by the duke of Cumberland. The English took their revenge

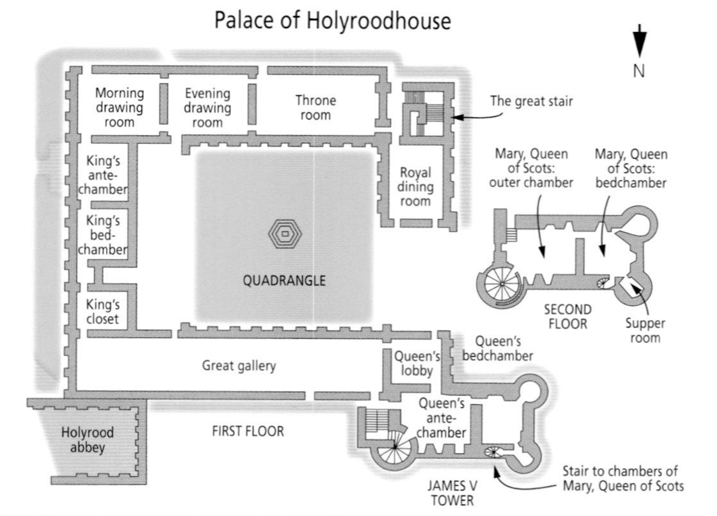

on his beloved Holyrood, twice ransacking the palace, a particular target being the portraits of Scottish kings and queens in the great gallery.

QUEEN VICTORIA

While the rebirth of Holyrood as a royal palace can be dated to George IV's triumphant visit to Scotland in 1822, it was during the reign of Queen Victoria that it was restored to former glories. Victoria loved Scotland and in 1848 she leased Balmoral in Aberdeenshire as a holiday home. For her journeys north, Holyrood palace was an obvious stopping-off point, both for her convenience as well as for reasons of state. As the palace interior was in a dilapidated state a huge programme of repairs and redecoration was put in place, and these were largely completed for the Queen's visit in 1850. Her consort, Prince Albert, took a keen interest in the palace exterior, the most notable addition of this period being the 1859 installation of the magnificent forecourt fountain (which can still be seen today).

THE PALACE TODAY

Both Edward VII and George V held levees and receptions in Holyrood and this led to it being recognised once again as the sovereign's official residence in Scotland. Indeed, in the twenty-first century, it is busier than ever. The Queen hosts a garden party every summer and its elegant rooms are used for many official purposes, including charitable events and investitures. It also plays host to dignitaries who are visiting Scotland, and, in 2010, the Queen received Pope Benedict XVI.

HOLYROOD HIGHLIGHTS

Holyrood is open to the public (fee payable) and it is well worth a visit for anyone interested in Scotland's history. Much of the exterior has been covered in the early part of this walk, so six of the inner/interior highlights are discussed below.

QUADRANGLE

From the forecourt, go through the triumphal entrance into the elegant, classical-style, quadrangle, which has a cloister-like layout, reflecting the palace's monastic heritage. Bruce's design incorporates three of the five classical orders – Doric, Ionic and Corinthian – on the different levels of the façade and the effect is stunning.

THRONE ROOM

Originally a guard chamber in Charles II's palace, this became the king's great drawing room for the visit of George IV in 1822. Wonderful oak panelling and many fine paintings of Scottish monarchs. Today it is used mainly for receptions and state visits.

THE DRAWING ROOMS

The evening drawing room was designed as a presence chamber, in which important visitors were received by the sovereign, while the morning drawing room was once the king's privy chamber, with access granted to only the most privileged visitors. Magnificent tapestries adorn the walls in both rooms.

GREAT GALLERY

This is the largest room in the palace and connects the king's apartments on the east side with the queen's apartments in James V's tower to the west. The most notable feature is the array of paintings, hung on all four walls, depicting Scotland's kings and queens, the result of a commission for artist Jacob de Wet, who carried out the work from 1684–6. Although the paintings were vandalised by English soldiers – you can still see the marks – they have been carefully restored. In 1745, Bonnie Prince Charlie held a ball in the great gallery.

ROOMS OF MARY, QUEEN OF SCOTS

The most atmospheric part of the palace, consisting, on the second floor, of the fateful supper room, the queen's bedchamber and an outer chamber. Mary received visitors in the outer chamber and this is where her famous meetings with Protestant reformer John Knox took place; it was also in this room that David Rizzio was stabbed to death and it is said one of his bloodstains can still be found on the floor.

HOLYROOD ABBEY

Thanks to repeated attacks and general neglect, there is only one part of the medieval abbey still standing: the church nave. Building work started on the church c.1195 and it is considered a fine example of Early English architecture. The composer Felix Mendelssohn visited the abbey in 1829 and was so moved by the sorry state of this magnificent building, and the feelings it invoked, that he would later compose his Scottish symphony.

Quadrangle, Holyrood palace

WALK 9
THE UNIVERSITY QUARTER

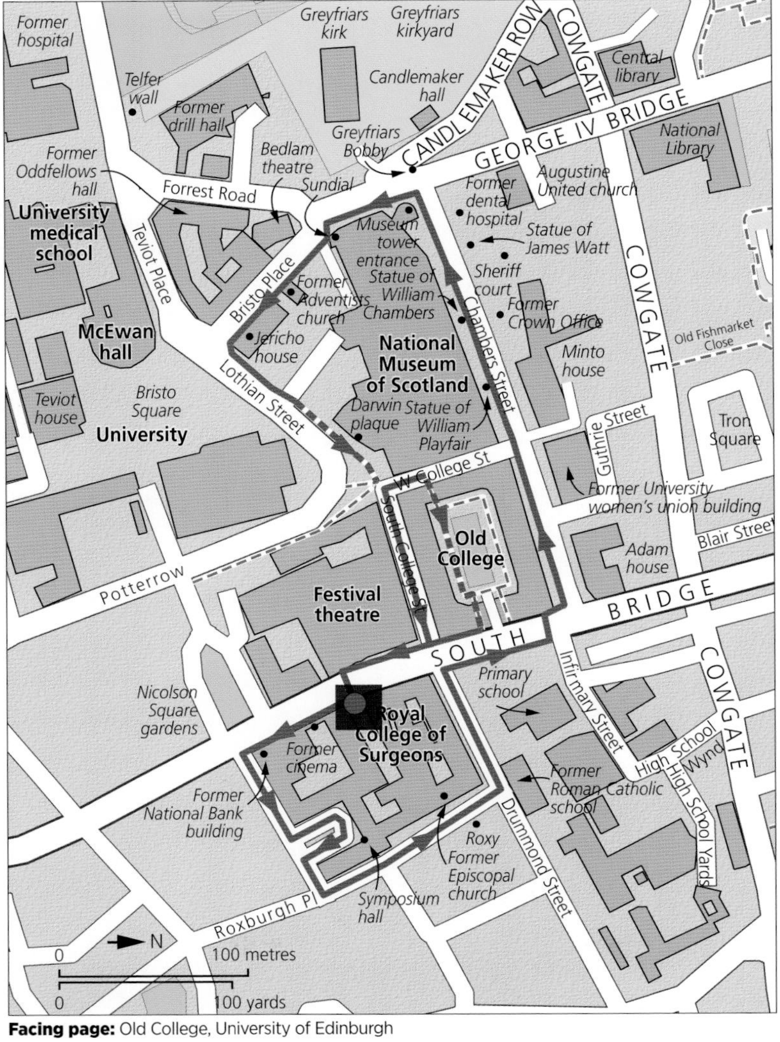

Facing page: Old College, University of Edinburgh

Start Surgeons' hall, Nicolson Street

Summary Beginning at the magnificent Surgeons' hall we move to the equally impressive Old College of Edinburgh University, before proceeding to Chambers Street, home to the National Museum of Scotland and many other fine buildings. It then moves back to the many historic buildings associated with the university.

Highlights Surgeons' hall • Sophia Jex-Blake story • Old College, University of Edinburgh • Murder of Darnley • Adam house • National Museum of Scotland * Teviot Row house • McEwan hall • Flodden wall • William McGonagall • Festival theatre • In-depth: Sir Walter Scott's Edinburgh

The Walk

We begin outside one of many grand buildings we see on this walk: Surgeons' hall on Nicolson Street, owned by the Royal College of Surgeons, an august body that was first given official recognition in 1505. Designed by the eminent Scottish architect, William Playfair, it is a Greek temple, complete with impressive portico and six huge fluted columns. Originally a teaching museum for medical students, the hall opened in 1832, and, following major renovation in 2015, it now houses three splendid museums: the Wohl pathology museum, the history of surgery museum and the dental collection.

There is a small charge to enter the museums and inside you will discover the equipment, specimens and curiosities from more than five hundred years of the institution. These include pioneering tools used by famous surgeons such as Joseph Lister, interactive exhibits demonstrating

Surgeons' hall, Nicolson Street

how the study of anatomy has changed, a notebook made from the skin of infamous murderer William Burke and the story of Sophia Jex-Blake.

Facing the giant columns of the Playfair building, turn right and walk along Nicolson Street.

On the left is the entrance to the Surgeons' hall complex and on the ground is a plaque celebrating the quincentenary of the Royal College of Surgeons. Through the entrance you can see a sculpture of hands, with a scalpel named 'From here Health', which was unveiled in 1994.

After the Surgeons' hall complex, the first buildings on your left are now businesses and flats but were originally the old North British Electric theatre, built in 1903. On the right, across the road, the building on the corner, at the start of Nicolson Square, is one of the few eighteenth-century tenements that survived the redevelopment of this area. In Nicolson Square gardens, near the gate, and inside the park, is the Brass Founders pillar. It is covered in coats of arms of many Scottish towns and cities and was created for the International Exhibition of 1886, blown down by a gale and resurrected in the 1970s.

When you reach the corner of Nicolson Street and Hill Place take a moment to appreciate the Free Renaissance-style, red-sandstone building on your left. It was built in 1898 for the National Bank of Scotland, which amalgamated with the Royal Bank of Scotland in the twentieth century.

Sophia Jex-Blake

Born in 1840, Jex-Blake was a tenacious campaigner for the right of women to play a full part in the medical profession. After working as a teacher, she found that her true vocation was medicine during a spell in the United States, where she worked in a New England hospital. She applied to Harvard University to study medicine but was rejected because she was a woman. In 1869, having returned to Britain, she applied to Edinburgh University to study medicine, and, after a long struggle, was accepted. There were, however, conditions: women students would be taught in separate classes, and, in addition, had to pay higher tuition fees than the men.

Even with the imposition of these onerous conditions many people were opposed to women being given the opportunity to study. Pressure was brought to bear from many quarters and matters came to a head on 18 November 1870 when a riot broke out. Several hundred protestors turned up at Surgeons' hall as Jex-Blake and six of her female colleagues (who became known as the Edinburgh Seven) arrived for an anatomy exam. The women were booed and jostled and pelted with mud, while one of the male students released a live sheep into the exam hall, causing yet more havoc. Predictably, the university reversed its decision to allow access to women medical students and despite taking legal action Jex-Blake was unable to qualify as a doctor in Edinburgh.

Even with this setback she never stopped campaigning, taking her fight to Parliament, where, after a long struggle, women who wished to pursue a medical career were granted certain limited rights. Then, in 1877, after a further period of study in Switzerland, Sophia Jex-Blake was granted a licence to practise medicine by the College of Physicians in Dublin. Returning to Edinburgh, she went into private practice, becoming the first woman doctor in Scotland, and in 1886 set up the Edinburgh School of Medicine for Women.

Brass Founders pillar, Nicolson Square Gardens

Tenement: former St Peter's Episcopal church

Turn left down Hill Place and left into Hill Square.

Around the square there are nineteenth-century tenements and the Symposium hall in the back-right corner. Built as a Free Church in the 1840s, it was converted forty years later into St Michael's Episcopal church and converted into a lecture hall and performance venue in the 1970s.

Walking around the square, turn left, follow the short distance down Hill Place onto Richmond Place and turn left again.

Continue along the road as it changes

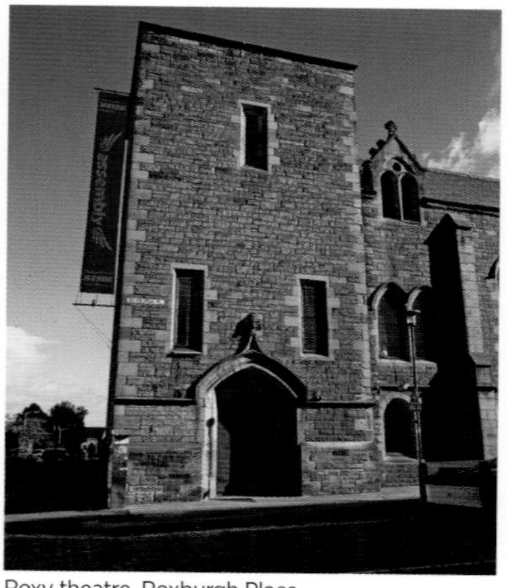

Roxy theatre, Roxburgh Place

into Roxburgh Place.

On your left is an interesting building, which appears to be just another eighteenth-century tenement. However, the bottom two floors have a different architectural style – note the arched, Venetian-style windows – to the flats above because this used to be St Peter's Episcopal church (1–3 Roxburgh Place).

On the right is the Roxy, a popular theatre venue (2 Roxburgh Place). Above its entrance is an angel, a St Andrew's cross and inscriptions that describe its original use, as a church and church hall of Lady Glenorchy's Free Church, south kirk. The Roman numerals date the formation of the original chapel to 1774 and the rebuilding to 1909. Lady Glenorchy was a patron of evangelical missionaries and the 'south kirk' designation is to distinguish it from another chapel her patronage created on Leith Walk.

At the end of the road look to your right. This is Drummond Street and it follows the line on which the Flodden wall ran. At the end of the street parts of the city wall still exist. You can also see the top of the University of Edinburgh buildings from the 1850s.

Cross the road.

These flats in front of us were converted from St Patrick's Roman Catholic school,

Flodden wall

built in 1905. Entrances clearly show the door intended for girls and its equivalent for boys. At the top of the building is a feature of many Edinburgh schools from this period, a relief of a woman teaching a young boy.

Turn left and head up Drummond Street.

On the right is the back of South Bridge primary school and, further along, the timber frontage of a restaurant that had been a pub for over 150 years. At the top of the building there is the date it was built, 1834, and a carving of a bridled horse.

On the other side of Drummond Street, there are eighteenth-century tenements but also a gated entrance to the Royal College of Surgeons complex. This entrance is where bodies from Edinburgh's mortuary are still delivered for use by the surgeons. That this practice still happens so close to where the infamous and totally ruthless criminals Burke and Hare once brought their murder victims is a reminder that Edinburgh's history is never far away.

At the end of Drummond Street turn right. Walk down to the traffic lights and cross over to the corner of South Bridge and Chambers Street.

The fantastically grand building that occupies this corner is Edinburgh University's Old College quadrangle. It was

Woman teaching a young boy, former St Patrick's school

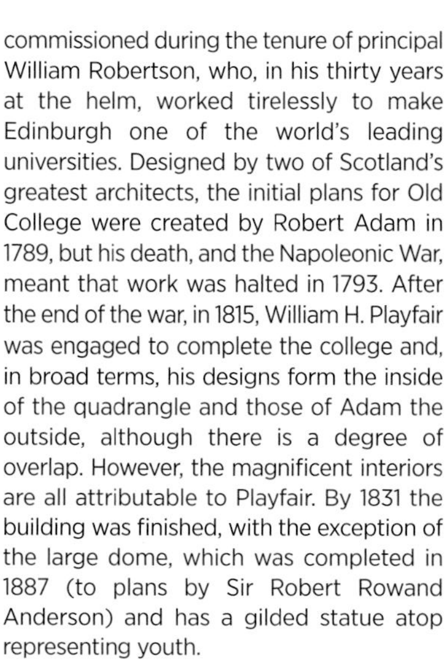

commissioned during the tenure of principal William Robertson, who, in his thirty years at the helm, worked tirelessly to make Edinburgh one of the world's leading universities. Designed by two of Scotland's greatest architects, the initial plans for Old College were created by Robert Adam in 1789, but his death, and the Napoleonic War, meant that work was halted in 1793. After the end of the war, in 1815, William H. Playfair was engaged to complete the college and, in broad terms, his designs form the inside of the quadrangle and those of Adam the outside, although there is a degree of overlap. However, the magnificent interiors are all attributable to Playfair. By 1831 the building was finished, with the exception of the large dome, which was completed in 1887 (to plans by Sir Robert Rowand Anderson) and has a gilded statue atop representing youth.

Old College is a masterpiece. According to Pevsner's authoritative architectural guide, 'there is nothing grander in Scotland' than Adam's entrance front on South Bridge – with the huge Roman Doric columns a particular delight – while the entry to the quadrangle is described as 'awe-inspiring'. Playfair, while adding his own touches of genius to the inside of the quadrangle, was always careful to respect the work of his

Quadrangle, Old College, University of Edinburgh

predecessor and the result is a delight. Often the quad is open during the day and you can enter it to get a better view.

The interior of Old College is also well-worth exploring. You will find the Talbot Rice art gallery there, which has three distinct exhibition spaces and is free. There are also the rooms used by the Speculative Society, founded in 1764 and dedicated to improvement in literary composition and public speaking; the 'Spec' has many distinguished alumni, including Sir Walter Scott and Robert Louis Stevenson. The pièce de résistance is undoubtedly the upper library, a stunning example of neoclassicism by Playfair. Stretching to 190 feet/58 metres, the library has a vaulted ceiling, tall classical pillars and eleven bays for books. It is no longer used as a library and today hosts dinners, speeches and receptions.

The Old College site has been home to a number of important buildings: Hamilton house, a mansion of 1552 owned by the duke of Chatelherault, old university structures dating from 1617 and a medieval cemetery. However, the best-known structure was the collegiate church and hospital of St Mary in the Fields, often referred to as Kirk o' Field. It was here that one of Scotland's most infamous, and unsolved, crimes took place: the murder of Henry Stewart, Lord Darnley, second husband of Mary, Queen of Scots (*see panel on facing page*).

Leaving Old College, turn left into Chambers Street and cross the road.

On the right is the neoclassical Adam house. It is also part of the University of

Adam house, Chambers Street

The murder of Darnley

Henry Stewart (or Stuart), Lord Darnley was an attractive prospect for any young woman in search of a husband, even a queen. Born in 1545, he was not only the son of an influential aristocrat, the Earl of Lennox, but also the great-grandson of a king, Henry VII of England. This put him second only to Mary, Queen of Scots in the line of succession to the English throne, while, through his mother, he was also a direct descendant of King James II of Scotland. To add to these powerful family connections, young Henry was tall, handsome, elegant and charming. His impressive lineage and personal qualities did not go unnoticed by Queen Mary and despite the fact that they were cousins, she fell in love with him. In 1565, ignoring the opposition of her advisers and Queen Elizabeth I of England, they married in the chapel of Holyrood palace.

Mary lavished titles and honours on Darnley. Before the wedding a public proclamation stated that Scotland would be ruled by a king and queen of Scots and he was also made Earl of Ross and Duke of Albany. However, after their nuptials, Mary refused to grant him the crown matrimonial – which would have given him the right to rule jointly and to succeed Mary after her death – and he was effectively relegated to the role of king-consort. This enraged Darnley, who, despite his charm and background was a petulant and arrogant young man, with a fondness for the bottle. He began to collude with Mary's many enemies, while at the same time Mary grew closer to her Italian secretary, David Rizzio, a friendship that infuriated Darnley. One night a gang of nobles burst into Mary's private apartments, an action that led to Rizzio being stabbed to death, with her husband's dagger used in the murder (*see Walk 8*).

After the murder of Rizzio, to their dismay, Darnley abandoned his fellow

Henry Stewart, Lord Darnley (artist unknown)

conspirators by appearing to seek a reconciliation with Mary. While appearing to go along with his entreaties, Mary now hated her husband, feeling that his actions could have endangered not only her life but also the that of their unborn son, the future James VI. Darnley's constant plotting against the queen, as well as his dissolute lifestyle, also provoked her wrath. At the same time, she had begun to rely more and more on a man who had shown himself capable of decisive political action, James Hepburn, earl of Bothwell, who would no doubt have seen Darnley as an obstacle to his own ambitions. The erratic Darnley had achieved the almost impossible task of making an enemy of everyone who counted in Scottish society. He was now in mortal danger.

In February 1567, after becoming ill, probably with syphilis, Darnley was taken by Mary to recuperate in the prebendary house attached to the collegiate church of St Mary, or Kirk o' Field as it was commonly known. After staying for a few days, on the face of it to look after her husband, the queen left Kirk o' Field to attend a wedding at Holyrood. On the night she left there was a massive explosion, whose force was so violent that it completely destroyed the house in which her husband was lodging. A few hours later the half-naked bodies of Darnley and his manservant were found in a nearby orchard. Given that the bodies were intact, and not charred or burnt, it was highly unlikely they had been killed in the explosion. The most convincing explanation is that Darnley became aware of a threat to his life and fled, but was then apprehended by assailants unknown, who then killed him and his servant, probably by strangulation.

Bothwell, a man with ambitions to be king, was thought by many to be the perpetrator, with either Mary's explicit or tacit support. Indeed, he was duly charged with murder, but acquitted after a show trial. Another theory is that the murder was carried out by a powerful group of nobles, exasperated by Darnley's treachery and dissolute lifestyle. Recent research even suggests that both Mary and Darnley were to be killed that night, creating a power vacuum that one, or more, of Scotland's nobles could fill. We may never be certain about who killed Darnley, or why, but we do know that when Mary married Bothwell in May 1567, just three months after the murder, there was outrage. An army was raised against her and Bothwell, leading ultimately to her surrender and abdication in favour of her infant son, James VI.

Edinburgh and this connection to education is made clear by the inscription, which informs us that Adam house was built in 1954 (Sir William H. Kininmonth). The Greek phrase translates as 'he who is educated has double insight'.

Also on the right-hand side of Chambers Street is no. 16, which has many carved heads of curly-haired, bearded men, with no two heads the same. It was built in 1879 and its most significant occupant was the University of Edinburgh Women's Union, which was established in 1905 and moved to this location in 1964. It is ironic that an organisation created because men were excluding women, should choose to have a building covered in male faces.

When we get to the corner with West College Street cross over and keep walking up Chambers Street.

Standing in front of us, at the beginning of a piazza, is a modern statue. Unveiled in 2016 as part of the National Museum of Scotland development this is William H. Playfair (1790–1857), the man responsible for

William H. Playfair statue, Chambers Street

National Museum of Scotland, the Victorian section

so many of the grand structures we have seen so far.

On our left is the museum itself, or at least the Victorian half. This building only became part of the national museum in 1998 when the newer half at the end of Chambers Street was completed. When it opened in 1866 it was known as the Edinburgh Museum of Science and Art and in 1904 it was renamed the Royal Scottish Museum. The Italian-palace design (1861) is by Francis Fowke and while the exterior is elegant it is overshadowed by the grand gallery inside. Rising through four storeys, and topped off by a glazed roof, the atrium of the grand gallery is a spectacular light-filled space, the visual effect greatly enhanced by the cast-iron pillars and balconies. The grand gallery houses the UK's single largest museum installation, the Window on the World, a 59 feet/18-metre-high display with more than eight hundred objects. At the top of the building there are groups of statues; those in the centre represent science and industry, to the left the people with animals signify natural history and on the right the figures are representations of the applied arts.

Crown Office building, Chambers Street

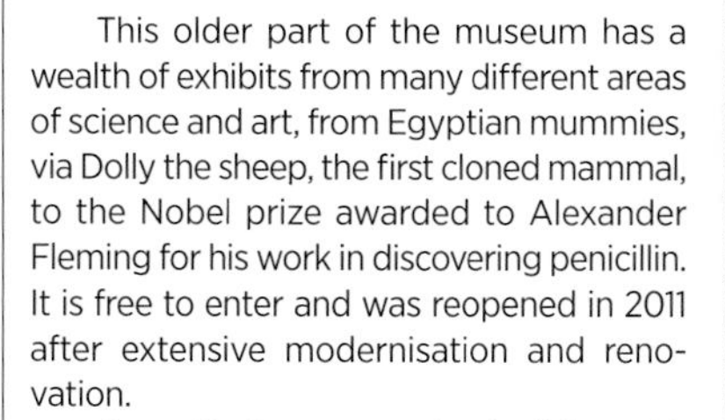

This older part of the museum has a wealth of exhibits from many different areas of science and art, from Egyptian mummies, via Dolly the sheep, the first cloned mammal, to the Nobel prize awarded to Alexander Fleming for his work in discovering penicillin. It is free to enter and was reopened in 2011 after extensive modernisation and renovation.

Opposite the museum is a building with a sign clearly saying 'Crown Office'. Today it is part of Edinburgh Sheriff Court but it was originally designed in 1872 by David Rhind for the Watt Institution, before being taken over by Heriot-Watt college (now a university). The building is covered in decoration, from carved flowers and stars to entwined lettering and human heads. At the top there is a naked boy hammering a block and either wing has a metal lion with a sceptre and a sword.

Just to the left of the Crown Office building is the entrance to the Sheriff Court and inside a small square is a statue by Peter Slater of the great engineer, James Watt, from 1854.

At the end of the piazza, there is

William Chambers statue, Chambers Street

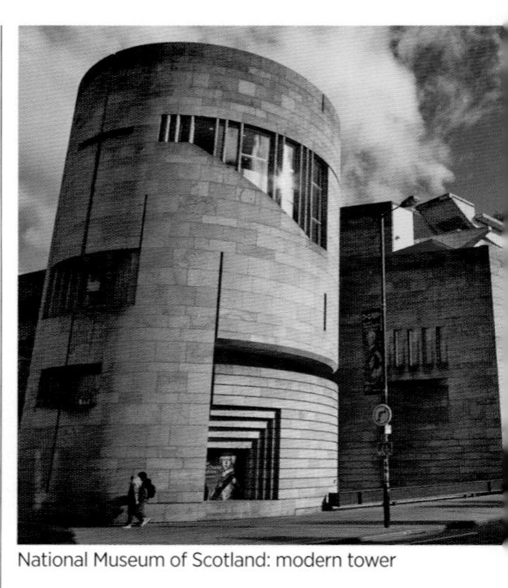
National Museum of Scotland: modern tower

another statue, that of William Chambers (1800–83), designed either by John Rhind or his son W. Birnie Rhind. It is, of course, for Chambers that this street was named. The plaques describe his life and work as Lord Provost, the highest position in the city. Chambers, who was a successful publisher, is also known for his small part in the story of Greyfriars Bobby. It is said to have been his influence that led to the dog being made property of the city of Edinburgh, thus saving its life.

As we reach the top of Chambers Street, to our left, we find the modern tower of the National Museum of Scotland.

This half of the museum details the history of Scotland and has many unique items, such as a carnyx (a boar-headed trumpet played by Celtic peoples), a leather tent used in the Roman invasion of Scotland and a harp owned by Mary, Queen of Scots. The highlight for many people is the Lewis chess pieces, which were found on a beach on the island of Lewis in 1831. Made from elaborately worked walrus ivory and whale teeth, these beautiful artefacts continue to fascinate visitors (of the ninety-three pieces found, eleven are in the NMS, with eighty-two in the ownership of the British Museum in London). The chessmen were made in Norway in the late twelfth, or early thirteenth, century at a time when Lewis was part of the kingdom of Norway. How they came to be on Lewis is a matter of conjecture but perhaps the most plausible theory is that a merchant was transporting them from his Norwegian home to Ireland and concealed them on the island for safekeeping.

In this part of the museum, you begin in the basement with Scotland's early history and then move upstairs and into rooms with more and more daylight to represent the mists of history being uncovered up to the present day. There is also a roof terrace that has four sculptures by contemporary artist Andy Goldsworthy (b.1956). Inspired by the work of 'father of geology' James Hutton (*see Walk 7*) the sculptures have holes into which you can look down to observe what Hutton would have called deep time. The terrace also gives you a great view of the city, and, on a good day, of Fife. It is perhaps not surprising that, outside of London, the

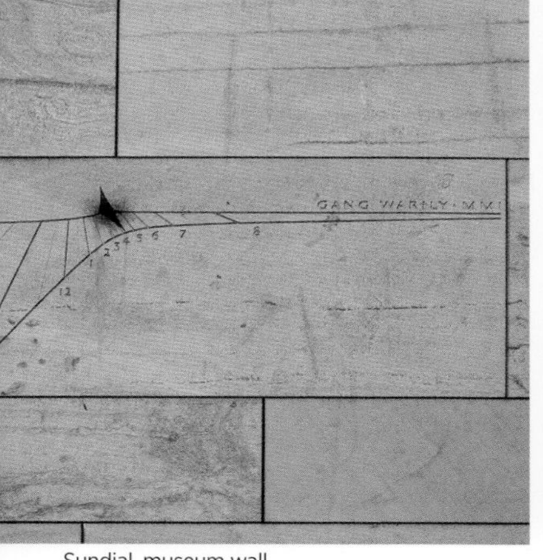

Sundial, museum wall

Bedlam theatre, Bristo Place

NMS is the most popular museum in Britain, with around two million visitors a year.

Opposite the museum tower, on the right-hand side of Chambers Street, is the old Edinburgh dental hospital and school. It was built in the 1920s and you can see its coat of arms, a winged rod with crossed elephant tusks, two entwined snakes and thistles at the bottom. The Latin motto translates as 'Not for Us but for All'.

Turn left at the corner of Chambers Street and follow the museum round. Just after you pass a pedestrian crossing on the right, stop and look up at the museum again.

About 10 feet (3 metres) above the ground, on the wall of the museum and close to the corner with Bristo Port, is a sundial. Set to GMT – so out by an hour during the summer months – the inscription appears to tell you to 'Gang Warily' at night, which suggests you should be careful after dark. However, it is actually the family motto of the head of the sundial society, which organisation suggested its inclusion.

On the left is Bristo Port, which today is mostly used as a goods entrance for the museum but was once an entrance to the city. The city wall ran past here, its gate controlling access into Edinburgh. In the eighteenth century, just outside these walls, was the Merchant Maiden hospital, founded in 1694 by Mary Erskine, a remarkable businesswoman who created a successful private bank out of the small estate she inherited from her second husband. A 'hospital' was the word used for any endowed institution and Merchant Maiden was effectively a boarding school for the destitute daughters of the city's merchants. The name of its creator lives on in the Mary Erskine school in Ravelston.

If you look up Bristo Port, you can see the painted sign of J. Donald & Co, china merchants here since the 1850s.

Cross over Bristo Port and go down Bristo Place.

The building on the other side of the road, in the centre of the fork, is now the Bedlam theatre (11 Bristo Place), the oldest student-run theatre in the United Kingdom. The name comes from the Bedlam asylum that once existed nearby, a grim institution that treated its patients like prisoners, forcing them into cells with stone floors

Jericho house, Bristo Place/Lothian Street

where they had only straw for bedding. The neo-Gothic structure was originally the New North Free Church (Thomas Hamilton, 1848), which was acquired by the University of Edinburgh who used it as a faculty building before giving it to the students.

Halfway along Bristo Place, at no. 2 we pass the Seventh Day Adventists church (Sydney Mitchell and Wilson), of 1900, originally a Baptist church but now a café and arts venue. At the end of the street, also on the left, is Jericho house (1 Bristo Place/55 Lothian Street), which was built in the 1830s as a Roman Catholic church but was occupied for a long time by the Jericho Benedictine Society, a Catholic order of monks based in Paisley, who ran the building as residences for homeless people.

The hotel on the right-hand side of Bristo Place occupies some buildings from the former Edinburgh city poorhouse as well as modern developments. Just along the street, also on the right, the plaque high up on the second-to-last building before the road ends states that Darien house stood here and was constructed in 1696. This name is confusing and probably a nineteenth-century mistake; the building described was the Bedlam asylum.

Turn left at the end of the road onto Lothian Street.

Bristo Square has two grand buildings you should always be sure to see: Teviot Row house and McEwan hall, both in Teviot Place. The Scots-style turrets and towers of Teviot Row house are impressive, and, as it was opened in 1889, it is the oldest, purpose-built student-union building in the world (Sydney Mitchell and Wilson).

Very close to Teviot Row house you will find McEwan hall, which takes its name from Sir William McEwan (1827–1913), MP for central Edinburgh MP in the Liberal interest and a noted philanthropist. After working in his uncle's brewery McEwan opened his own brewery, in Fountainbridge, in 1856. The business prospered at home and abroad (hence the famed McEwan's Export beer) making him, in the words of a biographer, 'one of Scotland's merchant princes'. He donated £115,000 to Edinburgh University to build a hall, which took his name, and, on its completion in 1897, he was awarded the freedom of the city. Although some have compared the shape to a blancmange, McEwan hall ((Sir Robert Rowand Anderson) is an impressive Italianate structure, D-shaped like a Greek theatre and perfect for the graduation ceremonies that are held there. The interior is opulent with fine painted decoration on educational themes, mainly by William Palin. The highlight is the fifteen murals of figures from the arts and sciences that make up the vast dome.

Walk down Lothian Street and as the road bends to the right cross over Brighton Street and on to the pedestrianised area. Parts of Flodden wall stood here until the museum was built in the 1880s and the stones embedded in the wall of the rising road to the right reflect this (photo p. 178).

Here on South College Street we walk past the back of the National Museum of Scotland (note the Charles Darwin plaque on the wall) and the back of Old College

Teviot Row house

McEwan hall

Embedded stones, Lothian Street

William McGonagall plaque, South College Street

Charles Darwin plaque

quadrangle. When you reach the corner of West College Street and South College Street you have a choice.

If it is open, you can walk a short way down West College Street to an entrance into the Talbot Rice gallery. If you go through this door you enter the courtyard of Old College and can walk past the gardens down onto South Bridge; from there you can turn right and arrive at the bottom of South College Street. The door is only open during museum opening hours so if it is closed, or you wish to investigate South College Street, go straight ahead and down the road with Old College on the other side of the street, to your left.

About halfway along South College Street, on the right, there is a nineteenth-century Presbyterian church that is now part of the University of Edinburgh. Further along, above a doorway, a plaque relates that William Topaz McGonagall – said to be the worst poet in the history of the English language – resided here. Although he was born in Edinburgh, in 1825, McGonagall lived most of his life in Dundee, before returning to his native city, where he lived out his final years. A handloom weaver by trade he also performed in the music halls of the day, reciting extracts from Shakespeare for his working-class audiences. Turning to poetry in his fifties his work attracted scorn and amusement in equal measure and when he recited his own verses on stage the audience would pelt him with rotten fruit and vegetables. His best-known poem is 'The Tay Bridge Disaster', which describes how a storm destroyed the old Tay Bridge in 1879 just as a train was crossing.

Festival theatre, Nicolson Street

Whichever route you choose we arrive at the bottom of South College Street, on the corner with Nicolson Street. Turn right and continue along Nicolson Street as we near the end of our walk.

The last interesting building on this walk is the Festival theatre on our right (13–29 Nicolson Street). This location can claim to be Edinburgh's longest-running theatre site, from Ducrow's music halls in the 1820s to the current building, which was originally constructed as the Empire theatre in 1928. The modern, glass-fronted renovation was finished in 1994 and it is a major part of Edinburgh's cultural landscape. With the largest stage in Scotland and seating for 1,900 it is the principal venue for the Edinburgh International Festival and the Edinburgh Film Festival, as well as being home to Scottish Ballet and Scottish Opera.

To finish the walk simply cross the road and we are at the Royal College of Surgeons again. If you wish to start the next walk turn around, walk past Old College, turn left up Chambers Street and cross the road to the statue of Greyfriars Bobby.

IN DEPTH

Sir Walter Scott's Edinburgh

Sir Walter Scott is everywhere in Edinburgh. There are streets, buildings, pubs and restaurants named either after him or for characters in his books. The city's most important railway station, Waverley, commemorates his series of novels of that name, while in the city's best-known thoroughfare, Princes Street, we find the majestic Scott monument, the tallest memorial to a writer in the world.

AN OLD TOWN EDUCATION

Walter Scott was born in College Wynd, in the heart of the Old Town in 1771, the tenth child of Walter Scott, a successful lawyer, and Anne Rutherford. As a child he contracted polio and was sent to his grandparents' farm in the hope that the country air would somehow benefit him (in fact, he would be permanently lame in his right leg). Returning to his parents' house – which was now at 25 George Square, as a wall plaque indicates – he was sent to the high school in 1779, before going up to Edinburgh University in 1783 at the age of 12. He studied Greek, Latin and philosophy and then, in a second spell, law, which enabled him to pass the examinations of the Faculty of Advocates. Scott also played a full part in the social life of the university, co-founding the Literary Society in 1789 and being elected to the elite Speculative Society a year later.

THE EDINBURGH LAWYER

Scott's first case was defending a drunken minister before the general assembly of the Church of Scotland, which he lost, and the truth is he was a middling advocate who commanded relatively modest earnings. His need to increase his income became more pronounced when he married Charlotte Charpentier, a French-woman, in 1797, their first child being born two years later. Looking around for a suitable berth, he applied to be sheriff of the county of Selkirk, and, in 1799, thanks largely to the friends he had cultivated at school and university, was appointed to the bench. This was a position he held until his death in 1832, the stipend of £300 per annum a useful supplement to his fees as an advocate. In 1806, he was able to secure an even more important position: principal clerk to the Court of Session, which brought with it a handsome salary of £1,300 a year.

EDITOR, POET, NOVELIST AND PUBLISHER

Scott's duties in the law were not especially onerous, which left him time to pursue his passion for literature. His first great success was as an anthologist. He had immersed himself in the oral culture and history of Scotland, particularly that of the south-east, and his *Minstrelsy of the Scottish Border* (1802) was a collection of skilfully edited traditional ballads, which proved to be a best-seller.

Scott was also poet of some distinction and his epic works – such as *The Lay of the Last Minstrel*, *Marmion*, *Rokeby* and especially *Lady of the Lake* – were warmly received by the public. As the royalties rolled in he was able to invest both in the firm that printed his books, James Ballantyne & Co. of Kelso, and in his Edinburgh publisher, Constable. These investments would, in due course, come back to haunt him.

Waverley appeared in 1814 and between then and 1832 he would publish twenty-three works of fiction, including *Ivanhoe*, *The Antiquary* and *Rob Roy*. His novels were wildly popular, making him the biggest-selling writer in the world. Now flush with cash he was able to build a lavish new house at Abbotsford, his estate in the Borders.

SCOTT AND EDINBURGH CASTLE

The Prince of Wales, the future George IV, was a great admirer of Scott's poetry and even offered him the poet laureateship, a position Scott thought ridiculous and therefore refused. However, the two became good friends, and, in 1818, the prince gave Scott permission to open a room in Edinburgh castle containing the Scottish crown jewels, which had not been seen by the public since 1707. The door was forced open and Scott was delighted to discover that the jewels were exactly as they had been left a century before. Amid great enthusiasm, they were put on public display, the beginning of a process that would see the castle become a major tourist attraction.

Scott also played a leading role in returning Mons Meg to Edinburgh castle. The mighty cannon, in Scottish hands since 1457, had been seized by Hanoverian forces after the Jacobite rising of 1745 and sent to the Tower of London.

BY ROYAL APPOINTMENT

In August 1822, George IV became the first British monarch to visit Scotland for 171 years, with Edinburgh the focus. The considerable pomp and circumstance was brilliantly choreographed by Scott, and included a ceremonial gathering of the clans, which helped make the wearing of tartan fashionable for lowland Scots, with the King playing his part by dressing-up in a costume made of bright-red, Royal Stuart tartan. The visit was a huge success – described as 'Scotland's greatest party' – and is commemorated by a statue (Francis Chantrey, 1831) of George IV at the intersection of George and Hanover streets.

THE EDINBURGH TOWNHOUSE

In 1826 the two firms most associated with the great man – Ballantyne's, the printer, in which he was partner, and Constable, the publisher, some of whose debts he had guaranteed – fell into insolvency. Scott's personal liability was £120,000, a vast sum for the time. He could have gone bankrupt but instead chose the honourable course by pledging his future literary earnings to creditors and thanks to his ferocious work ethic, almost all the money was repaid. His major regret was that his much-loved Edinburgh townhouse at 39 Castle Street had to be sold (Abbotsford was spared as it had been entailed on his son) and that he had to take rented accommodation while living in the city.

Sir Walter Scott

FRIARS

WALK 10
GREYFRIARS AND GRASSMARKET

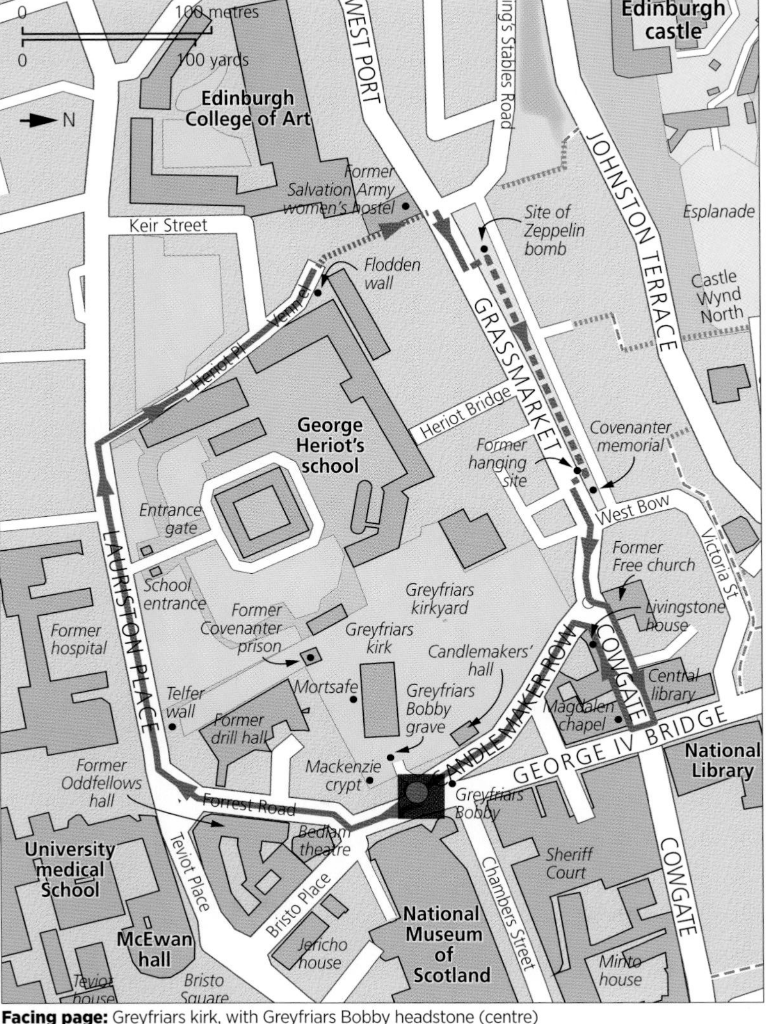

Facing page: Greyfriars kirk, with Greyfriars Bobby headstone (centre)

Start Greyfriars Bobby statue and memorial fountain, George IV Bridge/Candlemaker Row

Summary Starting at the Greyfriars Bobby memorial we move onto Greyfriars kirk and its fascinating kirkyard. Our walk then takes in the former Royal infirmary and George Heriot's school, followed by the Vennel, where we find both the Flodden and Telfer walls. The final section includes the lively Grassmarket and historic Cowgate.

Highlights Greyfriars Bobby fountain • Greyfriars kirk • Greyfriars kirkyard • Covenanters • Mackenzie poltergeist • Telfer wall • Former Royal infirmary • 'Jingling Geordie' and his George Heriot's school • Vennel • Flodden wall • Burke and Hare • Porteous riots • Zeppelin plaque • 'Half-Hangit' Maggie • Tam o' the Cowgate • Magdalen chapel • In-depth: 'Where couthy chiels at e'enin meet': Old Town conviviality

The Walk

The bronze statue depicts the famous Greyfriars Bobby, a Skye terrier that faithfully lay beside his master's grave for fourteen years. Atop a memorial fountain, it is the smallest protected building in the city and currently faces down Chambers Street. Originally, Bobby looked towards the grave in Greyfriars kirkyard but when work was done in the 1970s the statue was altered. Some say it was under instruction of the pub owner who wanted his business to be in the background of tourist photos. The bronze of Bobby is life-size, dates from 1873 and was designed by William Brodie following a commission from Baroness Burdett-Coutts, grand-daughter of the founder of Coutts bank. The baroness had been deeply affected by Bobby's story, and, in her capacity as president of the women's committee of the RSPCA, asked permission from Edinburgh city council to erect a memorial to the little terrier. The two shields on the marble column are the coat of arms of the city of Edinburgh and that of Baroness Burdett-Coutts (*see panel on facing page for Bobby's story*).

Behind Bobby is the entrance to Greyfriars kirk and its kirkyard, one of the most historically significant churches in Scotland (you will see a street sign, Greyfriars). Franciscan monks were first given the land around Greyfriars in the fifteenth century but their friary was destroyed during the Reformation. In 1562, Mary, Queen of Scots granted the town council the right to use the grounds of the former friary as a burial ground, and then, in 1602, a decision was made to create a new church here, the first to be built in Edinburgh post-Reformation. That church, Greyfriars, was completed in 1620, with a second church added to the west end in 1722, creating an old and new Greyfriars. In 1938, the two churches became one after the dividing wall between the buildings was taken down. The exterior of Greyfriars is simple yet attractive, with Gothic windows and buttresses, while much of the interior dates from the 1938 refurbishment. Look out for the magnificent Peter Collins organ, and, below it, a small museum.

Greyfriars kirk, south wall

Greyfriars Bobby

They say that the dog is man's best friend and Greyfriars Bobby, a little Skye terrier, is confirmation of that. When his master died the ever-faithful Bobby refused to leave his graveside, no matter the weather, keeping watch over it for fourteen years, and, in the process, became a legend. It is a story that has touched the lives of millions, not least because of the number of books, television programmes and films it has inspired.

The story begins in 1850 when John Gray, a gardener, arrived in Edinburgh to look for work. The only employment he was able to secure was that of night-watchman with the local police. To keep him company, he bought a dark-grey Skye terrier named Bobby and from then on, as he trudged the gloomy streets of the capital, 'Auld Jock', as he was affectionately known, was followed by his devoted pet. Sadly, in 1858, Jock died of tuberculosis and was buried in Greyfriars kirkyard. A few days later, locals visiting Greyfriars were surprised to see Bobby in the churchyard, watching loyally over his master's grave.

Touched by his faithfulness, people began to feed and pet Bobby. He quickly became a celebrity and as the years passed his steadfast devotion made him even more famous. However, Bobby was not the only ownerless animal in the city and in 1867 his life was threatened by a law ordering the destruction of stray cats and dogs. Disaster was averted thanks to the intervention of William Chambers, Lord Provost of Edinburgh, who intervened to make Bobby the property of the city, and legally therefore no longer a stray.

Bobby died in 1872 after being at his dead master's side for an incredible fourteen years and in his honour the fountain/statue by Brodie was hewn and placed next to the entrance of Greyfriars kirkyard. The bronze was positioned so that the little dog faced the grave of his master. As for Bobby, he was buried at the entrance to the kirkyard so that he would be close to Auld Jock. Finally, his collar was kept and is now on display in the Museum of Edinburgh on Canongate.

Many have questioned the veracity of the Greyfriars Bobby story, seeing it as a mixture of fact and fiction. There are many reasons to doubt the tale, as several historians have pointed out. The animal may have only returned to the kirkyard because it was being fed there; it could have been any one of a number of strays in the city at the time; Bobby would have been 18 when he died, exceptional longevity for a Skye terrier; and there is evidence that local businesses benefited financially from the huge number of visitors attracted to Greyfriars. Despite this, the story continues to be very popular, with locals and tourists alike choosing to believe in the romance of the dog who never left his master.

Greyfriars Bobby memorial fountain

If you have time take a walk around Greyfriars kirkyard. As well as the finest collection of seventeenth-century monuments in Scotland, you will find the graves of many eminent figures, so many that Greyfriars is often referred to as the Westminster abbey of Scotland. Facing the entrance is a granite stone dedicated to Greyfriars Bobby, while to your right there is a very useful board describing the historical figures interred here.

There are memorials on the church wall itself, including one to playwright Allan Ramsay, and close to it, one to George Buchanan, the great Renaissance scholar and critic of Mary, Queen of Scots. The oldest monuments in Greyfriars are along the east wall and include men who would have served James VI & I, for example his chief surgeon John Nasmyth. Close to the east wall, across the path, you will also find the simple 1858 headstone of John Gray, owner of Greyfriars Bobby. Further down the hill is the martyrs' monument of 1771, which honours those Covenanters who were killed after the restoration of the monarchy in 1660. Close to the north wall we can see the headstones of notables such as Gaelic poet Duncan Ban MacIntyre, James Craig, designer of the New Town (lying flat on the ground), and James Douglas, earl of Morton and regent of Scotland from 1572–80.

The west wall of the kirkyard, which follows the line of the old Flodden wall, has some of the most ornate monuments, many dating back to the seventeenth century. In the area behind the Flodden wall (left-hand corner) there is a plaque to William McGonagall, reputed to be the world's worst poet (*see Walk 9*). The gates next to McGonagall's plaque will give you the best view of George Heriot's school, one of the city's most impressive structures (which is covered in more detail below).

Along the south wall there is the handsome, circular mausoleum of Sir George Mackenzie (d.1691), a judge who became known as 'Bluidy' Mackenzie due to the number of Covenanters he sentenced to death. For centuries Sir George and his family rested in peace, until one fateful night in 1998, which saw the coming to life of the Mackenzie poltergeist (*see the facing page*). Close by, there is the mausoleum of the Adam family, which included three siblings who rank among Scotland's greatest architects: Robert, James and William. Next to the Adam memorial, there is the impressive Robertson mausoleum, which commemorates William Robertson, principal of Edinburgh University and a leading figure in the Scottish Enlightenment. Then, in an area known as south yard, you can see the headstones of James Hutton, father of geology, and Joseph Black, the great chemist.

Before leaving the kirkyard you should look out for the mortsafe. This was an iron cage that was buried around a body to allow it to decompose, thus deterring the gangs of body-snatchers. If a corpse was not fresh the anatomists at the medical schools would not buy it. Look for the mortsafe beside the path on the south side of the church building.

It was in Greyfriars kirk that one of the most important events in Scottish history took place – the first signing of the National Covenant. This was a document that reaffirmed the right of the Church of Scotland to be governed according to Presbyterian principles and without interference from the Crown. On 28 February 1638, the covenant was read from the pulpit of Greyfriars and then signed by the nobles and gentry present. The legend is that the signing was done on a gravestone in the kirkyard but, in fact, it took place inside the church and there is an inscription at the base of the pulpit commemorating the signing. After the first signing in Greyfriars, copies of the covenant were sent across the country and it is thought as many as three hundred thousand people appended their signatures. It was an event that would spark much conflict (*see The Killing Times on page 188*).

Greyfriars has another important link with the Covenanters. In 1679, after the

The Mackenzie poltergeist

The ghost associated with the Mackenzie mausoleum in Greyfriars kirkyard is said to be the most recorded poltergeist in the world. Since 1998, when it first appeared, people visiting the mausoleum have experienced bites, kicks, scratches and punches, while one unfortunate woman was found lying next to it, her body covered with bruises. While many will dismiss these stories as hokum, Edinburgh city council took no chances: it ordered that the mausoleum should be closed to the public, securing the entrance with a steel chain and heavy padlock. In 2000 a priest was asked to carried out an exorcism, in the hope that the attacks would stop; he was unsuccessful, and, feeling overwhelmed by the souls of the dead, he left. It is said the priest died of a heart attack a week later.

The Mackenzie mausoleum has always engendered feelings of dread. In past centuries Edinburgh schoolboys would egg each other on with the dare:

Lift the sneck [latch] and draw the bar,
Bluidy Mackenzie come out if you daur [dare]

However, recent events seem to have been caused by the desecration of the graves. The story goes that, on that fateful night in 1998, a homeless man, looking for a place to sleep, went into the Mackenzie mausoleum. Noticing an iron grate, he removed it, giving him access to a second chamber below. There was a row of coffins in the second chamber, which he decided to prise open, perhaps looking for valuables. Almost instantaneously, the wooden floor gave way and he fell into a deep pit. The pit was used as an illegal dump for plague victims and because it was well sealed many of the bodies were still decomposing. Scared witless, the vagrant scrambled out of the pit and fled. The theory is that, having been disturbed, Mackenzie is now taking his revenge on those who dare to visit the mausoleum.

Mackenzie mausoleum, Greyfriars kirkyard

Battle of Bothwell Bridge, its kirkyard became the site of the notorious Covenanters prison, in which 1,200 men were held in terrible conditions that some have compared to an open-air concentration camp. Some were executed while many of the prisoners died from their privations, thanks to overcrowding, a starvation diet and the spread of disease. Hundreds of the Covenanters were banished abroad, which led to one of the greatest tragedies in Scottish history. This occurred in December 1679 when a ship, the *Crown of London*, was transporting Covenanters to America, where they were to become slaves on English plantations. The ship foundered on rocks at Deerness, Orkney. Of the 257 Covenanters on board, 209 drowned, thanks largely to orders issued to the crew that the holds in which the prisoners were being held were

The Covenanters and the Killing Times

Few people today would be willing to risk their life for the sake of a religious principle, but that is exactly what the Covenanters did. These brave men and women were prepared to die a martyr's death rather than accept the king's authority on church governance. It is estimated by historians that some ten thousand Covenanters were killed in battle, judicially executed or subjected to other harsh punishments, such as being sent into exile.

While the Stuart kings had continually interfered with the Church of Scotland, the most divisive event occurred in 1637, when Charles I introduced *The Book of Common Prayer* to Scotland. There was widespread opposition, leading to the signing of the National Covenant in 1638. Charles was executed in 1649, following the English Civil War. His son, Charles II, was crowned king of Scotland in 1650, but only after accepting that Presbyterianism would be officially recognised in Scotland. However, when Charles was restored to the English throne in 1660, he reneged on the covenant and restored bishops to Scotland.

Following what was seen as the king's treachery, the period from 1661–88 was one of constant turmoil. Many of those who adhered to the covenant took up arms and were even prepared to kill clergymen associated with episcopacy: in May 1679, James Sharp, archbishop of St Andrews and a fierce critic of the Covenanters, was assassinated at Magus Muir in Fife. After being hit by a bullet, Sharp was dragged from his coach and skewered by his assailants' swords. The King was outraged by Sharp's murder and stepped up his campaign against the dissident Covenanters. It led to a number of pitched battles and the Covenanters gave a good account of themselves despite their lack of training and makeshift weapons. They were able to defeat government forces at Drumclog in 1679 but suffered a decisive loss later that year at the Battle of Bothwell

Death of John Brown of Priesthill by Thomas Duncan (1844)

Bridge, their four thousand-strong army overwhelmed by a force numbering some fifteen thousand.

Other severe measures were implemented by the Crown. Hundreds of ministers loyal to the covenant were ousted from their churches, forced to hold their religious services, or 'conventicles', in the fields. Meanwhile the King's men hunted down those considered disloyal, a campaign that was especially intense in the years from 1684–7, which became known as the 'Killing Times'. It was spearheaded by John Graham of Claverhouse, Viscount Dundee, nicknamed 'Bloody Clavers', an implacable foe of the Covenanters. In one infamous incident, in May 1685, John Brown of Priesthill, Ayrshire was captured by Claverhouse. Brown was questioned about his religious views and when he did not give the answers required, Bloody Clavers shot him dead in front of his wife and children. Another martyr had been created.

The conflict only ended in 1689 when William and Mary replaced the last Stuart king, James VII and II, which led to the Church of Scotland being re-established in line with Presbyterian principles.

not to be opened under any circumstances. The area in the kirkyard used for the prison is known today as south yard.

Leave the kirkyard by the main entrance. Facing the statue and the kirkyard turn left, cross the road, and head up Greyfriars Place onto Forrest Road.

On your right, quite high up close to the top of the building, you can make out a carved oak tree above 15 Forrest Road. This is the coat of arms of James Forrest, a butcher who resided in the area in the late eighteenth century. Further along, on the corner with Forrest Hill, the tops of the buildings have carved animal heads on the top gables, a wolf, a horse and a lion.

Turn right up and walk up Forrest Hill.

Look high up on the building on the corner to your right and the final carved animal is an eagle with the Latin phrase *HIS SECURITAS*, 'safety from these'.

At the top of Forrest Hill is an old drill hall, now part of the University of Edinburgh. The original building is from the 1870s, the frontage was added during alterations in 1904. Alongside the descriptive plaque are the Edinburgh City coat of arms and the badge of the Royal Scots.

Turn around and head down Forrest Hill back to Forrest Road and turn right.

Amongst the tenements on the opposite side of the road is the old Oddfellows Hall (J. C. Hay). The building dates from 1872 and is covered in wonderful ornamental carvings. At the top is a child, which represents charity, one of the functions of the fraternal society; there are also gargoyles and coats of arms, inscriptions and between the second-floor windows three women

Drill hall, Forrest Hill

Oddfellows hall, Forrest Road

representing faith, hope and charity.

Keep walking along Forrest Road and when it turns to the right, stop. This was where the New Port gate allowed people to enter through the city walls.

To the left, is the large, nineteenth-century Edinburgh medical school and across the road are two columns topped by unicorns. These were created around the time the public was gifted full access to the Meadows in the mid-nineteenth century after the Burgh loch, which had occupied the area, was fully drained. Draped around the mythical beasts are inscriptions, one has the motto of Edinburgh, the other that of Scotland.

Edinburgh medical school

Behind you the tenements above the bank are nineteenth century and you can find a gargoyle underneath one of the first-floor windows.

Follow the road as it turns right onto Lauriston Place.

On the right, you will pass a section of the Telfer wall. This wall was added to enclose an area of land, now used by George Heriot's school, which was outside the Flodden wall.

To your left is the former Royal infirmary, an extravagant essay in Scots Baronial by architect David Bryce. He consulted Florence Nightingale on the layout for the wards and surgical areas and his plans were heavily influenced by her 'pavilion' model, in which wards were narrower and had fewer patients, thus limiting the scope for cross-infection. Indeed, when the infirmary opened in 1879 it was hailed as the best-planned hospital in Britain. This area has recently seen the construction of flats and commercial properties, a development that has integrated the old hospital buildings. Behind the lodge at the entrance gates is the tall clock tower. If you choose to investigate the area further you can see above the doors of the main building are inscriptions praising the work the hospital does, on the left 'I was sick and ye visited me' on the right 'I was a stranger and ye took me in'.

Further along Lauriston Place on the right is the imposing George Heriot's school. On his death in 1624 the fabulously wealthy George Heriot left a bequest of £23,625 to build a 'hospital', or charity school. 'Jinglin' Geordie', as he was nicknamed, became rich as a goldsmith, jeweller and moneylender. He was a favourite of the royal family, being appointed goldsmith to Anne of Denmark, wife of James VI, in 1598, and then, in 1601, jeweller and goldsmith to the king himself.

The former Royal infirmary and the Quartermile development

George Heriot's school, north façade

When, in 1603, James added the crown of England to that of Scotland, Heriot followed his master to the court of St James, where he added greatly to his already considerable fortune.

While George Heriot's intention was to educate needy children ('puire fatherless bairnes' as he described them), the institution that bears his name is now one of Scotland's leading independent schools. As to the building itself, it is a fine example of Scottish Renaissance architecture, with the

Flodden and Telfer walls, Vennel

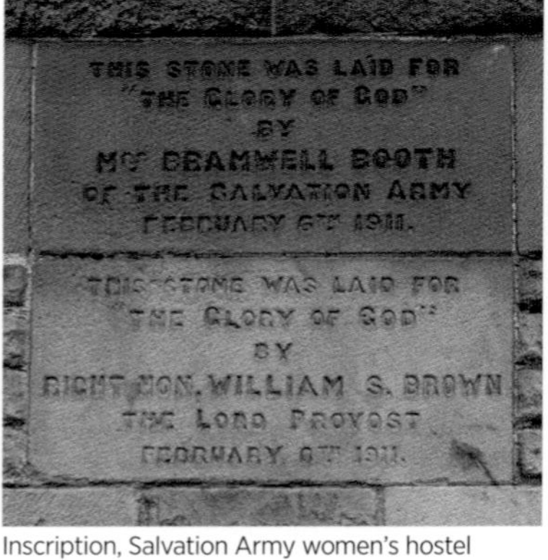

Inscription, Salvation Army women's hostel

main design by master mason William Wallace, and, following his death, additions by William Aytoun and Robert Mylne. The magnificent central clock tower on the north face is the highlight.

The ornate gateway has many carvings including gargoyles, stars, roses, grotesque heads and at the top a boy hitting an anvil with a hammer.

Keep walking along Lauriston Place until you reach Heriot Place. Turn right and head up Heriot Place with the Telfer wall on your right, passing another street sign, Vennel.

At the end of Heriot Place, you reach part of the Flodden wall and the shell of the only surviving tower. The wall has been altered as you can read by the nineteenth-century windows and is part of a Flodden trail that you can access via the information board. Construction of the Flodden wall started after the disaster of the battle of Flodden in 1513, at which King James IV was slain, with many in Edinburgh convinced that the English were about to take advantage of Scottish weakness and launch an invasion. The wall took decades to finish and the section we can see here is over 3 foot (1m) thick at the bottom and 20 ft (6m) high.

Walk past the wall and continue down the Vennel. A vennel is a minor street between buildings and this narrow path and staircase takes you past the nineteenth-century buildings of Brown's Place onto Grassmarket.

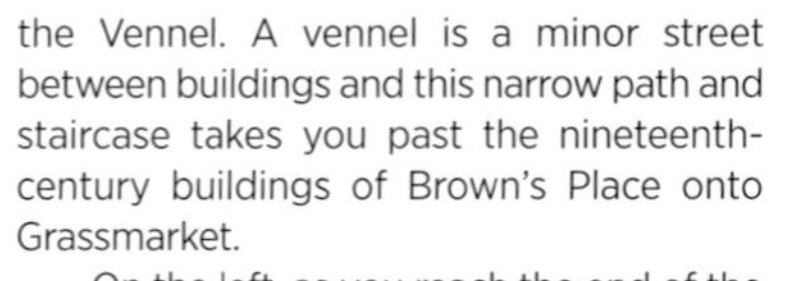

On the left, as you reach the end of the stairs, is the Art-Nouveau building of the old Salvation Army women's hostel, built in 1910 (inscription on wall, bottom of stairs).

At the bottom of the stairs we are standing at the site of the old West Port, another entrance into the city. The street to your left, named after the city gate, once had a street coming off it known as Tanner's Close. It was here that William Hare and his partner, Margaret Laird, had the lodging house in which he and his accomplice William Burke murdered their lodgers before selling the corpses to anatomy lecturer Dr Robert Knox (*see Burke and Hare panel on facing page*).

At the bottom of the stairs turn right and walk along the right-hand side of Grassmarket.

Archaeological evidence shows that the area around Grassmarket has been inhabited since the Bronze Age, three thousand years ago, but it was not part of Edinburgh until the fifteenth century, when James III gave permission for a weekly market. Today it is used for many different purposes. Many

Burke and Hare

In the 1820s, due to changes in the law, the number of people sentenced to death fell. While many saw this as progress it created a problem for the medical profession, which relied on executions to provide them with corpses for anatomy demonstrations. To meet the demand a new profession sprang up: that of 'resurrectionist' or graverobber. After a funeral, the fresh corpse would be spirited away by the graverobber and sold for anatomical study, much to the horror of the bereaved family. Edinburgh, having the most important university in Scotland for medical education, was at the forefront of this unfortunate trade.

While bodysnatching from a newly dug grave may have been reprehensible enough, two immigrants from Ulster, William Burke and William Hare, devised a more efficient, and macabre, way to harvest corpses. Instead of going to the trouble of robbing a grave, they simply murdered people they thought vulnerable and sold the bodies to the university. Burke and Hare arrived in Edinburgh at different times during the 1820s, having worked as navvies on the Union canal, where they may have met. In 1827, Hare was running a boarding house in Tanner's Close, in the West Port area, when one of his elderly lodgers, Old Donald, died, still owing Hare £4 for rent. To meet the shortfall, he sold Old Donald's corpse for £7 10s. to Dr Robert Knox, a distinguished anatomy lecturer at the university.

Realising the enormous potential, Hare, and his accomplice Burke, who lived in the same street, got down to work. It is thought that they killed at least sixteen people within twelve months, many of them from the margins of society, such as prostitutes, the homeless and even children. When another of Hare's lodgers, Joseph, became ill, they took matters into their own hands, plying the stricken man with whisky before suffocating him. This became their favoured method of dispatching victims, as it was difficult for the authorities to detect and also left the body unmarked for students to examine. With the money rolling in no one was safe, not even one Ann McDougal, a relative of Burke's mistress, Helen McDougal, who was disposed of without a moment's hesitation. The most brutal murders involved an elderly grandmother and her blind grandson: the woman was given an

The execution of William Burke

overdose, from which she succumbed, and then Hare killed the grandson by breaking the boy's back across his knee.

At the start of their killing spree the two Ulstermen were careful and methodical, selecting victims who were unlikely to be missed and then covering their tracks. But they had developed a taste for easy money and greed would be their downfall. Of their last three murders, two of the victims were well known locally, not least to the students who saw their corpses in Dr Knox's lectures: one was Mary Paterson, a prostitute; the other was 18-year-old James Wilson, a tall and muscular yet simple-minded lad known to all and sundry as Daft Jamie, whom Burke and Hare got drunk and then strangled with some difficulty due to his great physical strength. Although during a lecture Dr Knox denied the corpse was Jamie's he was quick to remove the head and deformed foot to conceal its identity. While the deaths of Mary and Jamie inevitably caused rumour and speculation, there was as yet nothing to connect Burke and Hare to any specific misdeeds.

It was the death of an Irish beggar, Mary Docherty, that led to their arrest. Invited to Burke's house, and offered a bed for the night, Mary was strangled after a late-night drinking session. However, her body was discovered the next day by a Mr and Mrs Gray, who were also lodging with Burke. Despite an attempt by Helen McDougal to bribe the couple into keeping quiet, the Grays refused and reported the matter to the authorities. Four arrests quickly followed: Hare and his wife and Burke and Helen McDougal. The problem for the Crown was proof; there were no witnesses to any of the murders and no such thing as forensic science as it is understood today.

Faced with all four of the accused getting off, the Lord Advocate offered William Hare a deal: turn king's evidence against Burke and Helen McDougal and be granted immunity from prosecution. Hare, reckoned to be the more devious and criminally minded of the two, did not have to be asked twice and so it was that Burke and McDougal were charged with the murders of Mary Paterson, Daft Jamie and Mrs Docherty. The trial started on Christmas Eve, 1828, and created huge interest among the public, with the courtroom so full that spectators risked suffocation. Hare, one observer noted, gave his evidence with a smirk, displaying barefaced effrontery.

The trial went on all day and into the night and it was half-past eight on Christmas morning when the jury was sent out to consider its verdict. It found Burke guilty of the murder of Mrs Docherty but decided that the case against Helen McDougal was not proven. The judge ordered that Burke would be executed on 28 January 1829 and that after the hangman had done his work his body would be publicly dissected. Despite heavy rain it is estimated that a crowd of between twenty and twenty-five thousand packed onto Lawnmarket to witness Burke's demise. Two days later a further thirty thousand then passed through the anatomy theatre to see his body laid out on a black marble slab.

In the aftermath, emotions ran high. People were angry that McDougal walked free from court, angrier still that Hare and his wife had faced no charges at all. The public was also dismayed that no one had been held responsible for the murders of either Jamie Wilson or Mary Paterson. As for Dr Knox, a hitherto respected and popular lecturer, his career at the university was effectively over. The newspapers of the day fiercely attacked him and a mob burned his effigy outside his house. Seeing no future in Edinburgh he moved to London. His role in the affair is remembered alongside Burke and Hare in a witty children's song.

Up the close and down the stair,
In the house with Burke and Hare.
Burke's the butcher, Hare's the thief,
Knox the man who buys the beef.

of the pubs and restaurants have spaces for alfresco dining and drinking and there are regular markets and festivals held in the vicinity. At times exhibitions have art, photography or boards with historical information placed around the square. The buildings are mostly late nineteenth century and built during an era of improvement and redevelopment of the cramped, unpleasant area.

Walk along Grassmarket. On our right is a nondescript entrance to a close that is off-limits to the public (at the time of writing the sign had been removed). This is Porteous Pend. John Porteous was the captain of the town guard in 1736 when a mob hanged him (*see Porteous panel overleaf*). It may be that the close is named after him.

When you reach the pedestrian crossing, cross to the centre of the square and turn right.

Where we are walking now was, in 1916, the site of a large crater after a Zeppelin dropped its bombs across the city; a plaque on the ground shows the exact spot. The twentieth-century hotel on our right is built where another bomb landed as the aircraft cut diagonally across the streets of Edinburgh. The hotel is built on what was the corn exchange, showing that Grassmarket's

Zeppelin plaque, Grassmarket

Captain Porteous plaque, Grassmarket

use as a market had continued for centuries; the cattle market was also not far away, on Lauriston Place. Next to the hotel, from nos. 37 to 41, is an old bakery but the brewery that sat on Heriot Bridge has now gone.

Further along Grassmarket, the trees end and the area opens up. On the right are a few closes that connect to each other and on the left some interesting buildings, including one of the surviving eighteenth-century buildings, currently over the Last Drop pub, and Grassmarket mission, above which entrance there is a plaque with more information.

As we near the end of Grassmarket, in the centre, is a gallows shape, the rough

Gallows site, Grassmarket

The Porteous riots

In the wake of the Act of Union of 1707 and the failure of the 1715 Jacobite rising many in Scotland were resentful of English influence in Scottish affairs, especially the high taxes. Excisemen were popular villains; they were either English, or, even worse, treacherous Scots in the pay of London. So, in 1736, when two smugglers were sentenced to death for attacking the collector of customs, they had the full support of the Edinburgh citizenry. With the city in a febrile mood it was a situation that would have to be very skilfully managed by the authorities.

John Porteous, captain of the city guard, was in charge, and at such a critical time it would have been hard to find a less-suitable candidate. As well as being arrogant and high-handed, Porteous had a sadistic nature and would brutally attack those in his custody. Not surprisingly, he was one of the most-hated men in Edinburgh. He was also incompetent: one of the smugglers, George Robertson, had escaped while being taken under escort to a service in St Giles cathedral, a serious lapse in security that enraged Porteous.

On 14 April 1736, the city guard, under the command of Porteous, escorted the remaining prisoner, Andrew Wilson, from the tolbooth prison to the gallows on Grassmarket. While there had been talk of attempts to free Wilson, the execution passed without serious incident. But when the body was being cut down, someone in the crowd threw a stone, striking the hangman in the face and causing his nose to bleed. Volleys of missiles from the crowd quickly followed, and an indignant Porteous called out to his men, 'fire and be damned'. Discharging his own piece, he shot dead a young apprentice, while his guardsmen killed several more, including spectators watching from upstairs windows. By the time calm had been restored there were nine dead spectators, with many more injured, some of whom required amputations.

Porteous was arrested, charged with murder, and, after a trial, sentenced to death. However, in a move that incensed the people of Edinburgh he was granted a stay of execution, pending a probable full pardon, after the intercession of British prime minister, Sir Robert Walpole. On 7 September 1736, a large mob took to the streets, baying for the captain's blood; the Porteous riots had begun. At the tolbooth prison on High Street, where Porteous was being held, after being unable to get through the doors with sledgehammers, the masked ringleaders set fire to them and forced their way inside. At first, they could find no trace of their quarry; terrified, Porteous had hidden up a chimney. After he was discovered, he was told he was to be taken to Grassmarket, the place where he had shed so much blood, and hung. Despite Porteous's desperate pleas he was seized by the arms and legs and dragged away. Minutes later, still in his nightshirt and slippers, he was swinging from a dyer's pole.

Despite a huge reward of £200 being offered no one was ever prosecuted for the murder of John Porteous. In London, Walpole was enraged by what he saw as mob rule, and, seeking revenge, he suspended Edinburgh's city council along with other punitive measures. It was an overreaction, costing Walpole much Scottish support in Parliament, and contributed greatly to his loss of the premiership in 1742. The great novel, *Heart of Midlothian*, by Sir Walter Scott, covers the Porteous riots in some detail.

'Half-Hangit' Maggie

One of the most famous stories from the Grassmarket gallows is that of 'Half-Hangit Maggie', a poor chambermaid, who, in 1721, was found guilty of concealing her pregnancy and hanged. Maggie was from Edinburgh but, after separating from her husband, moved to the Borders, where she found work in an inn. The son of the innkeeper took a fancy to Maggie and the relationship led to her getting pregnant, but, as she didn't want to lose her job, Maggie hid the fact that she was carrying a child. When the baby arrived, it was very weak and lived only for a few days. Maggie, unable to afford a proper funeral and desperate not to be caught, placed her dead baby in the river Tweed.

However, shortly thereafter, the baby's body was discovered, with locals immediately suspecting that Maggie was the mother. She was arrested, taken back to Edinburgh, put on trial and sentenced to die on the gallows. The hanging took place in Grassmarket on 2 September 1721 and she was pronounced dead. Maggie's body was placed in a cheap wooden coffin, loaded onto a cart and driven to Musselburgh, her home parish. The coffin was a makeshift affair that let in air and this, combined with the bumpy road surface, woke Maggie from the 'dead'. It is reported that her family got a terrible fright!

Her miraculous recovery was deemed an act of God and in consequence she was pardoned for her crime. Maggie lived for another forty years, and, reconciled with her husband, she had several more children. She was now a minor celebrity, with people calling out 'There's Half-Hangit Maggie' as she passed.

stones and inscriptions indicating that this was one of the three main hanging sites in Edinburgh. Pubs like the Last Drop refer to this dark side of history.

Walking past the memorial to those hanged, near the end of Grassmarket, is the Covenanters memorial, installed in 1937. Recent work has opened this area up with seating to make Grassmarket a more accessible open space.

To your right is a pedestrian crossing. Cross over, turn left, at the end of the road cross over Candlemaker Row to the start of Cowgate.

The name Cowgate (or Cowgait) goes back as far as 1335, with gate, or gait, meaning way or route, this being where cattle were driven to market. Although, like much of the Old Town, it declined markedly in the nineteenth century, especially after the construction of George IV Bridge and South Bridge, it was for centuries a very prestigious address, with one historian noting that, in 1530, 'the nobility and chief senators of the city dwell in the Cowgate'.

The building in front of us with the corner turret is Livingstone House (17–39 Cowgate). This was an extension of the Edinburgh Medical Missionary Society built in 1903 and with many carvings across the door. Some are eroded and hard to identify. Those that survive include a devil, many plants and what looks like a frog on a toadstool. The door that opens on Cowgate is also ornamented by shields.

On our left is the nineteenth century Free Church and above the door you can see a plaque in memory of William White, who bequeathed the funds to found the church. Further along that side of the road is the back of Edinburgh central library next to an arch of George IV Bridge.

Tam o' the Cowgate

One of Cowgate's most eminent residents was Thomas Hamilton, earl of Haddington (1563–1637), a real force in the land. Haddington, a favourite of James VI, was a lawyer who rose to become president of the Court of Session, Lord Privy Seal and secretary of state. However, he is perhaps best known for the sobriquet bestowed on him by James, 'Tam o' the Cowgate'. Haddington, or Tam, had a fine mansion in that street, in which he would entertain the rich and powerful, including, on occasions, the king.

Despite the high offices he held, Tam was no dry-as-dust statesmen. One night, relaxing in his luxurious house with a flagon of wine, he heard a commotion outside and saw that boys from his alma mater, Edinburgh high school, were fighting a group of older young men from the college (now Edinburgh University). Seeing that the schoolboys were getting the worst of it, the noble lord rushed outside and joined the fray on the side of his old school. With this distinguished figure leading the charge, the high schoolers drove the 'collegers' along nearby Grassmarket and out through the West Port gate. Haddington promptly locked the gate, forcing the college lads to spend the night in the fields, before returning to the Cowgate mansion to finish his wine. It is said that King James was greatly amused when told of his minister's exploits.

Walk further along Cowgate. Just past Livingstone House is the Magdalen chapel.

Magdalen chapel (41 Cowgate) may be small but it is one of the most atmospheric, and historic, buildings in the Old Town. The man behind it was Michael Macquhane (Macqueen), a merchant and moneylender, who, when 'greatly troubled with an heavy

Cowgate: Livingstone house (right) and Magdalen chapel (with steeple)

Stained-glass window, Magdalen chapel

disease, and oppressed with age,' sought by his good deeds to ensure eternal life. In 1537 he provided funds for the foundation of the chapel, which had two aims: firstly, it was to serve as a guildhall and chapel for the Incorporation of Hammermen, and, secondly, it was to be an almshouse chapel in which, as the founding charter states, bedesmen (poor men) 'should continually pour forth prayers to Almighty God'. After Macquhane's death the following year his widow, Janet Rynd, ensured the construction progressed until her own demise in 1553; you can see their initials inscribed around the shield above the door. Below that is an inscription from Proverbs 19:17 'He that hath pitie upon the poore lendeth unto the lord and the lord will recompence him that which he heth given.'

The rather uninspiring exterior of Magdalen chapel is due to remodelling in later centuries but the interior is a delight (and open to the public, see the information boards). The chief glory is the centre window, which has four roundels, and constitutes the only pre-Reformation stained glass in Scotland to survive in its original building. The roundels are: Lion Rampant; the arms of Mary of Guise; the arms of Michael Macqueen; the arms of Michael Macqueen impaled with those of his wife, Janet Rynd. Note, too, the splendid Jacobean timber

Above: Magdalen chapel, the tower and steeple

Facing page: The Old Town from Greyfriars kirkyard

panelling and the vaulted ceiling, as well as the tombstone of Janet Rynd.

It is often speculated that in the wake of the Reformation, the Magdalen chapel was used for the first general assembly of the Church of Scotland in December 1560 and while this cannot be confirmed it certainly hosted the general assembly of 1578. It was also important during the time of the Covenanters, being used not only for conventicles (prayer meetings) in the 1670s, but also as a place where executed Covenanters were brought to be dressed in their shrouds. Note the sword owned by the renowned Covenanter, Captain John Paton.

Turn back and return to the Cowgatehead, turn left and head up Candlemaker Row.

The candlemakers of Edinburgh were housed outside the city for safety and due to the unpleasant smells created. On the left we can see the back of the nineteenth-century tenements on George IV Bridge.

Cross over Merchant Street and continue up Candlemaker Row.

On the left there is the back of a nineteenth-century church, which has been converted into a pub, and, on the right, there are more nineteenth-century tenements. When you reach near the top of the road there is the Candlemakers' hall, which was built in 1722, as an inscription above a door testifies, but had a great deal of reconstruction in the nineteenth century.

At the top of the street we arrive back at Greyfriars Bobby and our walk is finished. If you have yet to try the first walk it starts just outside Edinburgh castle.

IN DEPTH

'Where couthy chiels at e'enin meet': Old Town conviviality

The Old Town has long had a reputation for bacchanalia and at no time was this tendency more pronounced than in the eighteenth century. A plethora of taverns, restaurants and private clubs sprang up to satisfy the bon viveur and they were rarely short of business. This conviviality was brilliantly captured by Edinburgh poet Robert Fergusson, who, in *Auld Reekie*, his epic poem of 1773, writes of his home city:

Where couthty chiels at
e'enin meet
[couthy chields – friendly lads]
Their bizzin' craigs and
mous to weet
[bizzin craigs – dry throats]

TRADITIONAL FARE

The typical tavern of the eighteenth century was a cramped, dimly lit building down a narrow close, the warm fire and cosy atmosphere attracting men and women from all strata of society. The most popular times were at noon, when the lunchtime meridian was drunk, and after eight o'clock. When business was over the folk of Edinburgh squeezed into a public house to enjoy a few hours of drinking before the beat of the ten o'clock curfew drum urged them home.

Alongside drinks of claret, whisky, brandy, rum punch, porter and ale, food was often served. This ranged from a simple stew to the menu of tripe, haddock and minced meat available at Douglas's in Anchor Close. Oyster cellars, known as laigh (low) shops, were very popular, not only for the raw shellfish and pints of porter, but also for the stimulating conversation.

Despite their onerous responsibilities it seems that lawyers and judges were particularly susceptible to the pleasures of the tavern. Charles Hay, a judge in the Court of Session where he used the title Lord Newton, was considered to be one of the 'profoundest drinkers of the day'. After a long night in his favourite tavern, Newton would drive home at seven in the morning, sleep for two hours and be in his courtroom for nine, where he would preside over the most complex cases of the day. Indeed, he took the view that he produced his best work when he had consumed no less than six bottles of claret.

LEGENDARY TAVERNS

Robert Fergusson's favourite establishment was Johnnie Dowie's on Libberton's Wynd, a street demolished during the building of George IV Bridge. Although there were two rooms with a very limited amount of light, Dowie's consisted mainly of a series of windowless rooms, which got smaller and smaller until the last was a mere box, wittily – but not inaccurately – known as the 'coffin'. Yet it attracted a distinctly upmarket clientele: judges, lawyers, businessmen and writers, including Robert Burns. The beer served at Dowie's was an undoubted attraction, the most celebrated being Younger's Edinburgh ale, which one historian describes as 'a potent fluid which almost glued the lips of the drinker together, and of which few, therefore, could despatch more than a bottle'.

Younger's ale may have played a part in the following anecdote. One night a customer walked into one of the rooms at Johnnie Dowie's, where he saw a group of young men lying in a heap on the floor, fast asleep and snoring loudly. 'Wha' may they be,

Mr Dowie?' the man asked. To which Dowie replied, 'Oh, just twa-three o' Sir Willie's drunken clerks'. The Sir Willie referred to was Sir William Forbes, one of Edinburgh's most important bankers.

Equally well-known was Jenny Ha's on Canongate, whose customers included the unforgettable 'Singing Jamie'. Sir Walter Scott recalled an inebriated Jamie drinking wooden bowls of brandy but still able to outrun anyone foolish enough to wager a bottle of claret over who could reach the next tavern quickest.

DRINKING CLUBS

There were dozens of drinking clubs at this time. Burns frequented the Crochallan Fencibles, which convened in the 'Crown Room' of Douglas's tavern on Anchor Close. William Dunbar was the 'Colonel' of the club, described by Burns as 'Rattlin' roarin' Willie'. Some clubs were the epitome of respectability; the Horn Order counted earls amongst its members while the Sweating Club would drunkenly attack passers-by at midnight.

The names of these members-only clubs often gave a clue about the nature of the gentlemen who joined them. The Cape Club, of which Fergusson was a member, met at the Isle of Man tavern and took its name from 'rounding the cape', when drinkers sought to evade the authorities when walking home after curfew. The Pious Club was a play on words; the group were not holy but gathered in a pie shop. The Oddfellows, who met in their hall on Forrest Road, chose to write their names upside down. The Boar Club's joke was that all of its members were boars, that their room was a sty and that the box it used for fines was a pig. The Dirty Club insisted on members wearing no items of clean linen.

Equally bizarre behaviour was exhibited by members of the Lawnmarket Club; they liked to spread false information, despite being a perfectly respectable group of woollen traders. They would visit the post office at seven in order to get foreign news but on Wednesdays there was no news from London so they would travel around public houses drinking brandy and making it up.

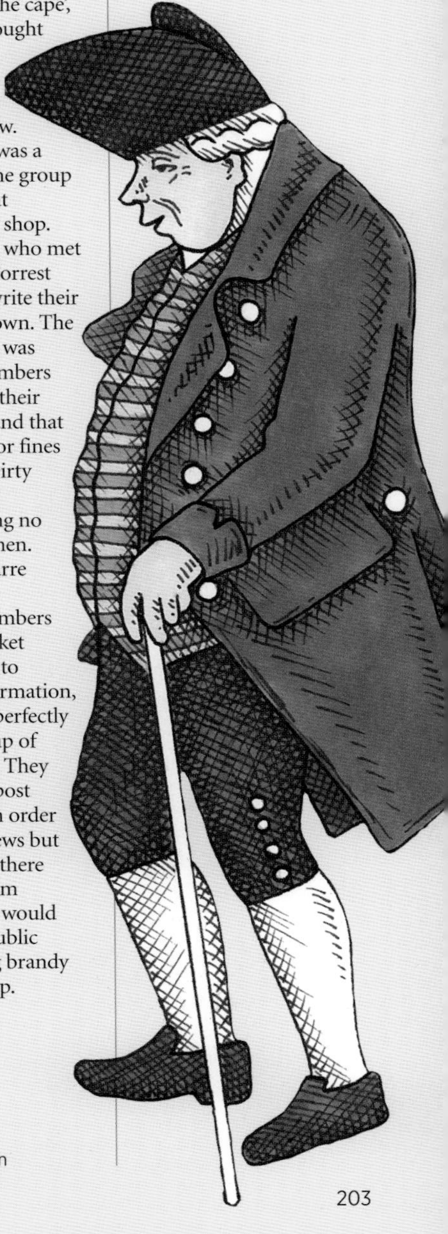

Johnnie Dowie, legendary publican

DISCOVERING
EDINBURGH CASTLE

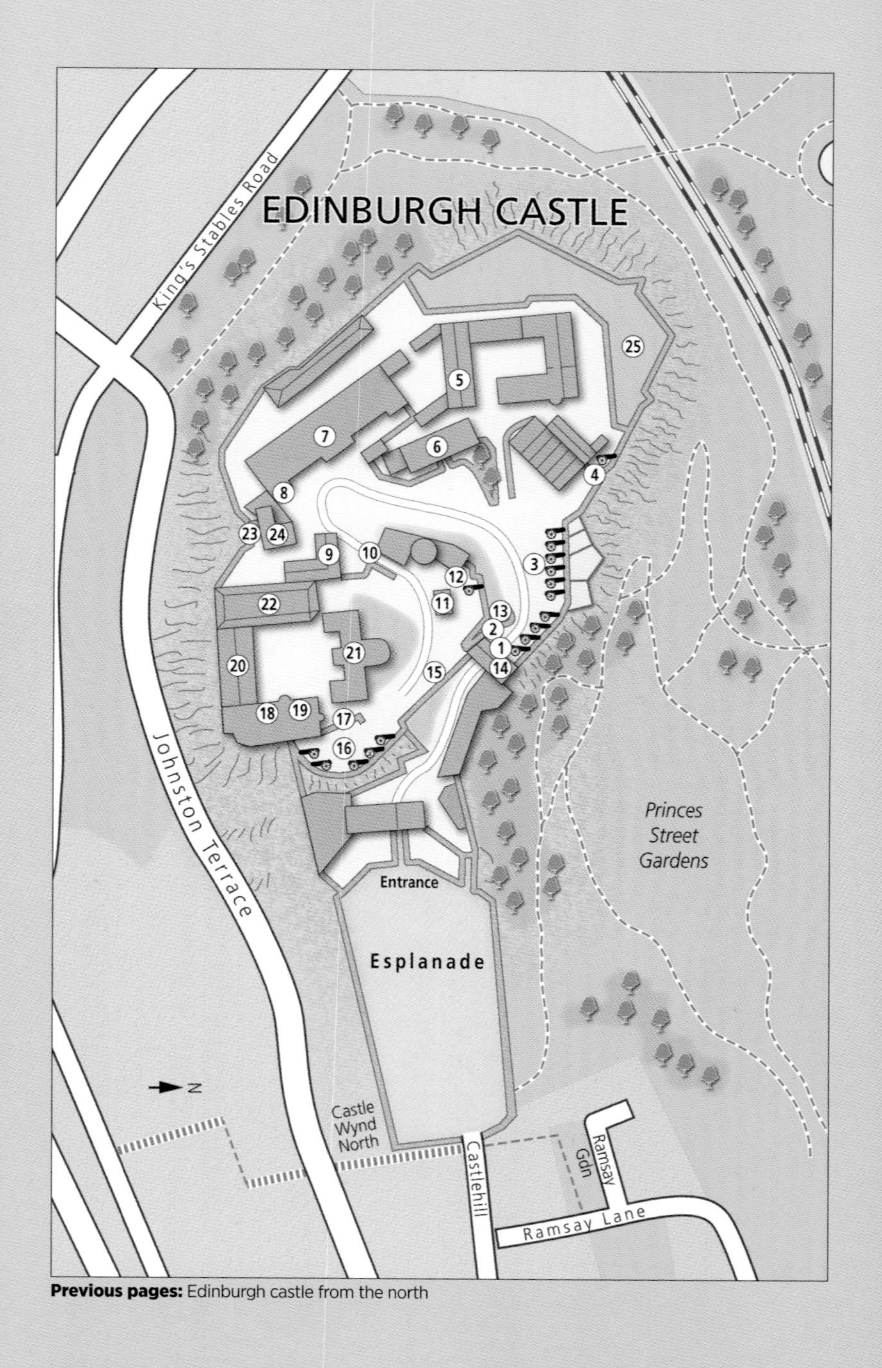

Previous pages: Edinburgh castle from the north

Map key

1. Portcullis gate
2. Lang stairs
3. Argyle battery
4. One o' clock gun
5. National war museum
   (Earl Haig statue close-by)
6. Governor's house
7. New barracks
8. Regimental museum: Royal Scots Dragoon Guards
9. Regimental museum: Royal Scots
10. Foog's gate
11. St Margaret's chapel
12. Mons Meg
13. Dog cemetery
14. Argyle tower
15. Forewall battery
16. Half-Moon battery
17. David's tower
18. Royal palace
19. Crown jewels/Stone of Destiny
20. Great hall
21. Scottish national war memorial
22. Prisons of war
23. Dury's battery
24. Military prison
25. Western defences

- For many Scots, the castle is *the* symbol of the nation. The location helps: atop an extinct volcano, sheer cliffs on three sides and 430 feet above sea level. Thanks to these natural advantages it dominates its host city in a way that is without parallel in Europe.

- There is clear evidence of human activity on the castle rock as long ago as 900 BC, during the Bronze Age. The Romans arrived in AD 78, and found a tribe they called the Votadini, later known as the Gododdin. The castle entered the historical record in the early seventh century as Din Eidyn, the stronghold of the Gododdin.

- By 1093, during the reign of Malcolm Canmore, there was a royal castle on the rock. In 1130 Malcolm's son, King David I, built St Margaret's chapel, which still survives within the castle walls. It is the oldest building in Edinburgh.

- Because of its strategic importance the castle was fought over constantly during the Wars of Independence between Scotland and England in the thirteenth and fourteenth centuries, changing hands four times.

- The 'lang siege' of 1571–3 saw supporters of Mary, Queen of Scots besieged by her own nobles. It resulted in much of the castle being destroyed, including the mighty David's tower, built in the 1360s by David II, son of Robert the Bruce. Following the siege, the castle is rebuilt.

- Today, the castle still has strong links with the armed forces but is more important for its museums and ceremonial functions and as the home of the world-famous Edinburgh military tattoo. Perennially popular with Scots and foreign visitors the castle welcomes around 1.7 million paying customers every year.

The one o' clock gun

CASTLE HIGHLIGHTS

Portcullis gate

Built to replace the Constable's tower, which, like David's tower, was almost completely destroyed during the 'lang siege' of 1571–3. This formidable entrance originally had four barriers – the iron portcullis and three pairs of wooden doors.

The one o' clock gun

Fired every day at 1 p.m. (except on Sundays, Christmas Day and Good Friday) the one o' clock gun was the brainchild of John Hewitt, an Edinburgh businessman who had witnessed a time gun in Paris in 1846. The first shot was fired in June 1861, helping ships in the Firth of Forth to set their maritime clocks. The firing has continued uninterrupted ever since, except for certain periods during the two world wars. The gun is located on the north face of the castle, on Mills Mount battery.

National war museum

The building that the museum now occupies was once an ordnance storehouse. Its outstanding collection tells the story of Scotland at war from the creation of the first standing army in the seventeenth century right up to the present day. Its most-famous piece is the 1881 oil painting, *The Thin Red Line*, by Robert Gibb, which portrays the renowned two-man-deep formation used by the 93rd Highlanders at the battle of Balaclava in 1854.

Outside the museum we find the bronze equestrian statue of Earl Haig (George Wade, 1922), which was paid for by a Bombay shipping magnate, Sir Dhunjibhoy Bomanji, and presented by him to the city of Edinburgh. Douglas Haig (1861–1928) was born in Charlotte Square, Edinburgh and rose to become the commander-in-chief of British forces in France during the First World War. He was a controversial figure and in the eyes of many historians his military strategy was one of the main reasons for the huge loss of life on the Western Front. His statue has attracted its own share of controversy: it once had pride of place on the castle esplanade, but, in

2009, it was moved from there to its current location. The official explanation was that it was a health-and-safety hazard to crowds attending the Edinburgh military tattoo, a rationale that was met with some scepticism by service organisations like the Royal British Legion.

New barracks

This enormous structure was constructed between 1796–9 during the Napoleonic Wars and had enough space to house an infantry battalion consisting of six hundred officers and other ranks. It is not considered one of the castle's architectural highlights, with Sir Walter Scott describing it as 'a vulgar cotton mill'. It still functions as a barracks and is also home to the regimental museum of the Royal Scots Dragoon Guards.

St Margaret's chapel

By the 1090s Malcolm Canmore (King Malcolm III) had built the first stone castle on the castle rock. He was a successful monarch, establishing a dynasty, the House of Canmore, that would rule Scotland for more than two hundred years. Equally revered was his queen, Margaret of Wessex, the sister of Edgar the Atheling, one-time heir to the English throne of Edward the Confessor. Margaret was a cultured woman who introduced many new customs to Scotland, including the speaking of English at court. She also had a great reputation for piety and established the pilgrims' route to St Andrews across the Firth of Forth at South and North Queensferry, places that are named after her. In 1093, already gravely ill, she heard of the death of her husband and son in battle, and, broken-hearted, died four days later. She was canonised in 1250.

St Margaret's son, David I, was another successful monarch who established Edinburgh as a royal burgh at some point before 1153. David continued his mother's work in reforming the Scottish church, bringing it into line with European practices, and, in her honour, he commissioned St Margaret's chapel. Located at the highest point of the castle rock, this modest building, with an interesting quadrant-dome roof, was built

St Margaret's chapel

Mons Meg

c.1130 and is the oldest structure in Edinburgh. It was used as a chapel for centuries, including by Mary, Queen of Scots, but by the nineteenth century had become a gunpowder store. In 1845 its original function was discovered by Sir Daniel Wilson, who supervised the necessary restoration work, the result being the building we see today.

Mons Meg

A few feet from St Margaret's chapel sits the great siege gun, Mons Meg. It was manufactured in 1449 in the Belgian town of Mons and given to King James II by Philip, duke of Burgundy as a wedding gift when James married the duke's niece, Mary of Gueldres. The gun arrived in Scotland in 1457 and was the pride of James's considerable arsenal; its massive size meant that 23-stone (150kg) cannonballs could reach targets two miles (3.2km) away. It saw action against the English at the siege of Roxburgh castle, where James II was killed, ironically by an exploding cannon. While Mons Meg could be an effective weapon of war, its size and weight were considerable drawbacks. Weighing more than five tons, it was hauled in a reinforced cart by horses and oxen, with the roads it traversed needing to be levelled by a gang of labourers as it trundled along. Inevitably, progress was slow, averaging about three miles (5km) per day. Another problem was the heat generated, which meant waiting hours for the barrel to cool before it could be reloaded.

Although Mons Meg was deployed by both James IV and James V, it was taken out of military service by 1550 and by the seventeenth century it was mostly used for ceremonial salutes. Then, in 1681, in a birthday salute for the Duke of Albany (later James VII) the barrel burst open, resulting in the great gun being mothballed. As part of the demilitarisation of Scotland after the Jacobite risings, Mons Meg was taken to the Tower of London in 1754. Fortunately, the gun's huge size saved her from being melted down, and, in 1829, to considerable fanfare, Mons Meg was returned to Edinburgh castle.

Dog cemetery

This little cemetery was created during the reign of Queen Victoria as a last resting place for dogs owned by officers and also regimental mascots. Among the latter are

Half-moon battery (to the right of castle)

Jess, a Black Watch pet, who died in 1881, and Dobbler, who went with the Argyll and Sutherland Highlanders to places like China and South Africa until his death in 1893.

Half-moon battery

The impressive curved wall of the half-moon battery dominates the southern and eastern perspectives of the castle. It sits above the

remains of David's tower, named after King David II, son of Robert the Bruce. David commissioned the tower, built 1368–77, and, rising to 98 feet (30 metres), it was the most prominent feature of the medieval castle. However, at the end of the 'lang siege' of 1571–3 the tower was almost completely destroyed by the armies opposed to Mary, Queen of Scots (the surviving parts of David's tower can still be viewed by visitors). Mary's forces inside the castle had been relatively secure until the arrival in April 1573 of an English force with a considerable number of artillery pieces. After splitting their siege guns into six separate batteries, the besiegers bombarded the castle's defences, causing a massive amount of damage to David's tower and other fortifications and facilitating an infantry assault. By the end of May, the garrison commander, Sir William Kirkcaldy, had no option but to surrender.

New defences for the vulnerable east side were needed and from 1573–88 the half-moon battery was constructed. It too would be damaged by a siege, in 1689, when Jacobite soldiers loyal to James VII defended the castle against the forces of William and Mary. The half-moon battery was repaired and this proved to be the last time significant damage was done to the fabric of the castle.

Crown Square

Crown Square is the main courtyard of the castle, and around it we find the most important buildings: the royal palace, the great hall and the Scottish National War memorial. The name 'Crown Square' refers to the 1818 discovery by Sir Walter Scott of the Scottish crown and other precious artefacts in the royal palace.

Royal palace

Begun in the 1430s as an extension to David's tower the palace was the royal residence in the castle. There is not much left of the original building, James I's great chamber, but the palace of the later fifteenth century has survived. There are many fine original features, including two fireplaces on the ground floor and three oriel windows on the east side. In 1617, prompted by a visit by James VI, the palace was remodelled and much of what we see today dates from that time, including the laich (lower) room and private apartments for the king and queen.

The most important event to have taken place in the royal palace was the birth, on 19 June 1566, of the future King James VI of Scotland and I of England. His mother, Mary, Queen of Scots, had been resident in Holyrood palace but two months before the birth she moved her household to the castle, four-poster bed and all. The tiny room in which Mary gave birth to James is on the ground floor of the palace and can be viewed by visitors. The last monarch to sleep in the castle was Charles I, the night before his Scottish coronation in June 1633.

Crown jewels and the Stone of Destiny

The crown jewels, sometimes known as the Honours of Scotland, consist of three main pieces. The first is the crown, made for James V in 1540 by Edinburgh goldsmith, John Mosman. The second is the sceptre, given to James IV by Pope Alexander VI in 1494. The third is the sword of state, created by an Italian craftsman and presented to James IV by Pope Julius II in 1507. All three pieces can be found in the crown room of the royal palace. They are the oldest crown jewels in Britain and were first used together for the coronation of the infant Mary, Queen of Scots in 1543. The story of the crown jewels reflects Scotland's turbulent history: from 1651–60 they were buried under Dunnottar castle to stop Oliver Cromwell from appropriating them and then, after the Treaty of Union in 1707, they were locked in an oak chest in the crown room. In 1818,

Previous pages: Crown Square

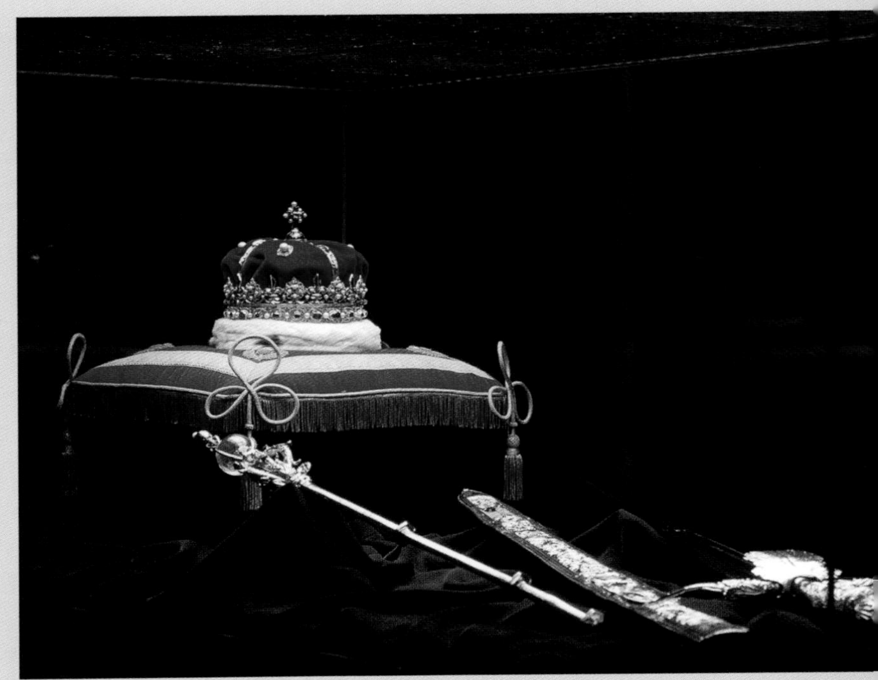
Cabinet containing crown jewels and the Stone of Destiny

thanks to Sir Walter Scott's friendship with the future George IV, the great novelist was given permission to enter the crown room and force open the chest. There to his delight were the crown jewels, just as they had been left 111 years earlier.

The Stone of Destiny, or Stone of Scone, is a simple, rectangular, sandstone block, decorated with a Latin cross. It was used for centuries as the seat on which Scottish monarchs sat to be crowned at Scone palace. Revered as a holy relic and reputed to have been used as a pillow by Jacob in biblical times, it is said to have reached Scotland in the ninth century via Egypt, Spain and Ireland. It became an important symbol of Scottish independence from England, with a succession of Scottish kings enthroned on it, the last being John Balliol in 1292. However, in 1296 it was removed by Edward I – the so-called 'hammer of the Scots' – and sent to Westminster abbey, where it was then placed underneath the coronation chair of England, which was made with this purpose in mind. Then, in 1996, after exactly seven hundred years in London, following a decision by the British government, the Stone of Destiny was returned to Scotland, and can now be seen in the crown room, where it is housed next to the Honours of Scotland in a glass cabinet.

Great hall

This imposing banqueting and ceremonial room is 95-feet (29m) long, 41-feet (12.5) wide and the walls are covered in displays of arms and armour. It was built for James

Great hall

IV in the early sixteenth century and despite being significantly remodelled by architect Hippolyte Blanc between 1887–91, it still has its original hammerbeam roof, considered to be one of the most important structures of its kind in Britain. The wooden beams are supported by carved stone heads and Scottish symbols. The great hall also has the famous painting, *The Fight for the Standard* by Richard Ansdell, on display (*see Walk 1*). In common with the rest of the castle the great hall was converted to suit the needs of the British military and was a barracks until the late nineteenth century, after which it was used as a military hospital. The other important structure in Crown Square, the Queen Anne building, was built in 1708 to house staff officers and stands on the location of the kitchens that once served the great hall and royal palace.

The Scottish national war memorial

The original occupant of this site was the castle church of St Mary, which, after the expansion of Holyrood palace by James V, was converted into a munitions store in 1540. The building was then demolished in 1754 and replaced by the north barracks. After the First World War, with the castle no longer required to house so many troops, it was decided to create a national war memorial, adapting the north barracks for the purpose.

The architect chosen was Sir Robert Lorimer and he was assisted by two hundred of Scotland's finest craftsmen and women. Work was carried out between 1924–7 and the magnificent memorial that was created is a fitting tribute to those who laid down their lives for their country. The exterior has sculpture that emphasises the 'just war', including human figures symbolising courage, peace and justice. Inside we come first to the hall of honour, which has bays honouring the Scottish regiments, the Royal Navy, the Royal Air Force, the merchant marine and those brave women who served as nurses and in other capacities. Leading off the hall of honour is the shrine, which, thanks to the quality of its artefacts, is unquestionably a masterpiece of public art. Most notable are the bronze friezes that go right around the walls of the shrine and depict scenes from the Great War, while the tall stained-glass windows also depict scenes from the war. The shrine has a granite altar, on which a steel casket has been placed. The casket contains the rolls of honour, which record the names of those who died in action in both world wars and in all conflicts since then. Overhead, a wooden figure, St Michael the Archangel, keeps watch.

Prisons

There are two layers of stone vaults below the great hall and Queen Anne building. Over the years they have served as stores, barracks and, most intriguingly, as accommodation for prisoners-of-war. The first prisoners arrived in 1758, during the Seven Years War with France, and, by the end of the war in 1763, more than five hundred men had passed through the castle gates into captivity. The vaults were used again during the American War of Independence from 1775–83, in which, rather bizarrely, some of the prisoners were Scots who had emigrated to America and had elected to fight for their new country against the country of their birth.

The busiest period for captured soldiers and sailors came during the Revolutionary and Napoleonic Wars of 1793–1815, with the large numbers being held causing overcrowding and squalor. Conditions were so bad that many prisoners tried desperately to escape. One escapee hid in a dung barrow, but when it was tipped over the castle walls by a jailer he was sent flying; he was later returned to the castle prison, bloodied and bruised and no doubt a little smelly! There was an escape bid on a much larger scale in 1811, when forty-nine prisoners got out through a hole cut in a parapet wall and lowered themselves down the cliffs using their washing lines. One unfortunate man fell to his death, while the others were soon recaptured and sent back. This 'great escape' was the last straw for the authorities and soon thereafter plans were made for a new prison away from the castle.

The spaces used as prisons have been imaginatively fitted out to give visitors an idea of what it must have been like for those held captive. You can also see graffiti carved by the prisoners as well as some of the artefacts made by them.

INDEX

THE CONTRIBUTORS/ ACKNOWLEDGEMENTS

The author

Euan MacInnes has lived and worked in and around the Old Town since 2002. After reading history at the University of Edinburgh, for which he was awarded the degree of MA (Hons), he has been employed as a guide for Cadies and Witchery Tours. During his fifteen years with the company he has led thousands of tour groups through the closes and courtyards of the Old Town, regaling them with the lighter and darker sides of Edinburgh's fascinating past and probing both well-known and more obscure places of interest. MacInnes lectures on the art of storytelling and has shared his deep knowledge of Edinburgh with a television audience. In an appearance on the highly rated BBC programme, *Antiques Roadshow*, he brought host Michael Aspel face-to-face with a gruesome business-card holder – it was made from the skin of the executed serial killer William Burke! (You will meet Burke in these pages.)

Euan MacInnes's first book *Edinburgh for Everyone* was a light-hearted but well-researched overview on the history of the city. He continues to tour, talk and write about Edinburgh, history and the Old Town he loves.

The designer

Mark Blackadder has designed more than three thousand books for publishers the length and breadth of Britain. He lives in the centre of Edinburgh and has a fine view of the castle from his office window.

The photographer

Malcolm Fife is both professional photographer and prolific author. Born in Edinburgh, where he still lives, he read geography at the University of Edinburgh, graduating with the degree of MA (Hons). He worked for Edinburgh City Council, where he helped produce printed material on the city's monuments and parks and was a contributor to the council's book, *Edinburgh's Green Heritage*. As a photographer he has supplied images to many companies, including the UK's leading photographic libraries. He has been a published author for many years and his titles include not only three volumes on Edinburgh's history and heritage but also a range of books on aviation-related subjects.

The illustrator

Doreen Shaw trained as a graphic designer at Cardonald college but has forged a highly successful career in illustration, her first love. She worked for a number of creative-design consultancies in Glasgow before starting her own business as freelance illustrator. Skilled in both traditional media and digital technology she has worked on a wide range of projects in the fields of educational information, sport, fashion, history and web visuals. Many high-end organisations have used her illustrations including the iconic Wedgwood company, the Lawn Tennis Association, the Scottish Parliament, the Scottish Government, the NHS, Rangers, Celtic and Manchester United.

The cartographer

Helen Stirling is an award-winning cartographer who has worked for a range of prestigious clients. She has a B.Sc (Hons) degree in geography from the University of Edinburgh and a postgraduate diploma in cartography from the University of Glasgow. After working for the Forestry Commission for several years, Helen Stirling turned freelance, and has produced mapping for Visit Scotland, Random House, Highland Council, North Coast 500 and Colin Baxter, among others. She has twice won the Wallis award (2007 and 2015) from the Society of Cartographers and in 2008 was honoured with an award from the British Cartographic Society.

First published in 2018 by
Fort Publishing Ltd,
Old Belmont house,
12 Robsland Avenue,
Ayr, KA7 2RW

www.fortpublishing.co.uk

ISBN: 978-1-905769-58-2

Design by Mark Blackadder

Cartography: Helen Stirling Maps 2018, contains Ordnance Survey data © Crown copyright and database right 2017

Photographs by Malcolm Fife and original illustrations by Doreen Shaw, apart from the following:
Alamy stock photos: pages 8, 45, 49, 55, 70, 73, 74, 79, 83 (l.), 84, 88, 91 (top r.), 93, 99, 102, 106 (l.), 111, 119, 128, 137, 147, 170, 171, 181, 193, 204–5, 208, 209, 210, 212–13, 215, 216
Bridgeman Images: p. 39
Getty Images: p. 35
Historic Environment Scotland: pp. 14–15, 17, 28, 61 (r.), 199
Press Association: p. 37
Other historic images: publisher collection

Photograph on pages 2–3: The Old Town from Princes Street, with the Royal Scottish Academy (*foreground*) and behind it New College on Mound Place. The spire that appears to be in the centre of New College is actually part of the Hub, now the headquarters of the Edinburgh International Festival, but once Tolbooth St John's church. It is an intriguing optical illusion. (*see Walk 2*)

Printed and bound in China by
1010 Printing International Ltd